BILL LOVE

On Restoring the
Crux of the Matter

Copyright© 1992
ACU Press, Abilene Christian University Press
All rights reserved. No part of this book may be reproduced, stored in a retrieval system, or transcribed, in any form or by any means, electronic, mechanical, photocopying, recording or otherwise, without prior written permission from Abilene Christian University.

Cover Design, *Pat Schrader*
Book Design and Typesetting, *Mel Ristau/Design*
Printed in the United States of America

ISBN 0-89112-151-X,Paper
Library of Congress Card Number 91-76128

First Edition   1 2 3 4 5

Dedication

IN LOVING MEMORY OF
GUY AND ERA LOVE
WHO INTRODUCED ME TO JESUS CHRIST.

Contents

PROLOGUE   xi

PART 1:
THE CORE GOSPEL IN THE NEW TESTAMENT
    Chapter 1: From the Beginning   1
    Chapter 2: Salvation For All   17
    Chapter 3: Unto All The World   29
    Chapter 4: Instruction For the Churches   41
    Chapter 5: A Scandalous Story   61
    Chapter 6: Avenues of Understanding   73
    Summary of Part 1   101

PART 2:
OUR RESTORATION PROCLAMATION OF   107
THE CORE GOSPEL
    Chapter 1: The First Generation   111
        (Alexander Campbell, B.W. Stone, Walter Scott,
        Benjamin Franklin, J.L. Sewell)
    Chapter 2: The Second Generation   157
        (T.W. Brents, T.B. Larimore, W.D. Frazee,
        J.S. Sweeney, J.W. McGarvey)
    Chapter 3: The Third Generation   185
        (E.M. Borden, A.G. Freed, J.D. Tant, R.C. White,
        N.B. Hardemann)
    Chapter 4: The Fourth Generation   211
        (G.C. Brewer, F.L. Cox, L.G. Thomas,
        F.E. Dennis, Foy E. Wallace)

Summary of Part 2   243

PART 3:
CURRENT PREACHING OF THE CORE GOSPEL   259
*(Frank Pack, Jim Howard, Jack Reese,
Wayne Dockery, Lanny Henninger, John Wright,
Paul Watson, Ken Durham, Tony Ash,
Rubel Shelly, Roy Osborne, Bob Hendren,
Lynn Anderson, Jim Woodroof, Dan Anders,
Charles Siburt, Rick Atchley, Dave Bland,
David Fleer, Mike Cope)*
Summary of Part 3   305

EPILOGUE:
THE WHOLE CHURCH SETS THE AGENDA   309

Appendix A: 311
Assumptions and Methodology Regarding
the New Testament

Appendix B: 315
Assumptions and Methodology Regarding this Study
of Restoration Preaching

Acknowledgements

My interest in this subject was fired by Fred Barton at Abilene Christian College where I was pursuing graduate work in 1961. Homiletics was my greatest interest and Barton was my major professor. He heard me preach at the College Church one Wednesday night. I called the sermon "The Polished Mahogany Cross," contending that the cross was much less attractive to people living in the first century than it is to modern people. Inspired by Jim Bishop's book, *The Day Christ Died*, I attempted to describe the crucifixion in vivid detail. Afterward I pressed Dr. Barton for an evaluation. Finally, he said, "Bill, how he died is not so important as that he died and why." He seemed to be saying: "Go, learn what this means." Those honest words of a good teacher outlived my ego wound and have stayed with me through the years. There is much about the cross that I have not learned but I am grateful to him for sending me on the journey.

So many have assisted me in the last few years of the book's preparation! Lisa White, a librarian at Abilene Christian showed me numerous kindnesses without which this project would not have been possible. R.L. Roberts, himself a walking Restoration library, helped me as he has so many others over the years. Bill Humble graciously made the holdings of the Sewell Restoration

Library available to me. Stafford North at Oklahoma Christian helped me find materials on Walter Scott. Jerry Rushford and Richard Hughes at Pepperdine University assisted me in finding information regarding W.D. Frazee. Bill and Lois Watson here in Houston gave me free access to their considerable library of Restoration materials. Several helped me with quantitative aspects of the book. Brad Bouldin and Bob Obenhaus gave invaluable assistance with computer programs. Danny Sheives helped design and Bill Morris prepared the charts. Joe Hightower reviewed the scientific data and Alec Schrader helped mark the limits and significance of comparisons made in the study.

Many have read parts of the manuscript and offered helpful suggestions. Ben Weibe, Paul Watson, James Thompson, Edward Fudge, and Leonard Allen read the section on the biblical materials and generously gave the counsel of their expertise. Daniel Massey read the story chapters and made perceptive comments. Mike Casey gave valuable advice about the design of the second part of the book, read the material and helped me past several difficult procedural problems. Richard Hughes read the historical section, saved me from several misinterpretations and shared sources not at my disposal. Lynn Mitchell also read the historical materials and added helpful insights. Four read the whole manuscript and wrote kind comments for the back cover: Leonard Allen, Harold Hazelip, Max Lucado, and Tom Olbricht.

I am especially indebted to the Bering Drive Church of Christ in Houston for the constant love and support they have given our family these last seventeen years. The elders and members have been most gracious in supporting this project, even granting a writing sabbatical in the summer of 1990. John and Gina Rebman provided the perfect hideaway. Pat Schrader went far beyond the call of her professional duty in designing the cover.

Nelda Billingsley graciously donated her services as proofreader. Judy Bouldin, our church secretary, has spent countless hours in painstaking preparation of manuscripts and sweetly enduring the many extra demands on her time and energy.

I also want to thank my family for their encouragement. Sheri and Mark supported their father's obsession, in good humor expressing some doubt that the book would be published before the Lord's return. Deanna has lovingly confirmed her husband's ministry over the years, endured my distractions, and graciously supported this project. To all of these loved ones in the Lord's family and in my family at home I am forever grateful. Most of all I praise him who came to serve and not to be served, to redeem us by his cross and to secure our hope by his resurrection.

Bill Love
Houston, 1991

Prologue

Nuclear energy is by far the most potent source of power yet harnessed by mankind. If one medium-sized chunk of coal weighing just over two pounds could be converted totally into energy by nuclear fission it would produce as much power as all the conventional power plants in the United States combined can generate in a month! The breakthrough happened when scientists came to understand what goes on when a neutron strikes an atom of uranium 235 causing it to divide and release energy in the form of heat. Long since we had understood how heat can produce steam and steam electricity. But a much more efficient method for producing the heat was now available. The secret of this new source of power resided in the core of the atom itself. That's why it's called "nuclear" energy.

While the nuclear reactor is necessary housing and instrumentation for the process, the secret of the power lies in the nucleus or core of single atoms of fuel. In the same way, the Christian religion is the necessary housing and instrumentation for an awesome power which changes lives and alters history. That dynamic changed Peter from the disciple who denied his Lord into a courageous proclaimer who witnessed to Jesus in the very city which crucified him just a few weeks before. That force at the center of the faith arrested young Saul of Tarsus on the road to Damascus, changed his whole theology, value system and mission and made him the first great Christian missionary. That something within the faith so affected the young playboy, Augustine, that he changed his ways, became a great preacher and theologian whose work changed the history of the church and western civilization itself. When this power broke Martin Luther in two the religious and political map of Europe was changed forever. John Newton, the slave trader, was converted by the force and praised God with his immortal hymn, "Amazing Grace." This power within Christianity has not only changed individuals, it has measurably impacted human society. The abolition of slavery and child labor, the elevation of women from the status of chattel, the recognition of civil rights for all people are just four of many advances in social justice which are indebted to Christianity.

Paul wrote the church at Rome that he was not ashamed of the gospel because it is God's power to save all who believe, both Jews and Gentiles. He prayed that the Christians at Ephesus would come to know "what is the immeasurable greatness of his power in us who believe, according to his great might which he accomplished in Christ when he raised him from the dead and made him to sit at his right hand in the heavenly places." He went on to say that God's awesome power not only saves individuals, it breaks down walls between races, converts enemies into a family of faith, provides witness to a whole universe of spiritual powers, releases individuals to be what God intended them to be, and sets in motion God's great cosmic plan: "to unite all things in Christ."

God has deposited his power at the center of the faith, in the core gospel. This book asks what that core is, how we in the Restoration Movement have understood and proclaimed it, and what present trends might predict for the future. In Part One I attempt an overview of the New Testament presentation of the core gospel. This survey will then be used as a base line by which to evaluate past Restoration preaching as it relates to the core gospel and to inquire about future directions for Churches of Christ. In Part Two I report research in the first four generations of Restoration preaching to discover how we have proclaimed the core gospel in comparison with the New Testament's emphasis. I will attempt summary, conclusions and analysis of our history regarding the core gospel down to mid twentieth century. In Part Three selected sermons of twenty current preachers are exerpted to show how the core gospel is being proclaimed among Churches of Christ today. Finally, questions will be asked about our future directions as a fellowship. If the reader wishes to encounter the central statement of this book he or she should begin at the beginning and read straight through to the end, resisting the temptation to skip ahead to something that looks interesting later in the volume.

Part 1
From The Beginning

Approach

If we are to discover what the core gospel is we must apply ourselves to loving God, as Jesus said, with our "whole mind." Our devotion to the investigation must be as great as the nuclear physicists' dedication to the study of atomic power. That kind of dedication carries with it a willingness to change one's mind as the data comes in. Have you ever wondered what Paul did for three years of silence in Arabia? Perhaps he was sorting through the new data, reworking his own theology and faith after his encounter with the risen Jesus. He had to revise every concept of his faith: God, man, creation, covenant, law, kingdom, messiah, salvation, hope. Our growing in the Lord is in essence like that. Painful as it is, the more we learn of him the more we are asked to adjust our thinking.

Looking at things in a different way is difficult. For example, one of the challenges to us in the Church of Christ is to discover again as adults what we learned as children: that the Bible is a storybook. For generations we have studied the Scriptures in pieces. The verses, paragraphs, chapters, and books offer so much rich meaning we may forget that all of it fits within the larger story of God and his dealings with mankind. Many of us have spent years learning how to study a text, digging into the original context, observing literary forms, examining words. We have learned to take each writing and study it on its own merits. The returns for that kind of study are enormous. From time to time we have been thrilled to tears because of golden insights discovered in the text. Over the years of such study one consciously or unconsciously forms his or her own biblical theology: bits of data and thought cluster around key subjects and ideas assume some relation to one another: God, man, creation, sin, redemption, Christ, church. That kind of theologizing is not only legitimate, it is necessary. All of this is well and good; we should never give up gains we have made in learning how to study particular books and individual portions of the Scripture. We are privileged all of our lives to ponder the great themes of the faith and their interrelations.

However, if there is an overall unity to the Bible, if it is not simply a random collection of sixty-six books, one must ask about the meaning of the whole. The study of individual books is not enough. If there is an over-arching story we must discover what it is. In addition to our study of particular texts, in addition to our examination of biblical themes, in addition to our prayerful thought about these matters, we must know that grand story if we are to experience the core gospel in its full power.

In this section of the book I am attempting neither textual analysis nor systematic theology nor the writing of history. The object is storytelling. The ancient Hebrew and early Christian narratives carry the storyline of the Bible.[1] In this chapter and the three which follow I am attempting to retell in broad outline that biblical story. Our aim is to discover the core gospel.

"In The Beginning"

While the earth was still "without form and void" God's Spirit moved over it calling order out of chaos, light from darkness, and life from inanimate matter. He did not have to do it. No one commissioned him for the project. God did not have unfulfilled needs of his own that only creating us would meet. God is love. For that and no other reason he created this universe. He made "man" in two models: male and female. The Creator made human beings the crown of creation and pronounced his handiwork very good. Within each person he placed his own image. We do not ask to which family Adam and Eve belonged, what their value was as persons, whether God loved them. It never occurs to us to inquire whether they were rich or poor, black or white, Jew or Gentile, Christian or non-Christian, educated or uneducated, young or old. God made them in his image. That's who they were: human beings made in the image of God whom he pronounced good.

The Fall

Creating them in his image meant putting within the man and the woman the power of choice. Adam and Eve could either talk with God or they could commune with the serpent. They had great potential for creativity or destructiveness. Because God planned their freedom from the beginning he knew that things would go wrong. He created them anyway, knowing they would break his heart, that there would be alienation between the Father and his children, and that getting them back home would cost him dearly.

God created for Adam and Eve the perfect paradise home; they had everything they needed. He said they could have free run of the garden, except for the tree of the knowledge of good and evil in the center. They were told not to touch it or they would die. Was the tree just an arbitrary power marker God laid down to make their lives miserable? Or was it a gracious statement of truth about human nature?

The serpent came along and engaged Eve in conversation. He appealed to her best side, her spiritual hunger to be like God. He began with the highest human aspiration and deepest need. Admiring the couple in their new home, he raised a question. "I hope no one is putting any restrictions on you! Wouldn't it be a shame in a place like this with fine persons like yourselves if you were limited in some way?" "Well, God did say we must not eat of the tree in the middle of the garden or we'll die." "You won't die," the serpent scoffed. "God's just guarding his own territory. He knows that if you eat of it you will be like he is, knowing good and evil. Can't you see that he is threatened by you? To protect his own turf he is keeping you from being all you can be, from knowing all you can know, and experiencing all you can experience."

With these new insights Eve looked again at the forbidden tree. Suddenly, it was the only tree in the garden. "What if the one who made us and gave us all this is not really on our side? Maybe he is trying to restrict us to protect himself. He may want our lives to be cramped and dull. The fruit does look good, it is beautiful! We have to eat something! Isn't life about learning all we can know? Why should we be limited, we can have it all! We'll never know until we taste it..."

Eve ate and gave some of the fruit to Adam and he ate. They did discover good and evil and received more knowledge than they bargained for: the guilt and shame of disobeying their gracious Creator. Then God came calling and they felt his disappointment and wrath. Adam blamed Eve, Eve passed the buck to the serpent. What was God to do? Legally he could throw the book at them. He chose rather to let them live and to win them back to himself. By their greed they had created a great gulf between themselves and God. They had chosen self over fellowship with God; they had opted not to obey their ~~Grateor~~ Creator. Becouse they defied their own limits they lost their pleasant home in Eden.

Never again would they walk and talk with God as before. Even though their disobedience grieved God he did not forsake them. The Father was determined to restore relationship if it took generations, even centuries. The challenge would be great: how could the loving and holy Father bring his selfish and sinful children back home without betraying his own nature or violating their freedom? He had a plan to draw his children back to him. And he wanted them drawn back, not driven. They were created in his image and he would not violate their freedom of choice.

God continued his gracious love to Adam and Eve. He made them clothes of skins to replace the pathetic leaves they had gathered to cover themselves. After Adam and Eve left their paradise home things went from bad to worse. One of their sons murdered the other and became a wanderer. Again, God was gracious, providing Cain a mark and protection from harm wherever he went. But as generations came and went people became more and more selfish until they had no consciousness of God at all. He had not given up on them, but he did wipe the slate almost clean by sending the flood. As before, God demonstrated his kindness, this time in providing Noah warning and instructions for the ark. God still planned to bring his children home. He remained firm in his resolve despite their pride. After the flood the hubris of God's children came back like a bad infection. They dreamed of building a tower up to heaven and went to work, presumably to storm the gates of glory and to take part ownership of the property. God had always given gracious gifts to heal his children's self-inflicted wounds. But this time, when the people arrogantly planned to invade God's space by their own cunning, he gave no mitigating grace. He confused the arrogant, as he has so often done since.

Covenant

Later God called Abraham to become the father of a chosen people. He would be an important part of the plan to bring God's children home. Through his family all the families of the earth would be blessed. God chose Abraham not because he was a saint. Twice he lied about his wife to save his own neck. God chose him for the same reason he created the human race in the beginning: because God is love and lovingly pursues his plan for reconciliation. He chose Abraham because this man would listen, trust and obey. He would say "Amen" to God's plan and then follow directions. God called Abraham from the security of his home in urban Ur of Chaldees to become a wanderer in search of a promised land. Abraham never really owned the promised land except for a little plot where he buried his wife.

When Abraham and Sarah were old God promised them a son through whom their destiny would be realized. They had no children and Sarah's child-bearing years were long past. Abraham wondered about God's promise when it didn't come true right away and tried to help God out by taking his handmaiden, Hagar, by whom he had a son. Finally, Isaac was born and the old couple were elated. But no sooner had the baby grown into a young man than God made an unbelievable request of Abraham. "Take your son up on the mountain and offer him as a sacrifice to me." Abraham carried out the instructions in every detail until, knife raised over his son, he was ready to give the most precious thing in his life to God. God held back Abraham's arm and spared his son. He had arranged a ram caught in a nearby thicket for a substitute offering. After all, Abraham did not have to sacrifice his son. But he had been tested and passed the test. That kind of trust would be necessary if Abraham's family would be God's instrument for reconciling all his children back home.

God repeated his promises to Abraham's son, Isaac and to Isaac's son, Jacob. The stories of Abraham's family are full of danger, romance and adventure. The resentful sons of Jacob sold their brother Joseph to a caravan of Ishmaelite traders on their way to Egypt. They knew they would never see him again. But God had another plan. Through God's intervention Joseph became Egypt's second in command. When the brothers came down many years later to buy grain during a famine, Joseph was reunited with his family. For generations they enjoyed an honored position in Egypt.

Bondage, Rescue And Covenant

After Joseph died and several generations of Egyptians leaders passed away his family lost their favored status and the Egyptians enslaved them. Then, even worse, they made them objects of planned genocide. The Hebrews cried out under the abuse of harsh taskmasters. God had not forgotten his chosen people and his plan to reconcile all his children to himself. He heard their cry and called Moses to be his redeemer. Moses was not perfect either: he had actually killed a man and fled Egypt to avoid punishment. The call was not good news to Moses. He was not eager to go back to face the music. He asked God, "Who shall I say sent me?" "I Am Who I Am" was the mysterious answer. The story which followed revealed some of the meaning. Moses had been called by the God who always was, always is, and always will be. That day God was saying to Moses: "You will never 'get my number,' be able to control, manipulate and use me. I have a plan; you're are an important part of it. I am going with you and will direct you. Nothing that happens from here out will be beyond my control."

God sent plague after plague upon Egypt until Pharaoh let the Hebrews go. The last straw was the death of the first born in every Egyptian home. Moses instructed the Hebrews to kill a lamb and wipe the doorposts of their houses with its blood so the death angel would pass over them. They would eat a meal together in readiness to depart. Ever afterward the Hebrews would eat the Passover annually in remembrance of their bondage, the sacrificial lamb, and God's mighty deliverance.

Moses led the people out of Egypt on a journey to the promised land. You would think they would have had a great, continuous worship service of God for all he had done. But, like Adam and Eve, these people were never satisfied. They were always grasping for more. God led them across the desert and endured their complaining all the way to Mount Sinai.

Moses instructed the people to wash their clothes and tidy up the camp. They were to meet the holy God. Moses went up on the mountain to receive God's instructions. Like a strong king who rescued a weak king, God reminded the Hebrews what he had done for them, promised to be their protector, told them what living under his reign would mean, and called for their undivided loyalty to him. All of that was contained in the covenant and Ten Commandments. His first commandment was that they would have no other gods before him. The loving God once again had taken the initiative by offering them covenant. He waited for their reply. The people pledged God their undying loyalty. God made covenant knowing full well that they would not keep their promise.

Later Moses went up on the mountain for further instruction. When he didn't return for days on end the people grew bored and restless. They got Aaron to make them a golden calf for a special worship experience. The calf was no big thing, just a visible reminder of their invisible God. It was no big thing to them, just an interim pastime, something to do. They knew their main God was meeting with Moses up on the mountain. He was the one who had rescued them from slavery. But they got carried away in the celebration and someone shouted: "These are your gods, O Israel, who brought you up out of the land of Egypt."

This was a big thing to Moses, even bigger to God. He had Moses call all the faithful to stand with him. They drew their swords and three thousand idolaters fell that day. The God who had rescued them was not only loving, he was also holy. He was serious about his plan and his people. That's how determined he was to work his plan and bring all of his children back to him. The Hebrews were rescued, called and given covenant, not to be God's exclusive club for their own enjoyment, but to be a model for the nations. In them God would demonstrate his goodness, holiness and power and what being his people could mean.

So God had Moses set up the priesthood, build the Tabernacle, and explain to the people his instructions for worship. He was a holy God, and they could not just waltz into his presence. Continuous sacrifices were required at considerable cost, to remind them of God's gracious rescue, of their sins, and of his covenant with them. Once a year the High Priest entered the Holy of Holies to make atonement. He offered the blood of a young bull for the sins of the priests and the blood of a he-goat for the sins of the people. He laid his hands on a second goat and sent it away into the wilderness, bearing away the sins of God's people. All of this was to teach and remind the people every year who God was, what it meant to be his people, that they were sinful and undone, that he loved them and had made covenant with them only by his grace. In addition, they were commanded to keep the Passover each year to remind them of their rescue from bondage.

Promised Land

After a two-year journey, murmuring all the way, God's people reached Canaan. Twelve spies were sent over the Jordan River to check it out. Ten of them returned saying no one in his right mind would attempt to take this land full of giants. Joshua and Caleb filed a minority report. They believed the Lord was with them and that fact made victory more than possible. But the people chose fear over faith. So God led them back into the wilderness where they wandered thirty-eight years until the faithless generation died. Their children finally crossed Jordan to claim the land. God still planned to bring all his children back home. But his plan would not work if his chosen people lost their identity and calling. So he ordered the total destruction of all Canaan's pagan inhabitants with their gods. That instruction seemed a bit extreme to the Hebrews. They did a large part of what he said. Surely he would be reasonable about the rest.

As they finished taking the land this group of second generation vagabonds faced the challenge of learning to farm and keep vineyards. They noticed that the locals had good crops and vines heavy with grapes. In response to their "how to" questions their neighbors gave helpful hints. "Well, you plant this way, cultivate like that, trim the vines so,...And, by the way, don't forget to worship the baals."

After all they had been through, God's people had no intention of leaving him for other gods. He had rescued them, made covenant with them, carried them across the desert and given them the promised land. But since that commitment was clear what harm could there be in tipping their hats to the fertility gods? Besides, the word was out that these strange worship services were exciting, enjoyable, and met certain basic needs. So they shrewdly chose the middle ground. After all, why not negotiate the most comprehensive insurance package possible? Their pagan neighbors had been more than friendly. Everyone knows that in the real world "you have to go along to get along."

Kingdom

The Hebrews were not yet organized as a single nation. The twelve tribes existed in a loose tribal league. After the people had settled for a few generations that quaint old arrangement seemed primitive and backward. If they were ever to take their place among the nations, if they were to secure their borders, they needed a king and a central government. The prophet, Samuel, explained that such a course meant betraying their covenant with God their only king. But, like Adam and Eve, they had the power of choice and exercised their options.

Their first king was Saul. He began well, but like so many, became the victim of his own success. The second king was Israel's greatest. Called from his humble work as a shepherd, young David was anointed king. Old King Saul, insane with jealousy and bereft of God's Spirit, chased young David about the countryside to eliminate him. But God blessed David with his

Spirit and eventually made him king. The young monarch became a military, political and religious leader *par excellence*. David would walk with God and exercise his considerable gifts as a writer of psalms to God's glory and for the benefit of his people. But when he was riding high David lusted after the beautiful Bathsheba, lay with her, tried to cover his sin, and eventually sent her husband to death in battle. God sent his prophet to call David to account; not even the king of Israel was exempt from the covenant and its commandments. As a result of his sin Bathsheba's baby died, David's home was torn apart, and his dream of building God a temple was denied him. God's plan for all his children would come about despite such selfish behavior. After this sordid chapter David's repentance and God's forgiveness made him whole. After all was said and done he was responsive to God's discipline, "a man after God's own heart." At the peak of his success David wanted to count his armies to measure his military might. God said no, that would mean placing his confidence in his own kingdom and not in God's. He did it anyway and again knew God's discipline. David learned the bad news and the good: he was not the teacher's pet, but he was God's man. He became the prototype of what Israel meant by a king. What God's people needed was another king like David, but better.

Beginning of the End

In some ways David's son was an even greater king. Solomon's kingdom was larger, he amassed greater wealth, he gained an international reputation for wisdom. But he also married foreign wives who brought with them their pagan gods. What enormously wealthy and politically astute king could deny temples for such gods when these wives applied the pressure? After all, Solomon knew they were not his main God. Ironically, at the apex of its power and influence the kingdom soon began to decline. He built a grand temple for God. On the one hand, the splendor of the edifice spoke eloquently of the glory and mystery of Israel's God. On the other hand, the temple would come to mean for many that God was nothing more than their national chaplain, that they had him enshrined in Jerusalem, and that nothing evil could befall them while they had this greatest rabbit's foot of all. Nothing could have been further from God's original plan.

After Solomon's death his kingdom was divided into two, the northern and the southern. Both kingdoms were cursed with a succession of proud and idolatrous kings. Only a very few cared about God's will. Before it was over most of God's people had lost any real consciousness of his presence in their lives. But God had not forgotten his plan. He sent prophet after prophet to remind the people of their covenant with him. They pointed back to the exodus and Sinai as indicators of who God was, who God's people were, of his hatred of idolatry and of his compassion for the poor and needy. It was no use. The people in both kingdoms became more and more impervious to God's word.

Isaiah was a prophet in the courts of the southern kingdom at Jerusalem. In a temple worship service one morning he saw God. The Sovereign of all things was high and lifted up, calling Isaiah to remind the people of their original mission. Isaiah saw a vision of all nations coming up to the house of the Lord, a homecoming for all God's children. Tragically, since God's people could not see the vision and cared nothing for his project they ignored Isaiah and were finally carried away into captivity. Isaiah saw God's love and salvation even beyond the suffering: redemption would come only through suffering. He composed songs about a suffering servant coming in God's name, one despised and afflicted, a man of sorrows and acquainted with grief; upon him would fall the chastisement of all. In short, Isaiah could hope only because God was sovereign and would certainly work his centuries old plan. Strange as it might seem to human wisdom, God revealed to Isaiah that his plan would be accomplished, not through Israel's glorious conquest and dominance as a nation, but through service and suffering.

Jeremiah, God's reluctant weeping prophet, saw and proclaimed the coming judgment. God called Jeremiah and stated his mission in international terms: "See, I have set you this day over nations and over kingdoms, to pluck up and to break down, to destroy and to overthrow, to build and to plant." Smug in the confidence that the temple was a talisman against all harm, the people ignored the warnings and persecuted Jeremiah. Through it all the prophet saw the promise that God would one day make a new covenant with his people, not one written on stone and forgotten, but one written on their hearts and lived out in their lives. Israel had completely forgotten its calling and mission and would suffer God's discipline. The warnings were to no avail. Both kingdoms fell and were carried away into captivity.

God had not forgotten his plan, his promise to Abraham, his covenant at Sinai. The captivity of his people would not be the end. God was still sovereign. He would see to it that a remnant would survive their self-inflicted wounds and return to their promised land. The remnant finally returned and rebuilt scaled-down versions of Jerusalem and the temple. Nothing happens outside of God's control.

The Old Testament story closes without the fulfillment of God's plan. God's people would have to wait. As we leave the biblical narrative we turn to history. In the second century before Christ, Palestine was for a brief period relatively free of foreign domination. Alexander the Great's kingdom was on the decline and the Romans had not yet come on stage. The Hasmonaean dynasty was founded in Palestine as a result of the Maccabean revolt against the Syrians in 168 B.C. The Hasmonaean leaders began with a strong loyalty to the Jewish people and their religious traditions and ended generations later having compromised their values to the world around them. During their reign the territory of Israel was expanded to include Samaria and Idumea. In 63 B.C. the Romans laid siege to Jerusalem and conquered the Jewish people in a scene of terrible bloodshed. Under the Romans a new family was set up to rule over Palestine: the Herods. The second of these rulers was in power as the New Testament takes up the story.

For generations God's people had looked wistfully back at David's kingdom and forward to another king who would come to revive their hope and reclaim their rightful place among the nations. Some who had remained faithful still clung to the hope that God would redeem their future, overthrow the wicked, convert sinners, restore the kingdom to the righteous and bring salvation to the world. By the time the New Testament story begins various sects had arisen each with its own answer as to how the Old Testament story would be completed. The aristocratic Sadducees who were cozy with the Romans and had much to protect were the "polish up the status quo" party. The platform of the Essenes was: "None is righteous but me and thee, and sometimes I wonder about thee." The Zealots took a more direct approach: "Praise the Lord and pass the ammunition."[2] The rabbis believed fulfillment of the Old Testament hope would come only when the Law and the traditions were understood, correctly expounded and faithfully adopted in the life of the people. Jesus of Nazareth came making quite a different claim.

Notes

[1] For the distinction see John L. McKenzie, *The Two-Edged Sword* (Garden City, New York: Doubleday/Image, 1966) pp. 83-94.

[2] For these characterizations I am indebted to Paul Watson.

Salvation For All   2

All four gospels tell us that the good tidings of Jesus Christ is a gospel for all nations. But Luke tells the story with the Old Testament story specifically in mind. When he listed the genealogy of Jesus it went back, not to Abraham, but to Adam. He reached all the way back to mankind's original problem and God's plan for bringing all his children home.

Luke's story begins in an obscure corner of the Roman Empire. A humble priest named Zechariah was in the temple at Jerusalem, going about his business. An angel of the Lord appeared, scaring him out of his wits despite the fact that the temple was God's house and one should not be surprised to hear from the Lord there. The angel told Zechariah that his wife Elizabeth would have a baby, even though she was barren and they were getting on in years. Zechariah couldn't believe it, tried to laugh it off, and was struck dumb until the baby arrived. Soon after this the angel Gabriel appeared to Mary, Elizabeth's cousin. The news was too good to be true. Mary broke out in a hymn of praise: "God has seen the low estate of his handmaiden, He has sent the rich empty away, has exalted those of low degree." Zechariah and Elizabeth had a baby boy and named him John.

This made a believer of Zechariah. He said, "God has rescued his people, as he promised long ago!"

Mary had her baby too, not in high class surroundings, there was no room for them in the inn. Nevertheless, the birth was accompanied by angels and a heavenly chorus who appeared to shepherds in the fields! Wise men from the east were notified and came bearing beautiful gifts! What a glorious event! On the eighth day they took baby Jesus to the temple for dedication. Like other poor folks they brought a pair of turtle doves for sacrifice. Old Simeon, full of the Holy Spirit, held the baby, misted up and praised God. "My life is complete, Lord, I have seen your salvation which you prepared in the presence of all peoples, a light for revelation to the Gentiles, and for glory to your people Israel!" Mary and Joseph didn't know what to think about that promise about the "Gentiles."

When Jesus was twelve he went with his parents to Passover in Jerusalem. They missed him on the way home and found him back in the temple discussing theology with the teachers of Israel. When asked for an explanation he said that he must be about his Father's business. And he wasn't referring to Joseph. Jesus had a sense of mission. He already knew the Father had something important for him to do.

Years passed and Jesus' cousin, John, came out of the desert dressed in camel's hair, telling the truth. It was such a novelty people came from everywhere. Luke says he was the one spoken of by Isaiah: "The voice of one crying in the wilderness: Prepare the way of the Lord...and all flesh shall see the salvation of God." Jesus came, stood in line like everyone else, and was baptized by John. When he came up from the water praying he heard a voice from heaven saying, "You are my beloved son in whom I am well pleased."

Jesus was led from baptism into the desert of temptation where Satan showed him short cuts to glory. "Become a bread king, feed them and they will follow you anywhere. But take care of your own needs first, you must be very hungry." "Dazzle them into the kingdom, jump off the pinnacle of the temple. Life is boring, people love to be entertained." "Just cooperate, stay with me and I can give you the world!" Jesus rejected each overture in turn. He would take no short cuts: his mission would be accomplished the hard way. Satan departed, for a time.

Jesus began his ministry in Galilee, calling disciples to follow him. He preached in his home synagogue at Nazareth, showing them from their own Bibles who he was, sharing his prospectus. He said he came to "preach good news to the poor" and that he would go beyond the borders of Israel. Had not Elijah gone to the widow of Zarephath and had not Naaman the Syrian found healing from Elisha? At this proposal his homefolk tried to throw him off a cliff.

In the synagogue at Capernaum he healed a man possessed of a demon and his fame began to spread. One day friends of a paralytic took the roof off a house to get him past the crowd to Jesus. Jesus honored their faith, told the paralytic his sins were forgiven and to get up and walk. Even though the man was healed the Pharisees were on their ear. "Who can forgive sins?" they wanted to know. It was a good question. Jesus said the Son of man had authority to forgive and heal. From the first Jesus never recoiled from heavy conflict with the religious leaders. This incident was not a good omen.

After calling Levi from the toll booth, he went home with him for dinner. No self-respecting rabbi would be seen with such a crowd. The house was filled with tax collectors, shyster lawyers, quack doctors and shifty-eyed used car salesmen. The Pharisees protested: "Don't you believe in the holiness of God? These people are not observant! How can you eat with them!" Jesus told them he hadn't come to heal the robust, but the sick. He wasn't a very good politician. He sometimes made remarks about old coats and new patches, old wineskins and new wine. Jesus even said he had authority over the Sabbath! Mixing with all kinds of people was vital for his plan.

The crowds loved him. He spoke with authority, no quotes or footnotes. He held out hope for the down-and-outs and a strong word of warning for the selfish comfortable. Jesus said anyone who followed him would have to love his enemy, give his neighbor the shirt off his back and learn to turn the other cheek. His followers would treat others as they would be treated. Most alarming of all was Jesus' rationale: "For God is kind to the ungrateful and the wicked."

Even though he was not "in the club," a Roman centurion dared approach Jesus because his servant was gravely ill. The Gentile said Jesus didn't need to make a house call, he could just say the word and heal from a distance. Jesus healed the servant and sent the Jewish scandal-mongers running by saying, "I haven't seen faith like this in Israel!"

Jesus' cousin, John, offended the wrong people and ended up in prison. Cut from the same cloth as thundering Amos of old, John had no use for a low-profile Messiah. He sent messengers asking Jesus if he was the one. "Go and tell John what you have seen and heard," Jesus said, "the blind receive their sight, the lame walk, lepers are cleansed, and the deaf hear, the dead are raised up, the poor have good news preached to them." Jesus then added: "Blessed is he who takes no offense at me."

The truth was almost everyone either took offense or found it a struggle to understand him. One day he was eating at the house of Simon the Pharisee. (He always worked both sides of the tracks. God loves his respectable children also.) A woman of tarnished reputation came in and made an outrageous display by anointing Jesus' feet. Simon was embarrassed. How could Jesus let this street woman touch him? "She loved much because she's been forgiven much," Jesus explained. Simon didn't get it.

Most people didn't get it. So Jesus told a parable about a sower and different kinds of soil. Only one of the several kinds of earth bore fruit. It wasn't just the Jews who rejected Jesus. He crossed the sea of Galilee into Gentile territory. A madman came running up, naked, raving, alarming the whole crowd. Jesus exorcised the demon. When the authorities arrived the man was sitting there clothed and in his right mind. They asked Jesus to leave. The whole town preferred the *status quo*. Who could control a teacher who did things like that?

Back in Jewish territory, he asked the twelve about public opinion. "Who do they say I am?" Various opinions were reported. Then Peter said it right out: "You are God's Christ." Jesus immediately told them to keep it to themselves, they didn't have the full story yet. Then he said if anyone wanted to follow him he must take up his cross daily and follow! How depressing! They had all seen crucifixions. Jesus obviously had a lot to learn about running for office!

More to the disciples' liking was the transfiguration experience. While Jesus prayed a splendid light shone from him. Moses and Elijah appeared. Peter said, "Lord, this is as good as it gets! Let's camp out here!" But a voice from above said, "This is my beloved Son, listen to him!" The transfiguration was a splendid event, for just a moment it was revealed exactly who this one was who had come to fulfill God's plan! But his splendor passed as quickly as it had come and his identity was again hidden for the time being.

Jesus took them back down the mountain to serve and teach. He told them not to tell what had happened, they didn't have the whole story. He had come to serve the common people, to bind up the wounded, and to bring all God's children back home.

Jesus knew he had to go to Jerusalem. That's where his Father's business would be transacted. He kept saying "the Son of man must go to Jerusalem." On the way he endured a whole series of misunderstandings. James and John, rejected when they went into a Samaritan village for groceries, asked Jesus if they could call down fire on the town. After all, they were only Samaritans! Jesus rebuked them for their self-centered ignorance. A man came up anxious to follow Jesus. "Foxes have holes, birds have nests...but the Son of man is a wanderer among men," Jesus answered. Another wanted to bury his father but Jesus said there wasn't time. The disciples must have winced at that. They didn't understand the Father's plan or how important it was to Jesus. Another man wanted to have a going-away party first. Jesus told him he could not plow while walking backwards.

One of the hardest things to understand was Jesus' attitude toward some of the really good people. One law-abiding Jew came, not so much to ask about eternal life as to claim its achievement. Jesus told a scandalous story of a Samaritan who didn't keep the law, almost never went to church, but did stop to help a man dying beside the road. Unlike the priest and the Levite who were late getting to church, no doubt to teach a Sunday school lesson on loving one's neighbor. If Jesus were telling the story in Jerusalem today he would probably make the hero a homeless Palestinian. The effect would be about the same.

The scribes and Pharisees had a stomach full of him by this time. Some of them came accusing Jesus of casting out demons by the power of Beelzebub. "That's nonsense," Jesus countered. "But if I am expelling demons the Kingdom of God has come and you haven't noticed. A strong man can keep his goods safe until a stronger man breaks into the house." Satan had not finished with Jesus when he left the desert of temptation.

Jesus shocked everyone with his parable of the Rich Fool. They all assumed that the wealthy were wealthy because they were good; that the cars, boats, and beach houses were rewards of hard work and clean living. Jesus told of a man who had everything and forgot that the real owner might ask for an accounting at any time. God called the successful man who had no time for him a "fool." Equally as disturbing was Jesus' embracing attitude toward all kinds of people. He even predicted that the great homecoming banquet in heaven would include men coming from the East and West to join Abraham, Isaac, Jacob and the prophets!

Some friendly Pharisees came to warn Jesus about danger from another side. "Better be careful. Herod is after you! Remember what he did to John." "No, the time is not right," Jesus said, "and it would never do for a prophet to die outside Jerusalem." Matters were obviously getting out of hand. Not only Herod, the religious leaders also had plans for Jesus. He told an outrageous story about a dinner host who invited the best people in town. Since they wouldn't give him the time of day he filled his feast with bag ladies, the homeless, vagrants. The "best people" were locked out.

None of this was lost on the powerful. Now they went on the offensive, asking again why Jesus ate with all kinds of riffraff and sinners. He could have answered: "Because I hate to eat alone." Instead, Jesus told three parables about a lost coin, a lost sheep, and a lost boy. None of the stories made any real sense. The woman ransacked her house to find one coin and then spent it and several more throwing a celebration! A shepherd left a whole flock of sheep to find just one! A father gave a party, not for his good boy who stayed ~~and~~ home and kept his nose clean, but for the rebel who had wasted his inheritance and ruined the family name! The older brother didn't understand. Who could blame him? "God's love is like that," Jesus was saying, "Spendthrift! Extravagant! You'll never understand it completely. The father really had two prodigal sons. He loved them both and wanted them both at the dinner table. I know you don't get it. But be careful, you can miss the party standing outside pouting."

Jesus befriended the worst people in town and offended the best. To the Pharisees who loved money he told the parable of the rich man and Lazarus. In the world to come their positions would be reversed because the rich man had lived exquisitely while Lazarus was starving at his gate. Like some collect stray dogs and cats, Jesus cared about Gentiles, women, even obvious sinners! Two men went up to the temple to pray, according to Jesus. One reported to God his achievements much as a junior lawyer would answer to a senior partner. The other wasn't even sure he belonged there and begged God's forgiveness. But he went home right with God and the good man didn't. Every time Jesus told such parables the guardians of the faith took offense. They were proud, not slow.

Jesus' gloomy forecasts about his future were getting worse and worse. He had some need to fulfill Israel's darkest prophesies. "...everything that is written of the Son of man by the prophets will be accomplished," he said. "For he will be delivered to the Gentiles, and will be mocked and shamefully treated and spat upon; they will scourge him and kill him, and on the third day he will rise again." The disciples didn't get it, didn't want to get it. They passed a blind man who cried out to see. Because that was what he wanted most Jesus gave him sight. The twelve didn't get the point.

Finally in Jerusalem, Jesus went to the temple, not, as the disciples hoped, to be crowned Messiah, but to upset everything. "This was to be a house of prayer for all nations! You have made it into a den of thieves!" Jesus shouted. Then he got physical and drove the moneychangers out. When the authorities challenged his authority Jesus told a fully loaded parable about a vineyard owner who sent servant after servant for an accounting from the tenants. Each servant was rejected and abused. Finally, he sent his son and they killed him. What would the owner do to them? The religious leaders felt the sting. They knew they had to eliminate Jesus. But quietly, he did have a following.

Jesus' disciples came to the Passover full of boyish anticipation. It had always been a warm family time of singing, laughter and celebration. Jesus ruined the mood by saying that one of them would betray him. They began debating who was the greatest in the kingdom. Jesus told them his kingdom wasn't like that. The greatest might not be the chairman of the board but the janitor.

Afterwards, they went to the Mount of Olives. Appropriate enough was this ancient site where olives were crushed into oil. He went to pray. Jesus didn't want to drink the cup of God's wrath on man's rebellion, ingratitude, and pride. He dreaded taking on himself the godforsakenness due sinners. For hours he struggled. Sweat fell like great drops of blood. The Father's plan to make a way home for his children was in the balance. Could this be the only way to preserve the holiness of God and the freedom of man? God had once spared Abraham's son, would he now not spare his own? "No" was the Father's answer. There would be no ram in the thicket this time. Jesus, himself, was the substitute for mankind. This was the crucial moment in God's whole plan. Again and again the man Jesus prayed, "Let this cup pass from me." He returned to his disciples and found them asleep. Agonizing again in prayer he asked if there was no other way. The Father said no. God's own son could not have his way. The ordeal was necessary if the Father's plan was to be fulfilled and a way made for his children to come home. Finally, in obedience to the Father and in love for all God's wayward children, Jesus yielded: "Not my will but thine be done."

Soon they heard the cries of a mob on the path below. In the torchlight one could see the glint of swords. Some carried sticks, other clubs. Judas was out front. He came up and gave Jesus a sugary kiss. "Is that the way you do it, Judas?" asked Jesus. "You betray the Son of man with a kiss?" The other disciples, still half asleep and full of self-righteous indignation, drew their swords. One tried to decapitate the servant of the high priest. "No more of that," Jesus said, "that's not what my kingdom is about." He then asked the armed mob, "Do I really threaten you this much? I have taught every day in the temple and you never laid a finger on me. Why are you so afraid of me?" Then, in a sentence, Jesus defined the whole situation. "But this is your hour, and the power of darkness." The serpent had returned in full force. The decisive battle between heaven and hell was at hand.

They seized Jesus and took him away. Peter followed at a distance. Some things look better from a distance. Peter, the "rock," began crumbling when a quiet maid asked about his connection with Jesus. Meanwhile, Jesus was inside facing the music. The Chief Priest, scribes and elders wanted to know if Jesus claimed to be the Christ. "If I tell you will you believe me? Soon now the Son of man will be seated at the right hand of Power." This was what they wanted and they took him to Pilate.

Pilate looked at Jesus and could see no threat to Caesar. He passed the political hot potato to Herod. He didn't want it, tossed it back. Pilate told the Jewish leaders he found nothing in Jesus worthy of death. Outside the chanting grew louder, more ominous. "Crucify him! Crucify him! Crucify him!" Law and order was now at stake. Pilate's record back in Rome wasn't that good and he needed to protect his army pension. He offered to scourge Jesus. That wasn't enough. They wanted his blood. So Pilate caved in. A cooperative effort of all God's children, Jews and Gentiles, sent Jesus to Golgotha.

Jesus was crucified. Between two thieves. "Father, forgive them, they know not what they do!" Jesus prayed. This kind of ignorance is not fixed by a night course at the university. They didn't want to know who he was and what he was about. Just as Adam and Eve didn't want to hear about the forbidden fruit. This kind of ignorance calls for repentance.

One of the thieves crucified with Jesus saw the absurdity: no one ever looked less like a king. The other asked Jesus to remember him in his kingdom. Jesus died. The veil in the temple split in two. That veil which Israel believed shut God in. That veil which did, in fact, shut Gentiles, women and sinners out. Only a few women among Jesus' followers stayed at the cross till the end. Jesus had fulfilled his Father's plan.

Early Sunday morning some of the women went to anoint Jesus' body. The news was too good to be true! When they found an empty tomb and were told Jesus was alive they ran to tell the disciples. But who can believe hysterical women? Later two men on the road to Emmaus were talking Camelot. A stranger joined them and before long he was opening their eyes to the Scriptures and all that had happened. Their minds were overloaded, their hearts were warmed by what he said. At supper he took bread, blessed, broke and gave it to them. Their eyes were opened and they knew him. Suddenly he was gone. Later he appeared to the disciples. Even while they were still reeling with the good news, Jesus commissioned them for their mission. They had the whole story now. He commanded them to wait in Jerusalem for the Spirit's anointing and then go out preaching to "all the nations" repentance and forgiveness of sins in their crucified and risen Lord.

Unto All the World 3

The disciples had thought Jesus' death was the end. God knew it was a part of the plan and that a new and exciting chapter in his story of salvation was about to be written. Luke tells the story in his second volume, Acts. Jesus spoke with the eleven before he ascended to the Father. Because they could imagine nothing greater, they wanted to know if he would restore David's kingdom. Jesus told them God would move on his own schedule, they should go to Jerusalem to wait and pray. They would be able to do nothing until the Spirit came upon them. Jesus would continue with his disciples by sending his Spirit to instruct believers about his cross and resurrection, about their discipleship, and to convict sinners and bring them home to God. In addition he gave them an overview of the program they would follow. They would be his witnesses in Jerusalem, Judea, Samaria and to the ends of the earth. The veil of the temple had been split. Jesus' death and resurrection had made reconciliation available for all peoples. God was now about to show the way back home to all his children.

As they waited and prayed God sent his Spirit on Pentecost. As on the first creation morning, God once again touched the earth with his Spirit to create life. His timing was perfect, Jews were present from all over the empire. When God sent his Spirit on the huddled disciples the whole city heard the commotion and ran to check it out. Mid-morning, Peter and the others began telling the story of salvation. Travelers heard it in their various tongues. Someone tried to brush it off. "It's no big deal. They've been into the Manischewitz already."

Peter explained they were not full of wine, full of themselves, but full of the Holy Spirit. It was all foretold by the prophet, Joel. The scope of what was happening was long ago indicated when the prophet said that "whoever calls on the name of the Lord will be saved." This was the fulfillment of God's age-old plan. Peter entered his main message by explaining how and why Jesus died. The cross was not just a tragic miscarriage of justice, an idealistic reformer caught in the wheels of the establishment machine. Nor was Jesus a martyr who offered himself in the hope that someone might see the cause and pick up the flag. In a single verse Peter's explanation of Golgotha is summarized.

> ...this Jesus, delivered up according to the definite plan and foreknowledge of God, you crucified and killed by the hands of lawless men.

It's hard to believe that God can work through the evil men do. Here Peter boldly asserted that the most dastardly murder ever committed fulfilled God's plan. Mysterious as it is, what happened on Golgotha was God's idea. The most important truth of New Testament teaching on the atonement comes into focus: it was God's plan, God's initiative, for God's purposes. Notice also that Peter said all God's children were represented in the Jews and Gentiles at Golgotha. The irony is strong: he saved all when all put him on the cross. Peter went on to say that God had raised Jesus up. It was not possible that death should hold Jesus. God was in control. Despite human impressions, despite

Jesus' own fears and dread, God's victory was never in doubt. Just as Jesus had repeatedly said "I must go to Jerusalem," God's victory over Satan, sin and death was a "must" for his plan. Even as great as King David had been, God did not raise him up. The resurrection was God's "yes" to Jesus' work, his stamp of approval on the way he opened the way for all God's children to come home. Even more, it was God's promise of life to all who would believe and respond to the story. Peter concluded with the keynote of the day, the keynote of the whole mission to the Jews: "God had made him both Lord and Christ, this Jesus whom you crucified."

The Spirit-filled message set off a chain reaction of guilt-repentance-forgiveness-new life in the listeners' hearts. When they cried out for instructions Peter told them how to receive the gift of Golgotha. He also said something about you and me he could not possibly have understood fully at the time.

> Repent, and be baptized every one of you in the name of Jesus Christ for the forgiveness of your sins; and you shall receive the gift of the Holy Spirit. For the promise is to you and to your children and to all that are afar off, every one whom the Lord our God calls to him.

Three thousand Jews from all over the world repented, were baptized into Jesus' name and received the Holy Spirit! The church was born. The community of faith continued in the apostles' teaching of the crucified, in fellowship and in observing the Lord's Supper together. Proclamation, baptism and the Lord's supper were the vital means by which faith could appropriate the gift of Golgotha. In fact, without the cross and resurrection there would have been no message and the two ordinances would have had no meaning. Because of the cross they declared that salvation is not a human achievement but the free gift of God. The cross described in the apostles' teaching, in baptism and communion created the fellowship. It was not the church which created the message, the core gospel created the church.

Just here we must pause to see the core gospel. Many wonderful things happened on Pentecost. The disciples were devoted to prayer. The Spirit descended. The church was born when three thousand were baptized. The fellowship was begun in bold witness, continued vibrant in prayer, remained constant in worship, shared their property for the good of all, all of which was informed by the apostles' teaching and preaching. It was wonderful to belong! But none of these features was the core gospel. In other words, Peter did not preach salvation by heritage, by prayer, by an experience of the Spirit, by baptism and membership in the church. Nor did he preach the Pentecost event itself. All of that was the necessary housing of God's power to save. Peter preached Christ crucified and raised by the plan and power of God for the salvation of all mankind. That was the core gospel. That was the nucleus of the gospel which changed the world.

No wonder they were filled with joy and love, willing to share all things in Jesus' name! While the initial excitement subsided after a while, they were never the same. They were not just Jews who accepted Jesus as Messiah, continuing on as before. Because the core gospel had exploded in their hearts they would forever see all of life differently.

What happened in the next few weeks and months was truly amazing! In the very city where Jesus was crucified only weeks before, his people witnessed, worshipped, shared, and grew in numbers and commitment to their Lord. The fledgling church was attacked. Peter and John went up to the temple to pray, healed a lame man, and preached the gospel. It was God's plan, they said, since the time of Abraham, Isaac, and Jacob that he would deliver up his servant Jesus for the sins of all. "The one you killed God raised up. You had no idea what you were doing. But God raised the Prince of Life in victory over the grave as the prophets had said." There it was again, the core gospel of the death, burial, and resurrection of Jesus. Jesus was called the "servant" of God. Who would not remember Isaiah's words: "he was wounded for our transgressions, bruised for our iniquities; upon him was the chastisement that made us whole..."?

The next day Peter and John were called on the carpet to face the same council that put Jesus to death. They boldly told the same story: "Whom you crucified, God raised up!" The authorities were amazed at these country boys standing there in their overalls and flannel shirts. They reminded them of Jesus in their boldness. Their confidence was not in themselves. In fact, they were plenty shaky in their own strength. The whole church went into prayer, quoting the psalms about rulers arrayed against God and his anointed and from Isaiah about the suffering servant who bore the sins of many. The Old Testament story defined Jesus' life and death and gave the disciples meaning in their suffering.

The leaders once again went to the temple to preach Jesus. Great crowds came to hear and many were baptized. The authorities threw the apostles in jail, an angel got them out, told them to go preach again in the temple. They continued with the same theme: "The one whom you crucified by hanging him on a tree God raised up." The new twist about the "tree" reminded every faithful Jew of that passage in Deuteronomy which said anyone who suffered capital punishment by hanging was cursed of God. The cross was a scandal. They said it right out loud. But God had raised Jesus up.

The authorities were not sure what to do; this new movement was growing in popularity every day. One of the table servants named Stephen went down to the synagogue, performed miracles and preached Christ. He was accused of blasphemy against Moses and was brought to trial. Before the whole town he told the Old Testament story of God's unfolding plan to redeem all peoples, emphasizing the stubborn and proud opposition of God's people along the way which had reached new heights in Israel's current idolatry of the temple. Stephen must have failed his Dale Carnegie course in public speaking if his conclusion is any sample:

> You stiff-necked people, uncircumcised in heart and ears, you always resist the Holy Spirit. As your fathers did, so do you. Which of the prophets did not your fathers persecute? And they killed those who announced beforehand the coming of the Righteous One, whom you have now betrayed and murdered, you who received the law as delivered by angels and did not keep it.

They stoned him to death for preaching Christ crucified. Young Saul of Tarsus heard the blasphemies as he held the garments of those "doing God's will." The death, burial, and resurrection of Jesus were not only that core gospel which the Spirit used to convert sinners and form the church, they were also the main defense of those early heroes of the faith as they stood up to fierce opposition.

Following Stephen's death savage persecution broke upon the church and they went everywhere telling the story. Interesting, isn't it, how God's ancient plan was being carried out? Through pain and suffering the faith burst the bounds of narrow Jewish nationalism and through the wall of racial prejudice. Jesus died and was raised to be the universal Lord of all.

The Spirit called another of those table servants, Philip, to a lonely road running from Jerusalem down to Gaza. He was nudged to join a lonely figure riding along in his chariot reading from Isaiah 53. The Ethiopian eunuch was a convert to Judaism, had made a pilgrimage to the holy city, and was on his way home. "Convert" inasmuch as any eunuch could be. According to Old Testament regulations a eunuch was never really allowed in the congregation of God's people. But he loved Israel's God and was as much a part of the activities as the law allowed. It was no trick at all for Philip to move from Isaiah's picture of the suffering servant to the story of Jesus. The eunuch was baptized into Jesus and for the first time was fully accepted as a member of God's people. God's plan to bring all his children home was working. The cross calls all kinds of people together.

As we said, Peter really had no idea of the far-reaching implications of his noble words on Pentecost. He was at Joppa, napping on a housetop patio when he had a vision of a sheet let down with all kinds of animals, "clean" and "unclean." "Rise, Peter, kill and eat," the Lord said. Peter would take some convincing. Three times it happened. "No, Lord..." (An interesting combination of words.) "No, Lord, you see I am kosher and have never eaten anything unclean in all my life."

But Peter wasn't in charge, God was. Before he knew it he was in the house of Cornelius, a Roman centurion facing a whole houseful of Gentiles waiting to hear what he had to say. He really didn't want to be there and made that clear. His welcome had been more than cordial. Cornelius and the others fell down at Peter's feet to worship him. Peter said, "Please get up, I am just a man like yourself." (All of us preachers would have done the same. It might have taken an hour or two but we would have gotten around to it.) Peter began with what for him was big news. He looked around the room and said, "Truly I perceive that God shows no partiality, but in every nation any one who fears him and does what is right is acceptable to him." At Pentecost he had proclaimed that the gospel was for all, now he was seeing it worked out in life. He told the story of Jesus, concluding with the same core gospel we have heard from the first:

> They put him to death by hanging him on a tree; but God raised him on the third day and made him manifest; not to all the people but to us who were chosen by God as witnesses, who ate and drank with him after he rose from the dead...To him all the prophets bear witness that every one who believes in him receives forgiveness of sins through his name.

The Spirit fell on the Gentiles as it had on the Jews at Pentecost and they were baptized into the name of Jesus. The same gospel of Christ crucified had been preached. Despite Peter's hangups, God was working his plan. The death, burial, and resurrection formed the heart of the message.

Meanwhile, God had tapped young Saul of Tarsus for a special mission to the Gentiles. On the Damascus road Jesus appeared to Saul. The carpenter lay preacher from Nazareth crucified for blasphemy was, after all, God's Messiah! This appearance of the risen and enthroned Lord exploded in Saul's heart, taking all his plans with it. For three years he would sort through all he had believed, adjusting everything to the new realization that God had come in the plain man from the hill country, crucified and risen.

God called Saul, now Paul, to go with Barnabas on a preaching mission. No one, not even Paul who was born in Tarsus of Cilicia, had ever dreamed that God would extend his kingdom to the whole Gentile world. God's purpose in calling Abraham had slipped entirely from Israel's memory. Everywhere Paul went he first entered the synagogue to tell God's chosen people of their messiah. Often he was thrown out on his ear. Then he always went to the marketplace, town square or public hall where he could tell the story to the Gentiles.

As different as Paul and Peter were in many ways their gospels at the center were precisely the same. At Antioch of Pisidia Paul preached in the synagogue. He told his brethren that the God of their fathers had worked his plan all the way down through John the Baptist to Jesus who fulfilled all the Old Testament prophecies. Jesus was hated, "hanged on a tree," and God raised him from the dead. They asked him back the next Sabbath to tell them more. But a large crowd assembled the next week. Defenders of the faith were present with their notebooks and tape recorders. Paul went on to explain that God's mission in the crucified messiah was "light to the Gentiles and salvation to the uttermost part of the earth." The Gentiles standing at the back of the room loved the message. The Jews hated it and ran Paul and Barnabas out of town. The events were repeated again and again wherever Paul went. His message was always the same: Jesus of Nazareth, God's Messiah, crucified and raised to bring salvation to all peoples.

It wasn't just the unconverted Jews who had trouble with this new, expansive mission. Many Jewish Christians objected. The church did not really have the matter settled until the Jerusalem conference met and confirmed that God was, indeed, acting among the Gentiles. The separation of God's people over the centuries had not been just for purposes of purity and preservation of the race. God intended his chosen to share with the world his gospel of forgiveness and new life in Christ.

Not that the conference made the slightest difference in the synagogues where Paul went to preach. In Thessalonica he preached, proving by the scriptures that it was becoming of the Messiah to suffer, that God raised him from the dead. God had won victory in Jesus! He went on about it for three Sabbaths until a mob was stirred up. They ran Paul and his companions out of town and attacked the leader of the synagogue.

Over at Athens Paul preached the same message to a completely different crowd. Those assembled met regularly to hear the latest philosophical theories. Paul acknowledged their interest in ultimate things, told them of the Creator God who needed no man-made houses, and went on to preach repentance in the one God had appointed and approved by raising him from the dead. The "what's happening now?" crowd laughed him out of court. A few believed.

Everywhere Paul went he established churches preaching the same gospel of Jesus crucified and raised. Along the way, in and out of scrapes, he wrote letters to the churches he had established. In those letters he applied the "word of the cross," exploring the implications of the core gospel for daily church problems.

Finally he ended up once more at Jerusalem. When his Jewish opposition learned that he was in town they rushed him and would have killed him except that the Roman cohort came to the rescue. Addressing the mob in Hebrew Paul told his own story. They listened until he mentioned his mission to the Gentiles and then they tried again to kill him.

As his Lord before him, Paul was shuffled from one magistrate to another. Even to the Roman Procurator, Festus, Paul made the core gospel clear. Briefing King Agrippa on Paul's case, Festus said the accusers "had certain points of dispute with him about their own superstition and about one Jesus, who was dead, but whom Paul asserted to be alive." Paul addressed the Jewish king, summarizing his case:

> To this day I have had the help that comes from God, and so I stand here testifying both to small and great, saying nothing but what the prophets and Moses said would come to pass: that the Christ must suffer, and that, by being the first to rise from the dead, he would proclaim light both to the people and to the Gentiles.

Legal recourse in Palestine became less and less an option. So Paul appealed to Caesar. And after a dangerous and eventful trip to Rome, Paul was kept in prison for some time where he continued telling the story even to the guards who watched him. Jewish leaders responded to Paul's invitation to come hear him out. He recounted the story of Israel that they all knew, laboring for hours "trying to convince them about Jesus both from the law of Moses and the prophets." A few believed, most did not. He lived there two whole years, visitors coming and going, Paul telling the story of the Lord Jesus Christ quite openly and unhindered.

Luke's two-volume story ends in an open-ended way. The central drama of God's age-old plan had begun with a simple priest in the temple at Jerusalem. At the end of Luke's story, we see a broken, remade Pharisee Christian proclaiming Christ crucified in the shadow of Caesar's palace! God's Spirit had moved with enormous power through the core gospel of Christ crucified and raised. It was a scandal to both Jew and Gentile, and, paradoxically it was the salvation of both. The word was out, the gospel is for all. God wants all his children back home and he has opened the way. The veil of the temple at Jerusalem was forever torn from top to bottom when both Jew and Gentile crucified Jesus and he said, "Father, forgive them. They know not what they do."

Instruction for the Churches

4

The churches Luke mentioned in Acts all had their own stories. We do not have the stories but we do have correspondence addressed to these churches while they were coping with life as communities of faith. We have seen how the death, burial, and resurrection of Jesus formed the core gospel which exploded in the hearts of sinners turning them into believers, how churches were established as a result, and how the first generation Christians used that same core gospel to explain and defend themselves against detractors from without. We now ask how the core gospel was used to instruct, inspire and correct these first Christian fellowships.

We begin with Paul's correspondence. One might ask where in his writings did Paul ever describe the crucifixion. A moment's thought will reveal that he never described the happenings of Golgotha. But in all his letters he spoke the "word of the cross." The Greek word, *logos,* has a double meaning. It means "message" or that which is communicated. It also means "logic," or the rationale of the communication. Paul had a message of the cross for the churches because he had a rationale or theology of the cross. He had come more and more to understand the implications of the death, burial, and resurrection for Christian living. In his classic study of the atonement, *The Death Of Christ,* James Denney emphasized how important it is for every proclaimer to develop such a theology of the cross, a "word of the cross." He rejected the sentiment which says: "Don't talk to me about theology, all I want are the facts. Just give the plain truth without any interpretation." According to Denney, the "word of the cross" is always theoretical. He did not mean that it is academic, abstract, or irrelevant, but that some understanding of the cross is necessary for faithful gospel preaching.

> The simplest preacher, and the most effective, is always the most absolutely theoretical. It is a theory, a tremendous theory, that Christ's death is a death for sin. But unless a preacher can put some interpretation on the death, unless he can find a meaning in it which is full of appeal, why should he speak of it at all? Is it the want of a theory that deprives it of its place in preaching?[1]

There was no want of a theory of the cross in Paul's preaching and writing. What follows are twenty-five samples of Paul's application of his "word of the cross" to everyday life situations in the churches and with individual Christians. Notice the richness of his many-sided understanding of the cross as he fed and led the churches.

1. "Who is going to run this church, the charter members or the newcomers?"

"All have sinned,...they are justified by his grace...in Christ Jesus, who God put forward as an expiation (propitiation) by his blood..." (Rom. 3).

2. "We have a proud heritage! We come from folks who took their religion seriously, obeyed God's commands and found favor in his sight because they worked hard at their faith. There is just no other way to get right with God!"

> "Therefore, since we are justified by faith, we have peace with God through our Lord Jesus Christ...while we were yet helpless, at the right time Christ died for the ungodly..." (Rom. 5).

3. "Enough of this negative stuff about 'sin!' We are saved by grace, we can forget all that guilt stuff. We are only human. God forgives, that's his job."

> "By no means! How can we who died to sin still live in it? Do you not know that all of us who have been baptized into Christ Jesus were baptized into his death? We were buried therefore with him by baptism into death, so that as Christ was raised from the dead by the glory of the Father, we too might walk in newness of life." (Rom. 6).

4. "I listen to the preacher spell out God's expectations of me and know that I am a miserable failure. Who can quarrel with the 'Thou shalts' and 'Thou shalt nots' of God's Word? If you take them seriously and really try to live up to them, you see very quickly that you don't have a chance to please God."

> "...you have died to the law through the body of Christ, so that you may belong to another, to him who has been raised from the dead in order that we may bear fruit for God...if Christ is in you, although your bodies are dead because of sin, your spirits are alive because of righteousness. (Rom. 8).

5. "How can I get along with my brother and his stupid ideas? God and I can't get him to see it our way!" "Who are you to pass judgment on the servant of another?...If we live, we live to the Lord, and if we die, we die to the Lord;...for to this end Christ

died and lived again, that he might be Lord both of the dead and of the living." (Rom. 14). Just as your personal salvation never depended on your own perfection, fellowship in Christ never depends on your straightening out your brother so that he agrees with you on every point.

6. "I really hate it when the preacher is out of town! Why do they let Brother Sidewalk preach? That man just opens his mouth and I want to scream!"

> "Is Christ divided? Was Paul crucified for you?" (I Cor. 1). The trouble all along has been that you have never seen anyone at church above and behind the preacher. Your worship is simply a human transaction.

7. "That 'Old Time Religion' 'Old Rugged Cross' faith may have been good enough for mom and dad. But they sent me off to college and now I live in the tough, sophisticated, real world. We don't study how to be crucified, we study how to survive and win!"

> "For the word of the cross is folly to those who are perishing...but we preach Christ crucified..." (I Cor. 1).

8. "My body and my life are my business. What's it to you if I have this affair? Get off my case. You will never understand why I do this. It's my body and my life!"

> "You are not your own; you were bought with a price. So glorify God in your body." It was Jesus' body and his life, too. He redeemed you, bought you back from slavery to sin. He has a right to claim your body for God's kingdom. (I Cor. 6).

9. "So you're saying my needs don't matter? What happened to 'free in Christ?' Why should I be hung up on what someone else

thinks? We are all adults here. Each person must take care of himself or herself."

> Your needs do matter. To meet your needs Christ died. He met your needs in a way you never could never have done by your own strength and cleverness. What makes your brother so special is that he is also one "for whom Christ died." (I Cor.8).

10. "So what's wrong with a 'social club' church? Where would you find a finer group for a club? You can't expect our group to relate to those other groups! We have nothing in common. No church this size has fellowship as a whole, you have to be part of a smaller group to belong. So why should the educated not stick together, the wealthy, the leaders in the community?"

> "For I received from the Lord...that the Lord Jesus on the night when he was betrayed took bread,...For any one who eats and drinks without discerning the body eats and drinks judgment upon himself." (I Cor. 11).

11. "Whether Jesus was actually raised is not the point. The truth is: 'hope springs eternal in the human breast' and 'truth crushed to earth will rise again.' The Christian hope revived, the early disciples believed that he lived on — that's what matters. The point is that one must have faith. His spirit lives on in us until we die. No one knows what is after the grave."

> "For I delivered to you as of first importance what I also received, that Christ died for our sins...,that he was buried, that he was raised...in fact Christ has been raised from the dead,...But thanks be to God, who gives us the victory through our Lord Jesus Christ." (I Cor. 15).

12. "You are about as exciting as an old shoe! Don't you know that this is the television age? If you can't hold people's attention they won't be back! Like it or not, they have to get excited to get involved. Other churches are growing because they lift people off the pew with dynamic worship services. We could have just as big a building as they have, have just as many members, just as big a budget. Why shouldn't we get our share of people coming our way?"

> "..if we are beside ourselves, it is for God; if we are in our right mind it is for you. For the love of Christ controls us, because we are convinced that one has died for all; therefore all have died. And he died for all, that those who live might live no longer for themselves but for him who for their sake died and was raised." (II Cor. 5).

13. "We went wrong when we got off into that 'grace' business! The truth is people have to have laws, rules, regulations! People cannot handle freedom. They will abuse it every time. All the talk to the contrary notwithstanding, we like to be told what to do."

> "Grace to you and peace from God the Father of our Lord Jesus Christ, who gave himself for our sins...I am astonished that you are so quickly deserting him who called you to the gospel of Christ...." (Gal. 1).

14. How can you accept just anyone into the church? Next thing you know we'll have the whole brotherhood mark us as odd, strange, way out, liberal! Don't you care what the others think?"

> "But if I build up again those things which I tore down, then I prove myself a transgressor...I have been crucified with Christ, it is no longer I who live, but Christ who lives in me; and the life I now live in the flesh I live by faith in the Son of God, who loved me and gave himself for me. I do not nullify the grace of God; for if justification were through the law, then Christ died to no purpose." (Gal. 2).

15. "We just begin making some progress and another 'issue' or 'cause' or complaint comes up. We fight from crisis to crisis. How can we ever get a great, consuming, overall mission?"

"Blessed be the God and Father of our Lord Jesus Christ,...in him we have redemption through his blood,...for he has made known to us...the mystery of his will...which he set forth in Christ as a plan for the fullness of time, to unite all things in him, things in heaven and things on earth." (Eph. 1).

16. "I guess it's time to start another church. We are so different! Besides that, I hear that only 'homogeneous churches grow'."

"You (Gentiles) were dead through the trespasses of sins,... we (Jews) were by nature children of wrath ...but God...made us alive together in Christ...for he is our peace who has made us both one and has broken down the dividing wall of hostility...and might reconcile us to God in one body through the cross, thereby bringing hostility to an end..." (Eph. 2)

17. "We know that we are supposed to serve one another. We've heard the story of Jesus' washing the disciples' feet. But how, in real life, dowe bring it off? Take, for example, this new thing about the roles of husband and wife in the family."

"Be subject to one another out of reverence for Christ. Wives, be subject to your husbands, as to the Lord...husbands, love your wives, as Christ loved the church and gave himself up for her,..." (Eph. 5).

18. "We have a nearly perfect church here. But there is that little thing between two ladies in the Ladies' Bible Class. People are starting to take sides. And there's a flap over the educational program, whether only those born and bred in the church have a corner on the teaching ministry ...they say everyone must come to the Lord just the way they did, only through all of their experiences and traditions."

> "Let each of you look not only to his own interests...Have this mind among yourselves, which is yours in Christ Jesus, who though he was in the form of God, did not count equality with God a thing to be grasped, but emptied himself, taking the form of a servant, being born in the likeness of men. And being found in human form he humbled himself and became obedient unto death, even death on a cross. Therefore God has highly exalted him and bestowed on him the name which is above every name,..." (Phil. 2).

19. "One day you hear about the "New Age" religion, the next you are bombarded with a salvation by works. What should one believe in a world like this?"

> "And you, who once were estranged and hostile in mind, doing evil deeds, he has now reconciled in his body of flesh by his death, in order to present you holy and blameless and irreproachable before him, provided that you continue in the faith,...see to it that no one makes a prey of you by philosophy and empty deceit, according to human tradition..." (Col. 1,2)

20. "I lived with my wife fifty-three years. She died last May 13. Tell me, preacher, where is she now? Will I see her again? Will I know her?"

> "For since we believe that Jesus died and rose again, even so through Jesus, God will bring with him those who have fallen asleep...and the dead in Christ will rise first..." (I Thess. 4).

21. "It's the open-endedness of life that gets you! Is God trying to wear us down? It's like a marathon. It's not the problems we have for a month or two, it's those that hang on for years without any promise of solution that get you down. Sometimes a person is tempted to ask just what kind of God he is! Is he really trying to save us or to damn us? Is he on our side?"

> "For God has not destined us for wrath, but to obtain salvation through our Lord Jesus Christ, who died for us so that whether we wake or sleep we might live with him. Therefore, encourage one another..." (I Thess. 4).

22. "Here on the mission field we don't enjoy the freedoms we knew back home. The government here keeps a watchful eye on us."

> "I urge that supplications, prayers,...be made for all men, for kings and all who are in high positions,...This is good, and it is acceptable in the sight of God our Savior, who desires all men to be saved and to come to the knowledge of the truth, for there is one mediator between God and men, the man Christ Jesus who gave himself a ransom for all..." (I Tim.2).

23. "I'm glad we have a time as fellow preachers to 'let our hair down.' Do you guys ever get so tired you wonder if it all matters? Isn't it really as pointless as trying to sweep back the ocean with a broom?"

> "Fight the good fight of faith, take hold of the eternal life to which you were called when you made the good confession...and of Christ Jesus who in his testimony before Pontius Pilate made the good confession." (I Tim. 6).

24. "I've about had it! Who needs this? What does it all mean? Others in other professions work hard too, but they have something to show for it. Even some 'big preachers' seem to

have rung the bell. Maybe I'm not cut out to be in the ministry..."

> "Be strong in the grace that is in Christ Jesus,...entrust to faithful men...the saying is sure: if we have died with him we shall also live with him..." (II Tim. 2).

25. "I know we are supposed to live holy lives. But admonitions to holiness sound better on Sunday morning than during the work week."

> "For the grace of God has appeared for the salvation of all men, training us to renounce irreligion and worldly passions, and to live sober, upright, and godly lives in this world, awaiting our blessed hope, the appearing of the glory of our great God and Savior Jesus Christ, who gave himself for us to redeem us from all iniquity and to purify for himself a people of his who are zealous for good deeds..." (Titus 2).

Before we move on please notice in how many situations Paul appealed to the death, burial, and resurrection of Jesus as the guiding star for churches and individuals. The point of this survey is that Paul considered nothing more "practical" than the word of the cross. Little wonder, then, that Paul would state clearly that the death, burial, and resurrection were for him the core gospel. He reminded the Corinthians what message had saved them, in which message their hope was anchored, and in which message they would find answers for their current struggles.

> Now, I would remind you, brethren, in what terms I preached to you the gospel, which you received, in which you stand, by which you are saved, if you hold fast — unless you believed in vain. For I delivered to you as of

> first importance what I also received, that Christ died for our sins in accordance with the scriptures, that he was buried, that he was raised on the third day in accordance with the scriptures, and that he appeared to Cephas, then to the twelve... (I Corinthians 15:1-5)

Curiosity makes us ask the question: was Paul's core gospel the matter of most importance for other New Testament writers? They certainly wrote in different terms, from different backgrounds, to different situations. But did they center as Paul did on the cross? We notice that Paul said he had *received* the gospel he handed on to the Corinthians. The core gospel was not Paul's invention but the secret of the faith from the first. What follows is an attempt to locate in several of the major books of the New Testament the authors' main concerns and to see how the cross of Christ answers those concerns in each case.

Matthew

The gospel of Matthew was probably written toward the end of the first century to Jewish Christians under persecution by the Jewish community. Friends and relatives were accusing them of leaving the faith, of abandoning everything sacred in Judaism in order to follow an upstart, self-proclaimed, crucified Messiah. Matthew writes to buttress their faith. They were assured that they had not forsaken the faith of Israel. Fifty-one times Matthew mentions the "kingdom." Jesus is the fulfillment of God's kingdom. Disciples under fire should remember that Jesus, too, suffered misunderstanding and death at the hands of God's own people. They should remember that he pronounced those who suffered "for righteousness' sake" "blessed."

Jesus' kingdom had both continuity and discontinuity with Israel's tradition. Regardless of the rejection, strangely through that very rejection which led to the cross, Jesus was the fulfillment of Israel's hope. There was continuity. Matthew even shaped his gospel in ways that would comfort these Jewish Christians. Moses had gone up on the mountain to receive the Law, Jesus went up on the mountainside to restate the Law from his deeper revelation of who God was. He reminded his listeners of the Law's instruction on murder, adultery, and divorce. He had not come to destroy the Law but to fulfill it. These early Jewish Christians had not left the kingdom of God, they were following God's Messiah. On the other hand, there was discontinuity of Jesus' kingdom with the religion of the Scribes and Pharisees. Precisely because they were Christians these Jews believed that Jesus' conflict with the Pharisees was a part of his mission. What happened on Calvary was not the tragic end of a noble dream. It was the fulfillment of God's plan. Now God's kingdom should include all nations. Jesus sent his disciples out to proclaim to the world God's kingdom in the crucified, resurrected Messiah. The cross was central.

Mark

It seems that Mark wrote in the second half of the first century to show Gentile Christians the meaning of discipleship. According to Mark's story, the first disciples were asked to follow Jesus "in the way." Discipleship is defined by who Jesus was and the way he chose to walk. The gospel begins: "This is the beginning of the gospel of the Son of God." For the first half of the story Jesus looked every inch the Son of God. He showed masterful authority, power and command.

At the center of the story Jesus turned toward Jerusalem and told his disciples that he must suffer and die. Peter objected and rebuked Jesus. Jesus rebuked Peter and told him he was working on the side of Satan. He then called out to all that anyone who would follow him must be prepared to take up his cross and follow. Twice more Jesus explained to the twelve that he was going up to Jerusalem to die and be raised. The third time James and John had so effectively tuned him out that they immediately asked if they could sit on his right hand and his left in the kingdom. Jesus explained that *service* would be the premier value in his kingdom, that *"even the Son of man came not to be served but to serve and to give his life a ransom for many."* The disciples were happy to hear him call himself the "Son of man," it reminded them of the glorious figure in Daniel's prophecy. But they hated to hear him combine that title with dark predictions of death. They loved the mountain of transfiguration but hated descending to the valley of service.

Jesus went to Jerusalem. As he approached the cross the disciples parted ways with him. He gave his life, not just for the Jews, but for "many." Mark clearly makes that point at the end when he recalled that the centurion saw how Jesus died and said, "Surely, this was the Son of God." The evangelist obviously wanted his readers to see that something had happened to the title "Son of God" along the way. Discipleship means following Jesus in obedience to God and in service to others. Disciples are those following the one who "came not to be served but to serve and to give his life a ransom for many." Mark's main point rests on Jesus' chosen mission to serve, suffer, die and be raised. Once again, the story centers in the cross.

John

I have attempted above to trace the story line and show the place of the cross in Luke's two-volume work, Luke/Acts. We now turn to John's gospel. It is the most complex of the gospels. John seems to have been written at the end of the first century to answer a variety of needs. At least in part, John writes for those who had trouble accepting both the humanity and divinity of Jesus. Some found it hard to find a place for the human, historical Jesus in the later church. The human figure wasn't "spiritual" enough. Others found Jesus human enough but had trouble believing his divinity and glorification. In John Jesus is presented as both human and divine, "the word became flesh and dwelt among us." God came to earth in Jesus to bring life and light to a world dying in the dark. To accomplish his mission God in Jesus would enter the darkness and into death itself. Early on in this story John the Baptist pointed to Jesus and said, "Behold, the lamb of God who takes away the sins of the world." In the golden text of the Bible, John 3:16, the evangelist sets it out clearly that Jesus was God's gift of life to all who would believe. But he was a man, he looked so common he had to be pointed out in a crowd. Judas kissed Jesus in the garden so there would be no mistaken identity. In these and many other ways John shows just how "human" Jesus was.

On the other hand, Jesus was the "word made flesh" who came to fulfill a divine mission. This average-looking man was, in fact, the "lamb of God." At the end, on the cross, Jesus said, "It is finished." God's paschal lamb had been offered for the sins of the world. Those who had walked with him clearly saw his humanity. But they often missed the "signs" of his divinity. One must believe in "the word made flesh" if he is to receive "life," John's word for salvation. After relating the seven signs of Jesus' divinity, John comments that no one really believed. (12:37)

They may have believed in Jesus as teacher, wonder worker or prophet. But that kind of belief would not lead to life. They did not believe in him as the "word made flesh." Thomas would show the kind of belief that leads to life. Only after the final sign would Thomas fall to his knees and cry: "My Lord and my God." He confessed faith in his risen and glorified Lord when he saw the scars, the sure proofs of Jesus' earthy and bodily suffering. The risen one had obviously been crucified! The crucified had obviously been raised! God had taken on human form, had died for the world and has been raised victorious over death! John is saying that one can find "life" only by believing in the human and divine "Word of God." One must see him lifted up on the cross, lifted up from the grave victorious over death "with scars," and lifted up in the church's proclamation of "the word made flesh" to save the world. The cross is central to John also. "If I am lifted up," Jesus had said, "I will draw all men to me."

Hebrews

Having reviewed Paul's writings above, we now turn to the book of Hebrews. The Christians addressed in this letter were tempted to let go of their faith. Whether because of boredom, fatigue, or fear of persecution they were losing their grip on the gospel. They may have been inclined to return to Judaism, a safer religion in their time and place. The Hebrew writer stresses God's unique, final work in Jesus Christ. There would never be another salvation. Jesus was both High Priest and sacrifice. His work on Golgotha provided access to God's throne. Jesus had come to stand in the congregation of God's people with them, to be one of them and to overcome for them the fear of death. Because of his life and death he was their perfect High Priest who empathized with every Christian's temptation and heartache. His atoning work followed and completed the lines of the High Priest in the Old Testament who annually on the Day of Atonement carried the blood of sacrifice into the Holy Place to atone for the sins of the people. Jesus entered the throne room of heaven with atonement in his own blood. In his flesh he had suffered great anguish, crying out with loud cries as he tasted the bitterness of giving up self and his own way in obedience to the Father's plan. Letting go of so great a salvation would be the ultimate foolishness. No other such atonement could ever be made. Of all the points the writer used to show the uniqueness of the faith none is so central as Jesus' sacrificial death on the cross.

I Peter

First Peter was addressed to "exiles" who felt away from home and displaced in every way. Peter assured them that they had a sure hope, an inheritance secure in the heavens. Meanwhile they "belonged" in God's "house," his family on earth, because they had been redeemed by the precious blood of Christ. In his cross Jesus was also the example for slaves suffering under hardship, and by extension, for all Christians suffering because of their faith. Peter is probably the one, through Mark's gospel, his sermons in Acts, and I Peter who introduced the pictures of Jesus as the Suffering Servant of God. Quoting Isaiah, he reminded the exiles that Jesus "himself bore our sins in his body on the tree, that we might die to sin and live to righteousness." Their suffering was to be viewed in the light of Jesus' suffering. He reminded his fellow elders that he was a witness of the sufferings of Christ. One cannot help but notice how Peter had changed. At Caesarea Philippi nothing was more odious to Peter than the thought of Jesus' suffering. He was willing to give his life to prevent it and he "rebuked" Jesus for even mentioning the possibility. But by the time he wrote I Peter that which had been most offensive to him had become the center of his theology, the anchor of his faith, the ground from which he instructed the church and its leaders.

I John

John wrote to people who believed in Jesus' divinity but not his humanity. They believed in his glory but not in his suffering. How could God, himself, suffer? Some taught that Jesus did not really die on the cross, he only "seemed" to suffer. These doubts naturally cut the root of the disciples' confidence that they were the beloved children of God. John wanted his readers to know that Jesus came and really suffered in the flesh to provide life in his death for all who believe.

John said that God is light, that if they walked in the light they would have fellowship with one another and the "blood of Jesus" would continue cleansing them from all sin. All of this is possible because of Jesus' death: "...he is the expiation for our sins, and not for ours only but also for the sins of the whole world." John confirmed these Christians in their faith by reminding them they were, in fact, the children of God. The life within them was greater that the world and they would win the victory over any dark powers they encountered. They should remember that "God is love." In specific reference to Jesus' life and death John said: "...not that we first loved him but that he first loved us." As in the gospel of John, life here is offered in the one who is lifted up to save the whole world.

Revelation

John's Revelation was given to him toward the end of the first century to shore up the faith of Christians under persecution. It appeared that Rome's power was absolute and evil. For John the curtains of heaven were drawn briefly so he could see God reigning sovereign over all creation and history! Featured center stage, beside God on his throne was the crucified and risen Lamb. The Christians needed assurance that God was in control, that survival was not the ultimate question, that God would have the last word.

It is hardly accidental that the book of Revelation is last in the canon. The biblical story ends where it began, with God. In the beginning the loving Father created his children. When their greed and pride cost them their paradise home he pursued them in his love and planned for them a way back home. Jesus opened the way by his self-giving at Golgotha. Now at the end of the story as many of God's children as had accepted his salvation surrounded the throne in a great homecoming. The story ends in triumph! God had worked his plan! The redeemed sing praises to God and to the one who redeemed them with his blood.

> 'Worthy is the Lamb who is slain...To him who sits upon the throne and to the Lamb be blessing and honor and glory and might for ever and ever!' And the four living creatures said, 'Amen!' and the elders fell down and worshipped.

Summary

To this point we have attempted to trace the story of God's plan to redeem his children and bring them back home. From the proud sin of Adam and Eve in the garden all the way through the Old Testament the story of God's loving rescue mission unfolds. God called Abraham to make his family a blessing to all peoples. His chosen people in the Old Testament were sometimes faithful, more often not faithful. Seldom did they remember the mission for which they had been chosen. Prophet, priest, and king were God's instruments for leading his people. Through glorious rescue and covenant they were galvanized into his people. But because of unfaithfulness they were carried away into captivity. The Old Testament ends without God's revelation of his final method of salvation for all mankind.

In his gospel Luke picked up the universal love of God theme, presenting Jesus the universal savior. He served and died because of his love for the outcasts. God raised him in victory. In his second volume Luke traced the waiting of the disciples, the coming of the Spirit, the proclamation of the crucified and risen messiah, the birth of the church, its early struggles and the persecution which propelled it to its mission. The book ends in Rome where Gentiles are welcomed along with the Jews into the kingdom of Christ.

Proclamation of the crucified and risen Lord brought an assortment of God's children back home to him. Writers of the New Testament letters had the continuing task of edifying, correcting and instructing these communities of faith. For them that word which had saved souls in the beginning and had given birth to the church, that which was the sure ground for the defense of the faith was also the fountainhead of edification. Without the cross of Christ there would have been no church, no mission, no New Testament. God truly demonstrated his love and power to save in what happened on Golgotha, at the open tomb and in the word of the cross. This brief telling of the biblical story has isolated for us the core gospel. The death, burial, and resurrection of Jesus and the word of the cross truly formed the nucleus of God's power to reconcile the world to himself.

A Scandalous Story 5

Joseph S. Harvard, a Presbyterian minister in Durham, North Carolina, tells how the filming of a movie in that university town caused quite a stir. The movie version of The Handmaid's Tale by Margaret Atwood was filmed in and around Durham. Duke University was a primary location. The movie included one scene in which women were put to death by hanging. The gallows were set up in front of the Duke Chapel. Will Willimon, Dean of the chapel, told of numerous phones calls protesting the violation of "the sacred beauty of our chapel." Letters were written to local papers and a heated community debate ensued over the appropriateness of gallows in front of the chapel. One Duke staff person commented in the student newspaper: "I don't understand what all the fuss is about. Maybe the people who are upset have not noticed the cross at the center of the chapel."[1]

It's not really too hard to understand, is it? Which of our congregations would look kindly on a gallows erected on the front yard? Who wants to be reminded in such a graphic way what the cross was all about? The cross is a loved symbol in our society. Gold cruciform jewelry adorns rock stars, athletes, and millions in the general population who claim no discipleship to Jesus. But the cross in the first century had no aesthetic appeal whatsoever. Paul said the "word of the cross" was "folly" to those who were perishing. The Jews demanded signs and the Greeks were looking for wisdom, "but we preach Christ crucified, a stumbling block to Jews and folly to Gentiles..." If we stay faithful to the New Testament we must say that the story of the cross was offensive to all. If we stay faithful to the core gospel there remains something deeply disturbing about that message today.

Jesus, Himself, Was A Scandal

The life, words and ministry of Jesus were so offensive that he ended on a cross. According to Matthew it all began when King Herod felt threatened by the babe of Bethlehem and slaughtered the innocents to retain power. Mark tells how Jesus' home folk at Nazareth "took offence," were scandalized (the same word in Greek Paul used regarding the word of the cross) at his preaching. "Who is this carpenter's son come home, putting on airs, claiming to be somebody?" As Luke reports it, they loved him and were proud of him at first. Then they turned on him because he would not work a miracle for them and especially because he defined his mission of salvation in terms of Elijah and Elisha's outreach to those outside Israel. John the Baptist also had his questions. He expected a Messiah in the mold of Elijah or Amos who would come in reforming zeal. He was not prepared for Jesus' ministry of compassion and healing for all kinds of people.

Jesus' own disciples were offended once they began to get the drift of his message and mission. At Caesarea Philippi Peter could not believe what he was hearing when Jesus said, "The Son of man must suffer..." Peter took him by the lapels, talked down to him, commanded (as Jesus had commanded demons) Jesus to reconsider. Jesus told Peter he was the one who had a demon, the demon of human understanding in opposition to God's plan. Peter and the others never agreed to Jesus' program. Not until after the resurrection did they begin putting the pieces together.

So it is small wonder that Jesus' enemies resented him. The Jews and Romans alike were put off by Jesus. In his book, *The Crucified God,* Jurgen Moltmann explores the factors that brought about the historical event of Calvary. I am indebted in much of what follows to Moltmann's work.[2]

To The Jews Jesus Was A Blasphemer

They had him dead to rights under the Law as they interpreted it. Discarding rigid traditions of ceremonial cleanliness, Jesus ate with all sorts of people. He touched lepers, spoke with women in public, ate with sinners, and regularly had contact with Roman Centurions. He played fast and loose with the rabbis' Sabbath regulations. Healing on the Sabbath and allowing his disciples to pluck and eat grain seemed an obvious flaunting of the fourth commandment. When challenged Jesus enraged the best people in town by saying, "Man was not made for the Sabbath, but the Sabbath for man." He added, "...for the Son of man is Lord of the Sabbath."

Rumor had it that Jesus had talked about tearing down the temple, Israel's central shrine and most sacred place of worship. Worst of all was Jesus' repeated claim to be God's only son. "The Father and I are one," he said. "If you have seen me you have seen the Father." "If you reject me you reject my Father who sent me." He taught his disciples to pray beginning, "Abba, Father," a personal, intimate way of addressing God no pious Jew would have dared use.

The day inevitably came when Jesus stood before the High Priest to give an account. It all came down to a single question. "Are you the son of the Blessed?" "I am," Jesus answered, "and you will see the Son of man sitting at the right hand of Power, and coming with the clouds of heaven." That was it! What else need be said? Here was an ordinary looking man, a carpenter's son, an unlettered layman who had led his followers to disregard the law, despise the temple, approach God in a familiar way, claiming to be the son of God in some special sense!

Not that technical legal charges against Jesus were by any means the whole story. He had called his accusers "whited sepulchres full of dead men's bones." He had warned the people about their leaders' hypocrisy, pointing up the gap between their preaching and their practice. He called them "blind guides" and publicly repudiated their whole system of doctrine. They had a personal score to settle with Jesus.

We must be careful not to generalize about the scribes and Pharisees. Nicodemus and Gamaliel represented the best Judaism had produced. We noticed in Luke's story that certain Pharisees came to warn Jesus about Herod. We should not think of all scribes and Pharisees as stuffed-shirts who were not serious about their faith. Typically, they prayed three times a day, gave well over ten percent of their gross income to the temple and in alms to the poor, and carefully observed the traditions. In addition, they took seriously their role as teachers and guardians of the faith. They believed that eternal life was the reward for studying the Torah. Protecting Israel from the dilution of the faith by contact with other worldviews was their life's work. They loved God with all their heart as they knew him. In many ways they were model citizens, the "best people in town."

So why did large groups of them want Jesus out of the way? Jesus called them hypocrites. They were probably unaware that they demanded of others what they could not perform themselves, that they were idolatrous about the temple and the Law, that they were self-serving in their protection of the traditions and ignorant of God's great plan given in promise to their father Abraham. It was precisely because they were good, good in themselves, that Jesus was a scandal to them.

To The Romans He Was A Troublemaker.

The Romans could not have cared less about the niceties of Jewish law. But they were big on law and order. In order to keep their Empire intact, to maintain power, to enhance commerce they kept restless elements in society under control. Governors appointed by Rome were charged first of all and above all with keeping the peace.

Rome was quite ecumenical when it came to religion. The government preferred for local peoples to continue serving whatever gods they chose. It kept them happy, quiet and productive. The Romans, themselves, were broad-minded about the gods. One could be a faithful citizen and believe in a variety of gods or in no god at all. But the gods were to serve Rome. The government would not endorse any religion which caused civil unrest or promoted another "king." Nothing was more certain to cause unrest among the people than a popular prophet calling himself a king. Caesar would brook no rivals.

The Jewish leaders understood this, and how to use the policy when push came to shove. The Roman attitude was well personified in Pilate. He was a fair man, at least according to the code of his Equestrian rank. His kind prided themselves in fairness under the law. Rome was an empire under law. Pilate tried several times in various ways to free Jesus. He could see nothing in him which posed any real threat to Rome. Jesus was clearly being assailed by religious rivals who wanted him out of the way. Pilate may have enjoyed toying a bit with the pesky Jewish leaders. He was not disposed to turn Jesus over to a lynch mob just to clear his desk. The Jewish leaders knew where the pressure point was. After Pilate would not bend to mob outrage or protests of blasphemy, they went for the jugular. "If you do not do as we ask, you are no friend of Caesar's."

They had said the magic words. Pilate cared about fairness and justice, but not at his own expense. So when it came right down to it he said to Jesus, "Better you than me, fella." Like the Jews, Pilate needed a legal charge. Since Jesus called himself "king" the charge of treason and insurrection would do nicely. The Romans crucified Jesus as a troublemaker, a rebel.

For all concerned, Jews and Romans, Jesus was crucified because he disturbed their way of life. He threatened all they prized most and put their ways of life in jeopardy. Nothing is more dangerous than challenging a person's way of life, his security and lifestyle.

Here is the irony. At the foot of the cross, the Jews and Romans were more alike than they were different. From different worlds, different world-views, different cultures, languages, religions—they were still the same. Neither was willing to let Jesus threaten their *status quo*. From the story of Adam and Eve on, the Bible says that all human beings are infected with self-serving pride. The cross shows what human pride would finally produce. As Paul would say: "all have sinned and fall short of the glory of God." On Golgotha all classes, religions, and races became one. The crucifixion was a cooperative effort between rivals who had a common enemy.

Where Was God?

One who believes in the God of the Bible must ask the question. Surely the one who created all that exists out of nothing by the word of his mouth, who parted the Red Sea, who set King David on the throne and determined the destinies of empires could have rescued his only son.

How could this happen? It's certain beyond any doubt that, whatever the Jews and Romans felt toward Jesus, he could not have been crucified without the Father's consent. Is this not the ultimate scandal of what happened on Golgotha, that God himself was party to the event? How could God let this happen? Always the God of love and justice, champion of the abused and downtrodden, how could he allow this crime of crimes? It is scandalous!

We recall that comforting passage from Romans 8: "He who did not spare his own Son but gave him up for us all, will he not also give us all things with him?" "Gave him up," or as some translations have it "delivered him up" is not the language of accidental death or of tragedy in the classical sense. Here, as in Acts 2, it is sacrificial language from the Old Testament. God "delivered Jesus up" for us. What Abraham did not have to do with Isaac, God did with His own son for us! It was God's plan from the beginning to make a way back home for all his children.

Corresponding to the Father's will was the Son's willing obedience. The gospels show Jesus walking resolutely toward Jerusalem, knowing all along what would happen. In the garden, after hours of struggle to avoid the ordeal, Jesus submitted his will to the Father's: "Nevertheless, not my will but thine be done." He went to the cross because the matter had already been decided, there was no other way.

The "Word Of The Cross" Was Scandalous

It follows that the news of a crucified God would also be offensive. The story of the cross was and is offensive in at least three ways.

Offense Against Good Taste.

One does not comment at a fine dinner party: "Did you see the documentary the other night on capital punishment? It was really gruesome, they showed an actual electrocution. The high voltage jolted his body, his hair stood on end, smoke arose from restraints on his arms and legs, he became as rigid as a poker!" We just don't say such things in polite company. Few if any of us have seen an execution, or want to witness one. We don't even want to think about it.

People in the first century felt the same way about crucifixions. Cicero is quoted: "Let even the name of the cross be kept away not only from the bodies of the citizens of Rome, but also from their thought, sight, and hearing."[3] Sophisticated Romans avoided crucifixion scenes. The bloody public executions may have provided cheap thrills for the most depraved in society.[4] It may have been considered fair enough reward for insurrectionist slaves or criminals convicted of treason. But certainly no upper class Roman would stop to see it, consent to a citizen's death in that fashion, or mention it in polite company.

The Jews felt the same way for different reasons. Crucifixion was, after all, the Romans' form of execution. The Jews preferred stoning. They also found public nakedness shameful. The last thing they could imagine was their own Messiah stripped naked and crucified like a common criminal. "Cursed is anyone who hangs on a tree" was the quote which came quickly to mind. King David was the prototype of the Messiah. He dispatched his share of Israel's enemies. But no informed and faithful Jew could imagine David scorned, spat upon, stripped and crucified. The cross was an offense against good taste. There was nothing aesthetically appealing about a first century crucifixion.

Offense Against Human Pride.

The word of the cross said God sent his son and Jesus gave his life because we were helpless and hopeless. Jesus came not just to be an advisor, example, companion, and friend. He came to *save* the lost.

It's offensive to need saving. In everyday life we are offended at the insinuation that we are inadequate and helpless. None of us wants a Boy Scout helping us across the street. My daughter, in her mid-twenties, likes to kid her dad about his getting older. Once when she found me resting on the couch before dinner, she took me by the arm and said: "Come on, now, dad. It's time for dinner. We go this way, I'll show you to the table." My reaction? "No! Get away from me! Don't rush me into my dotage!"

It's always the same. Services we buy for ourselves are welcome. They are status symbols. Most of us could adjust to a maid and a gardener. But it's a different matter if the teenagers from church come to clean our houses and mow our yards free of charge because we cannot do it ourselves. Our gratitude would be mixed with embarrassment and even a little resentment at our situation.

"While we were yet helpless, at the right time Christ died for the ungodly." There was a time when Paul would have choked on that word, "helpless." Young Saul of Tarsus had everything going his way. He was on a fast career track and making good time at the front of his class, he obviously had a bright future. He must have treasured the praise and encouragement from Rabboni Gamaliel! The perks, prestige and power that renowned teacher enjoyed were not lost on young Saul of Tarsus. What a rude reversal he experienced on the Damascus road! How terrible it was to discover that all he had thought about God was wrong! How upsetting when he came to realize that he could never know enough, do enough, feel enough, or be enough to merit God's acceptance! How disturbing to be told that Jesus was his only hope! Along with all of that, the whole program and schedule for his career was shattered in favor of the life of a missionary. The gospel is always bad news first. The cross is God's scalpel. Having one's chest opened is always painful, even if a master surgeon is doing the heart transplant for our survival. To admit that we cannot stand on our own record before God is insulting. Confessing that there is absolutely nothing we can do to fix our alienation from Him, to remedy our sickness, to heal the injury we have done others leaves a bitter taste.

When we look long enough at the cross we get the message. God is not just saying: "Look how much I love you." He is also saying: "Do you know this rescue mission has been my plan from the beginning? Will you admit that I have given you every blessing you enjoy, life itself is a gift from my hand? Can you see what your human pride and greed come to? Do you know that when you go into business for yourself you make me your enemy? Can you see that there was absolutely nothing you can do to heal our alienation? Will you let me fix it for you?" How wonderful to be so loved! And yet how hard it is to take! We have not yet really seen the cross until we are somewhat offended, chagrined, embarrassed by it all. Part of the offense of the cross is its commentary on our human condition.

The Ultimate Scandal.

Above we said that the ultimate scandal of the cross was God's allowing and sending Jesus to die such a death. Even that does not indicate the full dimensions of the ultimate scandal. What does the cross say about God himself? What implications follow for his children who worship him and would be like him?

Often those of us who do pre-marital counselling stress how values determine behavior. What one values most determines how one spends his or her time, money, and energy. Whatever we believe in as ultimate is our god. More than that, we become more and more like our gods.

The Jews and Romans agreed on very little. They were from different worlds. They worshipped different gods. And yet, they agreed on one thing: whoever "god" is he is lifted up, full of prestige, knowledge, power, riches. God is served by all and serves no one. They could go to worship their various gods and sing wholeheartedly "O To Be Like Thee." Who does not want to be lifted up, full of prestige, knowledge, power and riches? Who does not enjoy being served, and secretly believe the service is deserved?

What could be more upsetting than a story about one who lived in the White House and gave it all up to live in a log cabin? What would that do to the American dream? Perhaps the only story more offensive is this one about a God who gave up the splendor of heaven to come down to earth to wash feet and die on a criminal's cross. Peter wasn't just thinking of *Jesus'* dignity when he refused to let his Lord wash his feet. What can one do with this God on his knees with towel and basin? Who wants to become like a God who says: "I came not to be served but to serve and to give my life a ransom for many," "A servant is not greater than his Lord, if I washed your feet you ought to wash one another's feet," "The greatest of you will be the servant of all," now "take up your cross daily and follow me"?

If Jesus Christ reveals who God is, if the cross more than any other event in history reveals the heart of God, then our most cherished ideas of God are wrong! The ultimate scandal of the cross, of the "word of the cross" is that it redefines God. He is not just a God who *is served*, he is also one who *serves*.

NOTES

[1] Joseph Harvard, A Book Review of *A Theology Of The Cross*. by Charles B. Cousar, Journal For Preachers, Winter, 1990. pp. 36,37.

[2] Jurgen Moltmann, *The Crucified God* (New York: Harper, 1978), pp. 126-145.

[3] Moltmann, p. 33.

[4] For an analysis of the ordeal of crucifixion from a medical point of view see: Edwards, Gabel, and Hosmer, "On the Physical Death Of Jesus Christ," Journal of American Medical Association, March 21, 1986, pp. 1456-1463.

Avenues of Understanding 6

Our New Testament survey revealed that the cross determined the content of earliest Christianity. Those who evangelized unbelievers, defended the faith, and taught the church had a handle on this core gospel. We have seen that Paul spoke of the "word of the cross," by which he meant the message and implications of what happened on Golgotha. Other New Testament writers did the same, each in his own way. We have attempted to see how scandalous the core gospel was.

In addition to the canonical writings a storehouse of rich insight into the cross comes down to us in the Christian literature of twenty centuries. We are privileged to enter that storehouse and carry away with us priceless treasures. But must we only receive these insights from others? Is it possible for us to develop a theology of the atonement for ourselves? The familiar old Chinese proverb says: "Give a man a fish and you feed him for a day. Teach a man to fish, and you feed him for a lifetime." The richest insights of non-canonical Christian literature provide nourishment for the day. The best insights have come ultimately from the scriptures themselves. If we want nutrition for a lifetime we must learn to find the meaning of the cross in the Bible itself.

The question here is about method. Is the Bible concerned with this "how to" question? Not overtly, the Bible is not in the modern sense a "how to" book. Nevertheless, it provides us ways to get hold of the atonement. The New Testament teaching on the atonement is found in narrative, parable, epistle, argument, vision, etc. We are most comfortable with direct instruction, the "application to life" kind of material found in the epistles. However, if we want to learn to "fish for ourselves" we must explore all avenues to a better understanding. So far as the atonement is concerned two of these ways are of supreme Importance but too seldom travelled. These are story and picture. Or we might say, narrative and metaphor.

Reading The Story

Our attempt in chapters one through four to trace the biblical narrative reminds us that the core gospel may only be discovered when we recall God's story with mankind. The centerpiece of the larger narrative is the story of Jesus. Consequently, we must learn to read and appreciate story. Just here we may encounter some resistance within ourselves. It's easy to assume that story is a less sophisticated medium of communication than an epistle. "Stories are for children, aren't they?" Children do love stories. None of us has ever heard a small child say at bedtime: "Please review that syllogism about the happy life." "Tell me again those three points you explained about human nature." "Can you recite that poem again?" "Tell me a story!" is the plea. But children are not the only ones, adults love story, too. Novels, plays, and movies will never to go out of style. Every speaker can testify to the almost magical effect of storytelling. From the youngest to the oldest we love stories. Perhaps most significant of all: whether in pride or despair we never tire of telling our own stories.

Sometimes we underestimate the power of story in our lives. We often imagine that we are living life only by logic, reasoning, and analysis. Admittedly, all of that is important. But we receive our real vision of life from story. Our grandparents and parents grew up hearing Parson Weems's story about George Washington and the cherry tree. It was a story to teach honesty. And there was "The Little Engine That Could" which taught perseverance. Horatio Alger fired the imagination and made generations work hard to claim a part of the American Dream. One can rise from "rags to riches."

The same power of story is with us today. Over the years I made it a hobby to notice what people are reading on airplanes. Several years ago, when I first noticed, they were reading, *Jonathan Livingston Seagull.* Later it was the life story of Lee Iacocca. When I first wrote this chapter I noted that people were reading Donald Trump. We can be sure that another hero of American business will soon replace this idolized success figure. The writings of such a person are appreciated not because he is a brilliant or a perceptive writer, but because the readers want to know his story and the secret of success for themselves. Stories grip us down deep, fire the imagination, define our ambitions, and send us on our way.

Michael Goldberg, a rabbi who studied in a Christian seminary, wrote a book he entitled: *Jews And Christians, Getting Our Stories Straight.* He observed that both Jews and Christians have a "master story." For the Jews it is the exodus, for Christians it is the cross. "These stories "not only inform us, more importantly they *form* us," observed Goldberg.[1]

The first time I read Goldberg's observation it rang a bell. I was first drawn to God when my mother read to me *Hurlbut's Story of the Bible.* These many years later I still remember vividly the adventures of Joseph, David and Goliath, Daniel in the lion's den, the Prodigal Son, Jesus on the cross, and Paul's missionary journeys. In each case colorful pictures illustrated. I can still see Joseph's coat of many colors, Daniel and the lions, Jesus on the cross. The Bible is the original and best Bible story book. It's a story with a beginning, a middle, and an end. As the story begins mankind loses its fellowship with God and it ends with God redeeming his children back to himself. These features are not there by chance. The Bible is a storybook, complete with pictures.

An understanding of the atonement must begin with the Old Testament story and continue on with Matthew, Mark, Luke, and John. Too often we skip the gospels as if we had mastered them as children in Sunday School. In the story line each gospel provides insight into the center of our faith. I say "story line" because they are stories to be read as stories. We should see how the story begins, proceeds, and ends, asking what the narrative tells us about God? Jesus came into contact with a full cast of other characters: disciples, the "crowds," his enemies, the Romans, and others. The gospels contain profound insight into human nature. We should read the narratives asking in each case what Jesus did and said that took him to the cross, what others did that had him crucified, why God delivered him up for us. The first level of study has to do with the history of Jesus, what he said and did.

On a second level, one should ask what each gospel writer was saying to his readers a generation or more later. All four gospels in their unique ways reveal Jesus as God's son. Guided by the Holy Spirit, each writer chose to relate certain incidents in the life of Jesus and not others. Each evangelist was guided to show those aspects of Jesus life and death which spoke most directly to his readers' needs.

This understanding determines the way we must read the gospels. Each gospel must stand on its own feet and be studied that way. "Harmonizing" the gospels washes out the vivid and distinctive revelation in each. In reading each on its own terms we ask what the writer was saying. Why does he choose certain events and teachings and not others? Why does he emphasize this word and not that one? Why does he stress certain factors which led to Golgotha while another evangelist stresses another set of factors? Why does Mark build his story around Jesus' journeys, especially the journey to Jerusalem? Why does Matthew stress Jesus' relation to the Jewish law and religious leaders while Luke pictures Jesus as universal savior? Why does John show that "the word became flesh" while the others do not put it that way? Each story must be studied on its own. Each gospel is a gold mine of insight regarding the atonement.

For purposes of understanding the core gospel it would help to think of the Bible and the gospels the way we think of other stories. We think of a play, a movie, or a novel as a *whole*. What is the main plot? What are the sub-plots? Who are the main characters, what are they like, who is the hero and who the villain? What are the points of conflict and tension? How is the story resolved? What does the story mean to our lives? What will we remember most about the story and why? We are blessed in the Church of Christ today with more and better biblical scholars than ever before. We should seek their insights into the biblical narrative. Perhaps they, in turn, would be enriched by more conversation with our many fine scholars in literary criticism.

Observing The Pictures

"A picture is worth a thousand words" the saying goes. Another less well known observation says: "Give me the Gettysburg

Address, the Twenty-Third Psalm, and the Beatitudes and you can have any picture ever painted." All three together contain less than a thousand words. But this is a false debate. One cannot use words without painting pictures. Words, even the most logical words, paint pictures.

Take, for example, the epistle to the Romans. Here is one of the most carefully reasoned writings in the Bible. One might expect logical discourse without visual imagery. But look at just a few of the many pictures in the first six chapters:

> "Paul a *servant* of Jesus Christ..."

> "For God is my *witness*..."

> "I have intended to come to you that I may *reap* some *harvest*

> "Blessed is the man against whom the Lord will not *reckon* (accounting term) his sin...

> "Circumcision was a *seal* of righteousness"

> "We were *baptized* into his death...

> "Our old self was *crucified*..."

> "The *wages* of sin is death, but the *free gift* of God is eternal life in Christ Jesus our Lord."

As the New Testament evangelists and writers of epistles conveyed the "word of the cross" they used a variety of pictures or metaphors. These visual images communicate understanding, stir the imagination, evoke feelings, and galvanize the will. If we would understand the cross from the New Testament point of view we must learn to appreciate metaphors.

In the early thirties Charles Reynolds Brown, Dean Emeritus of the Yale Divinity School, addressed the students. Much of what he had to say was published in book form under the title, *Have We Outgrown Religion?* His audience fancied themselves sophisticated, secular and enlightened. Many felt they had outgrown the Christian faith because they considered themselves "rational, scientific thinkers." Brown challenged their attitudes.

> What do we think of a man who faces rainbows and sunsets, and awful grandeur of the ocean in a storm or the lovely autumn colors on our hillsides (when they look as if a thousand sunsets had gone wreck in the treetops), saying to himself, 'What is all that to me?' What should we think of a man who looked upon the paintings of Raphael and Rembrandt, or who sat listening to some superb orchestra playing Schubert's *Unfinished Symphony* or some magnificent chorus singing *The Messiah* saying 'What has all that to do with me?' What would we think of a man who turn the pages of *Hamlet* or *Macbeth*, Tennyson's *In Memoriam* or Goethe's *Tragedy Of Faust*, saying 'What do I care about all that?'
>
> We would say at once "He is a moron. He is abnormal. He is incomplete. He is 'not all there.'" If he finds nothing in himself which responds to those varied forms of appeal, it does not condemn the ocean and the sky; it does not condemn the artist, the writers and the musicians, but it does everlastingly condemn him.[2]

The problem is not always a matter of intellectual pride. Sometimes we can be blinded by a rationalistic and quantitative mindset. Someone has said there is a kind of person who can look at Niagara Falls and comment: "H_2O." I suppose there is a kind of person who looks at Grand Canyon and thinks: "This is a prime example of soil erosion," or at the starry heavens on a clear night and thinks only: "$E=MC^2$". Some believe every mystery of life will yield to measurement and logic, that anything worth knowing can be reduced to a syllogism or formula. Our modern age speaks in computer language and demands that we "cut through to the bottom line." I suppose the life, death and legacy of Jesus could be reduced to the language of a police report:

> "Male, caucasian, about 30 years old. Alleged victim of mob, executed over religious differences and to avoid civil unrest. Some claimed that he came back to life, call themselves by his name as "Christians."

Who can argue with the facts? But does that kind of report tell the whole story? No, much more happened than can be reported on a police blotter, or in a thousand page book of the finest historical research. The gospel cannot be communicated just in report language. That takes story and picture. This fact demands that we learn to appreciate the pictures if we are to get a better grasp of the meaning of Golgotha. We must engage our imagination as well as our analytical skills, our "right brain" as well as our "left brain." Just as our literary scholars can help us with story, our art professors might help us study pictures.

What follows is a brief overview of eight main New Testament pictures of the atonement. Each metaphor shows us some aspect of God's great salvation at Golgotha. We do not pretend here to understand or explain fully these metaphors of the atonement. But we can identify them, claim them, hang them in our living area where they can begin speaking to us.

"Suffering Servant"

Jesus' "way" was service and suffering for man in obedience to God. It led to a cross. Many today call such a life "sick" and "masochistic." It is true that one must learn to love himself or herself properly. Jesus was not a masochist. He had appropriate self love and self esteem as we can see in John's gospel. In chapter 10 he said the Good Shepherd would lay his life down for his sheep. But he made one thing clear. "I lay it down and I take it up. No one takes it from me." In chapter 13, Jesus "knowing that the Father had given all things into his hands, that he had come from God and was going to God," got up and washed their feet. Only one secure in his own worth and relationship with God can afford to serve the way he served. Then, in chapter 18, when the servant of the High Priest slapped Jesus he replied, "If I have spoken wrongly, bear witness to the wrong, but if I have spoken rightly, why do you strike me?" Jesus was no doormat. He knew well the value of the gift he was giving. That giving did not come easy. But the main point is that he did give it. He had not come to preserve himself for himself. He came to serve others in obedience to the Father and for the kingdom.

The disciples loved to hear Jesus refer to himself as the "Son of man," the title he chose for himself from the book of Daniel. The name conjured up images of power, conquest, dominion. Peter, James, and John were eager to follow such a leader. As we observed in Mark's gospel, they had ambitions which only someone like the Son of man could satisfy. But there was another Old Testament image, the "servant" of whom Isaiah sang. "...he was despised and rejected by men; a man of sorrows, and acquainted with grief;... he was wounded for our transgressions, he was bruised for our iniquities..." This picture was the exact opposite of Daniel's powerful "Son of man." So Jesus' words "the

Son of man must suffer" were shocking. Nothing could have been further from the hopes and desires of the disciples than a suffering servant Messiah. They could not even conceive of it. Leander Keck observed that they could no more think of a non-military Messiah than we can think of a non-military general.[3]

Years later John told the story of the Last Supper in a way different from the other gospels. There is no institution of the meal at the supper. He remembered something else. When the disciples were too full of themselves to serve one another, Jesus arose, put on the apron, took the towel and basin and began washing their feet. It was not really just about washing feet and serving one another. Jesus was acting out a parable by which his death could be understood. He took the towel and basin to do the servant's (slave's) work.

Isaiah had pictured the "Servant of God" as one who achieved three things. First, he yielded his will to the Father's. Second, he suffered in the place of, instead of, as a representative of others. Third, his suffering would renew their covenant with God. When we ask what happened on Golgotha and what it means, the first and most important picture for us to study is that of the Suffering Servant.

This picture was soon de-emphasized in the early church, has always been the least popular, and will always remain so. It pictures in vivid colors the scandal of the cross. The early church soon began to say the Suffering Servant had, after all, also been raised in glory to be triumphant over death. Many today find any discussion of the cross and suffering service depressing at best and sick at worst. Evidently, our human nature finds it too hard to focus on the servant. The crown is always more attractive than the cross. Nevertheless, the Suffering Servant is the essence of Jesus' mission and his way of teaching the meaning of life. This least popular of all the metaphors is also the most powerful in breaking our selfish pride. In no other picture of Jesus on the cross can we see more clearly the core gospel in all its power.

Martin Luther called the church back from a *theologia gloria* (the God high and lifted up ruling over a proud church absorbed in self-deification through knowledge and works) to a *theologia crucis* (the God who came down as servant to die on a cross to call to himself a servant church).[4]

Priest And Sacrifice

Forgiveness is a gift, not a right. An unfaithful husband might come home and say: "Dear, I know I have not been exactly true to you. I have been thinking about it and have decided to set it straight. I plan to give more money to the church and to volunteer at the cancer hospital. Just wanted you to know that I have admitted my problem and that I have fixed it." How would she respond? She might reply: "Wait just a minute! You are simply pronouncing yourself forgiven? You haven't even confessed to me that you're wrong! You can't just forgive yourself. You get real and honest and we will talk about where to go from here!" Any woman who has any self-respect would react that way.

If such wrath is legitimate in human relations how much more is God's wrath justified in his relation to mankind. Emil Brunner, the Swiss theologian, has written that God's wrath is "infinite divine self-respect, without which his love would not be divine love but sentimentality."[5] God has wrath upon man's pride because he takes himself seriously and he takes his creatures seriously. If he did not love us, if he were not concerned to be true to himself our behavior would not matter to him.

Men and women of all time and places have needed a priest and a sacrifice. Also rooted in rich Old Testament scripture are the pictures of Jesus as priest and sacrifice. From the beginning God had asked man to sacrifice. Later, when the Hebrews made covenant with God at Sinai he made the same claim on them. Along with the Law, God gave his people a priesthood and a sacrificial system. He would not allow his selfish children just to saunter into his presence, pronounce themselves "okay" and promise to atone by a little community service. His arrangement of priest and sacrifice was serious spiritual education. Even the casual observer would have to notice the rigorous procedures through which the priest passed before offering the sacrifice. Who would not pause at the sight of an innocent lamb's throat slit, its blood shed for the sin of human beings? Something was said there about the seriousness of the worshipper's problem. The release from guilt in such a process also said something about God's grace and steadfast love.

In several of the New Testament writings God's action on Golgotha is pictured in terms of the priest/sacrifice metaphor. At the beginning of John's gospel John the Baptist pointed to Jesus and said, "Behold, the lamb of God who takes away the sins of the world." On the cross Jesus said, "It is finished." Later Paul recalled the same picture when he wrote to the Corinthians, "For Christ, our paschal lamb has been sacrificed." As we saw the end of the story of salvation as told in Revelation, the scene around the throne of heaven where all of creation sings praises to the One upon the throne and to the Lamb.

The book of Hebrews supplies the most extensive treatment of this metaphor. The writer portrays Jesus as both High Priest and sacrifice. The great salvation provided when Jesus entered the Holy of Holies with his own blood was unique, matchless, and never to be repeated. By his priesthood and sacrifice these early

Christians had been given access in worship to the very throne room of heaven. How could they let go of such a great salvation! The pictures in Hebrews elaborate the metaphors used by John and Paul. This picture reminds us that we are not good enough to approach God on our own, we come to him through the cross "in Jesus' name."

Expiation/Propitiation

In Romans 3:25 Paul says that God put Jesus forward as an "expiation" or "propitiation" for all, Jews and Gentiles alike. In I John 2:2 and 4:10 where John described what God did to take away our sins he used the same word. As the various translations indicate, scholars disagree about the best rendering of the Greek. Neither "expiation" nor "propitiation" immediately conjures up a picture for today's English reader.

The word "expiation" means "to cleanse," "to wipe clean," or "to blot out." It pictures what happened to our sin and guilt on Golgotha when Jesus offered himself on our behalf. A modern example of expiation might be helpful. Those of us who are familiar with word processors know that by the touch of a single key words on the screen can be completely and forever "deleted." They simply do not exist any longer. That's expiation.

"Propitiation" means "covering" or the "place of covering." It, too, speaks of the result of the High Priest's sacrifice for sin. In some pagan religions the Greek word meant the result of sacrifices worshippers made to buy off bloodthirsty, capricious, angry gods. To avoid such connotations many translators have used "expiation." But other scholars have insisted that we must not lose the word. A powerful metaphor of the atonement is lost if we throw it away. But what shall we do with the word's blemished past? The single most important fact of the New Testament doctrine of atonement comes into play here. Everything depends on Who is giving the sacrifice, Who is doing the atoning. The New Testament makes it clear that God gave the sacrifice and made the atonement. Forgiveness was not a reward for man's sacrifice. It was God's idea from the beginning. He took the initiative and did the atoning. Whether God loves mankind has never been in question. All the pagan overtones disappear when we remember that God came to us, lived with us, died for us in Jesus. The cross was not man's idea and offering to win God's love. The cross was the greatest gift of God's love to redeem mankind.

But why should we keep the word, "propitiation"? What unique picture does it provide? In this metaphor we are ushered into the Holy of Holies of the tabernacle. Before us sits the ark of the covenant. The lid of the ark of the covenant is called the Mercy Seat. It is the *place* where God meets his people to forgive their sins. On the Day of Atonement the High Priest comes into this holy place and sprinkles the blood of sacrifices on the Mercy Seat. God had prescribed it. It is his provision of a *place* where the sins of the people can be forgiven. This Old Testament picture is used in the New Testament to describe the cross. The writer of Hebrews described the *place* where the Old Testament priest took the blood of sacrifice as the *hilasterion.* (9:5) The same word is found in I John 2:2 and 4:10 to describe the atonement. It is the same word Paul used in Romans 3:25 translated "expiation" or "propitiation."

Far from being like the bloodthirsty, temperamental, angry gods of the pagans, the God of the Bible in his great love and grace provided both the *place* and the *means* of our atonement. He, himself, was present on Golgotha to redeem us. When we are baptized we meet him at the cross, the *place* where we are forgiven. When we come to communion we return to Golgotha, the *place* we meet him for cleansing and new life.

Reconciliation

"God was in Christ reconciling the world to himself" is Paul's picture of the cross in II Corinthians 5. This sentence portrays a peace-signing after a long and bitter war. It is not first of all peace of mind, but cessation of hostilities. At Appomattox Generals Grant and Lee signed papers ending a long, bloody, and bitter family conflict. The signing of papers marked the end of open, military hostilities. Terms were spelled out and agreed to. The war was over. The peace was not fully appreciated and internalized by North and South for some time. But hostilities had officially ended.

What happened on Golgotha was an end of hostilities between God and man. In sending Jesus to die, in Jesus' willing death God reconciled himself to man and provided a way home for all his children. The Father had honored Jesus' prayer, "Father, forgive them." Together Father and Son had made that forgiveness possible. It was all God's doing.

When the Father allowed Jesus to be crushed under our burden of our guilt, alienation, and godforsakenness "he made him to be sin" for us. (II Corinthians 5:21) In the cross God solved his two age-old problems posed by the fall of mankind. How could the holy God remain true to himself and receive home his sinful children? And, how could he respect human freedom and still draw his children back home? He did it by taking the sin and alienation into himself. Neither his holiness nor his love was lost.

> Only at the Cross of Christ does man see fully what it is that separates him from God; yet it is here alone that he perceives that he is no longer separated from God. Nowhere else does the inviolable holiness of God, the impossibility of overlooking the guilt of man stand out more plainly; but nowhere else also does the limitless mercy of God, which utterly transcends all human standards, stand out more clearly and plainly. That God can be both at once, the One who 'is not mocked,' and the One who 'doth not deal with us after our transgressions'; that neither aspect is sacrificed to the other, or can be subordinated to the other as a mere attribute; that God is equally the Holy One who asserts His unconditional claims, the One whose glory may not be given to another, and the Merciful One who gives Himself to the very utmost limits of self-emptying — this fundamental theme of the whole Bible is the message of the Cross, the truth which is not to be separated from the fact, but in it alone, in this actual happening, is the truth.[6]

Reconciliation is an accomplished fact in the heart of God. He completed it on Golgotha. So Paul in Romans 5:1-11 could write some of the most comforting words in all scripture: "Since we are justified by faith we have peace with God." He went on to say how it happened: "...while we were yet helpless, at the right time Christ died for the ungodly." God made the peace treaty, signed, sealed, and delivered it to us for our acceptance. We accepted his peace at baptism and celebrate it every Sunday at the Lord's Table. The cross is reconciliation. Because of it we are back at home with our Father forever. Our peace with God in the cross is the basis upon which we can find peace with one another (Ephesians 2:14-17) and peace within ourselves. (Philippians 4:7).

Redemption

Since the beginning of the biblical story human beings have been portrayed as captives, as prisoners. "Ransom" is the price in money paid for a slave's release, or sometimes the price paid in bloody conflict for the rescue of captives. The result of ransom is "redemption" for the ones set free.

Once again, the stories explain the pictures and *vice versa*. The Hebrews in Egypt were slaves held by the physical force of their masters. In the time of Amos, Israel was enslaved to the "good life," oblivious to the plight of the poor. They were blind to the coming doom of God's judgment on their self-indulgent lifestyle. In Jesus' day poor wretched souls were possessed of demons and evil spirits. Their lives were not their own. His enemies, the Scribes and Pharisees, were enslaved to their own understanding of God and their own vested interests. All human beings in all ages are slaves to sin and death.

In Mark 10:45 Jesus answered his disciples who were enslaved to ambition. He had just explained for the third time that he was going to Jerusalem to suffer, die, and be raised. Jesus explained his mission: "For the Son of man also came not be served but to serve, and to give his life a ransom for many." Their favorite topic of discussion was "who is greatest in the kingdom?" Jesus promised to break their bondage to self-centeredness. He would "ransom" them, pay the price for slaves on the auction block and set them at liberty of his kingdom. He would incur the losses of battle necessary to free the captives.

New Testament ethical admonitions were often framed in this redemption metaphor. Paul reminded the Corinthians that they were purchased by Christ. "You are not your own; you were bought with a price. So glorify God in your body." (I Corinthians

6:19,20) Peter used the same picture in I Peter 1:18 and following. The "exiles" saw persecution on the horizon and were afraid. Peter comforted them with the reminder that God had purchased them and they were his own.

> You know that you were ransomed from the futile ways inherited from your fathers, not with perishable things such as silver and gold, but with the precious blood of Christ, like that of a lamb without blemish or spot..."

Even in our world where the slave block is never seen, when few of us have been held hostage, these pictures still have powerful appeal. Alcoholism, workaholism, drug abuse, sexual additions and all other kinds of escapist behaviors torment people and keep them enslaved. The most basic, subtle and cruel of all captivities is slavery to self. All of us know that imprisonment. In the ancient Greek myth Narcissus was enslaved to himself. Contrary to popular opinion, worship of self does not enhance one's life, it de-humanizes its victim. It turns us into something other than human. Jurgen Moltmann pointed to our only hope.

> The knowledge of God in the suffering of the cross of Christ destroys man who abandons his humanity, for it destroys his gods and destroys his supposed divinity. It sets him free from his inhuman *hubris*, to restore his true human nature. It makes the *homo incurvatus in se* once again open to God and his neighbour, and gives Narcissus the power to love someone else.[7]

Before The Judge

In 1975 I was privileged to attend a series of lectures by the well-known German preacher and theologian, Helmut Thielicke. He spoke of life, death and judgment. The professor mentioned the play by Jean-Paul Sartre, *The Flies*. In that drama Orestes at one point shouted, "I am my own freedom!" asserting that he would have nothing more to do with his past but would start life all over again. Thielicke cited Colossians 2:14 to the effect that Christ has dealt with the believer's past in a different way: the bill of indictment was nailed to the cross. One does not pretend or try to deny his or her past, Jesus has taken upon himself our past. To explain Thielicke recalled a dream he had of his appearance at Judgment Day. God the Judge began by asking the identity of the defendant. Before anything else could be said, Satan as prosecuting attorney answered: "This is the one who has not loved his neighbor, has been proud and selfish, has injured others and could not repair the damages," and so on. Thielicke knew the accusations were all true. That was, indeed, his past, his identity. Then Jesus, the defense counsel stepped up to the bench and replied: "All of that is true, Father. But it is not true. His identity now is that he is one of my disciples. He is no longer to be identified just with his own past, he has a new identity in me." On that basis the Judge acquitted the defendant and welcomed him home.[8]

What a great thing if one day we had so absorbed the core gospel that we could have such a dream! Nothing could be more biblical. This courtroom picture of the cross is in the biblical word, "justification." For many of us any dream of judgment would be a nightmare terrifying beyond description.

Paul loved to use this courtroom metaphor to show what Jesus did for us on Golgotha. In Romans 3 he reminded the small community of faith that they had no right to quarrel over who should run the church. Gentiles were sinful because of their godless, self-centered past. The Jews were sinful because they saw the Law as a status symbol and their religious practices as meritorious and deserving of God's rewards. Paul made it clear: "all have sinned and fall short of the glory of God." They all stood hopeless before the judgment seat of the holy God.

But the Judge himself had made provision for their acquittal. Because of the cross they had all been justified. Jew and Gentile had been justified equally in the cross. Their hopelessness in themselves and their justification in Christ was the only ground upon which they could deal with their various claims to prominence in the church.

No wonder the book of Romans has had such a powerful impact in the history of individuals, of the church, and of society as a whole! Nothing is so liberating as the sure knowledge that we are right with God, that we are secure in his love for eternity. Our faith, like our works and our knowledge, is always imperfect. The love of God at Golgotha is strong, steady and forever sufficient. While our faith, hope and love wax and wane, the cross is eternal, solid and forever. There will never be a time when Jesus has not died for you and me. Such confidence also allows Christians to suffer hardship and develop Christian character. Paul concluded his discussion in Romans 6 by showing how by his cross the "second Adam" finally erased the curse of the "first Adam."

> Then as one man's trespass led to condemnation for all men, so one man's act of righteousness leads to acquittal and life for all men. For by one man's disobedience many will be made righteous. Law came in, to increase the trespass; but where sin increased, grace abounded all the more, so that, as sin reigned in death, grace also might reign through righteousness to eternal life through Jesus Christ our Lord.

How desperately we need to believe that we are truly justified in the cross of Christ! An elderly Christian woman on her deathbed was terrified and said, "I just don't know, I don't know if I've done enough!" Paul would assure her that she had not done enough. Could she have done enough Jesus need never have come. But Jesus had done more than enough and she had already accepted his gift. Despite her fears she was justified in the blood of Christ and safe with God for eternity.

Our Pattern

Preachers know they must apply their messages in one way or another to the real, felt needs of the people. Every good teacher uses examples. All of the pictures of the atonement discussed above have application for our daily lives. The cross of Jesus was not simply an historical event which redeemed our lives. It is also the living model after which we are to live our lives as Christians.

In choosing the cross Jesus is our example. Peter wrote his first epistle to "strangers and exiles," reminding them of the "living hope" they had because of what Jesus has done for them on Golgotha. Jesus gave them an example. "For to this you have been called, because Christ also suffered for you, leaving you an example, that you should follow in his steps" (I Peter 2:21).

The picture is in the word "example." All of his readers would easily recognize the image Peter meant to evoke in their minds. A child of five or six sits at a table, learning to write the alphabet. With clear dots the letters are already outlined on the page. All the child has to do is "connect the dots." It's a matter of tracing what is already there. Peter is saying that we do not know how to cope with life, we are not asked to make it up as we go along. Jesus went before us, showing us the way.

Without using the same Greek word, the same picture is clearly seen in other New Testament passages. Immediately after Jesus told the twelve for the first time that he was going up to Jerusalem to die Peter objected. After their lively debate and Peter's painful correction, Jesus called out to the whole crowd, including his disciples:

> If any would come after me let him deny himself and take up his cross and follow me. For whosoever would save his life will lose it; and whoever loses his life for my sake and the gospel's will save it. For what does it profit a man, to gain the whole world and forfeit his life? For what can a man give in return for his life? (Mark 8:34-36)

Jesus does not call us just to give up something, he calls us to deny self. Self is sneaky. It will wear any costume to stay on center stage, even its "Sunday best." Religion is the ultimate vehicle of self-aggrandizement. In his book, *How Can I Find God?*, Leslie D. Weatherhead said the problem is not so much where or how to find God but whether we will allow ourselves to be found by God.[9] He spoke of the "bunkers," those favorite hiding places where moderns like to hide from God: the busy life, the intellectual life, social activism, and in nature. Last on the list of bunkers was the religious life, man's deepest and best fortified hideout. That's where the Scribes and Pharisees were hiding from God. The life and death of Jesus is the only explosive powerful enough to crack the bunker of selfish and respectable religiosity. Only by imitating his self-giving life can we truly know God and find life.

The cross is not only the pattern for our individual lives, it also gives us the model for our life together in the church. In Philippians 2 Paul told the church to imitate Jesus who, though full of his own dignity and rights, emptied himself even to the point of the cross and God raised him up. Only the community of faith which takes seriously Jesus' death, burial, and resurrection as its model can truly be what God intends it to be. We are not asked to make life up as we go along. We are asked to look at the servant life of Jesus, at his cross and resurrection and to pattern our lives after him.

Victor Over Satan And Death

Christians sometimes think of the cross as a tragedy, a defeat over which God barely won victory at the last minute in the resurrection. It is true that the resurrection was a resounding victory. Had Jesus not been raised there would be no Christian faith. But the cross was itself a triumph. When we fail to see the several ways in which Jesus won victory on Golgotha we tend to de-emphasize the cross. It becomes only the disaster from which God rescued his son.

In the seven pictures of the cross just viewed we can see aspects of God's victory. The Suffering Servant metaphor shows victory over ambitious pride. Jesus won over his self-preservation instincts in offering himself as the sacrifice for our sin. In becoming our propitiation, he won victory for us over all our restless wandering to find access to and a place of mercy before God. He won over our alienation from God by becoming in his own body our bridge back to our Father. Jesus triumphed over all that holds us captive when he ransomed us at Golgotha. He won victory for us over our "past" by nailing it to the cross, securing our justification, and giving us a new identity in him. Jesus pioneered for us, winning for us over suffering, heartache, loneliness, godforsakenness and death and calling us to follow. All of these were triumphs Jesus won for us in choosing the cross.

In addition to these, I would point up three aspects of his victory that are especially relevant in our day. In choosing to come here and die for us Jesus overcame the curse of meaninglessness. Modern men and women are as burdened by the pointlessness of their lives as they are by sin and guilt. So many Americans knock themselves out to be "successful." They appropriate all the prescribed symbols of success, losing meanwhile their integrity, their family, and their joy of living. They are left to ask: "For what? What does it all mean?" Whatever else Jesus' life was, it was not pointless. His life and death were the most meaningful the world has ever known. He won a glorious victory over futility. In choosing to follow him we also find salvation from meaninglessness.

Second, Jesus won victory over enslaving self-interest. He taught his disciples to pray: "Thy kingdom come, Thy will be done." Jesus' words of submission in the garden locate for us the central struggle of our lives: "Not my will but thine be done." My instinct is to resist the whole cluster of ideas in that sentence: that God's will and mine are separate and distinct, that his kingdom and purposes are at odds with my kingdom and purposes, that the Father said "no" to his only Son and that I should also expect a negative answer from time to time, and that Jesus "learned obedience through what he suffered." All of that is totally foreign and deeply disturbing. Jesus submitted to the Father's will in order to bring all his children home. As a result you and I have salvation. No greater victory can be seen in the cross than Jesus' willingness finally to say: "Not my will but thine be done."

Third, the gospels portray the cross as victory over Satan and death. Luke especially emphasized this aspect of the story. After the temptations, the Devil departed "for a while, for another time." These temptations arose again and again. In Luke 4 we see Jesus tempted to please the homefolk at Nazareth. But he would not cater to prejudice even for the approval of those who knew him best. At Capernaum they loved him so much they begged him to stay, settle down, become their chaplain and have a forty year ministry with all the fringe benefits. But he came to preach the kingdom from place to place and to touch all sorts of people. In Luke 11 Jesus was accused of casting out demons by the power of Beelzebul, the prince of demons. He asked if a house divided against itself could stand. Then he told the parable of the strong man whose possessions were safe until a stronger man came along. He was obviously referring to himself as the one stronger than the Devil. Jesus defined his whole mission as the decisive battle of God with the rebellious angel, Satan.

Jesus' conflict with Satan came to its climax in Luke 22. In the garden Jesus struggled with the Father's will. The mob came to arrest Jesus. Peter tried to protect him with a sword. That was not Jesus' way. Then Jesus turned to the mob and asked them why they came with swords and clubs. Had he not taught them openly in the temple day by day? Could they not have arrested him there? Then Jesus explained what was really happening: "But this is your hour, and the power of darkness."

Jesus was betrayed, forsaken, railroaded, abused, scorned and crucified. He cried out, "Father, forgive them" and died. The decisive battle was over. It was obvious to his disciples that Satan had won. They would just have to face the ugly truth.

God raised Jesus up in victory over all that hell could do! Resurrection was victory indeed! Jesus had triumphed by taking on the Devil and the legions of hell. He had won in choosing the cross.

His victory would make Christians strong in the face of lions and death at the stake. It would steel Martin Luther in the face of the Roman church. Negro slaves in the Old South would gain strength from singing, "Were you there when they crucified my Lord?" Today men and women all over the world "hang on" and "see it through" because Jesus chose the cross. Not just the resurrection, Jesus' cross was victory!

> Since therefore the children share in flesh and blood, he himself likewise partook of the same nature, that through death he might destroy him who has the power of death, that is, the devil, and deliver all those who through fear of death were subject to lifelong bondage." (Hebrews 2:14,15)

There are serious problems with a faith based only on the resurrection. When we have only a resurrection faith we see suffering as abnormal, exceptional, something to be avoided at all costs. We deny human suffering and try to pretend that it has no place in life. Or we look for victory in all the wrong places. The modern church, like the modern world, is worshipping beautiful idols: self-fulfillment, self-esteem, self-enhancement, pleasure, prestige, power, possessions, success, religion on the grand scale, and especially excitement. Worship at these altars stimulates the devotees' self-centeredness, blinds them to the crucified, makes them too tender to serve in the real world, and ultimately leaves them spiritually empty.

The more we absorb this portrait of Jesus' victory in his life, death, and resurrection the less we are obsessed with physical fitness, the illusion that we must remain young all our lives, and physical survival at all costs. The more we know of his cross the more we know that it's okay to be used up and to die for something worthwhile. Such a commitment is the only thing that makes life worth living.

> Fear not, I am the first and the last, and the living one; I died, and behold I am alive for evermore, and I have the keys of Death and Hades. (Rev. 1:17,18).

NOTES

[1] Michael Goldberg, *Jews And Christians, Getting Our Stories Straight.* (Nashville: Abingdon, 1985), p. 13.

[2] Charles Reynolds Brown, *Have We Outgrown Religion?* (New York: Harper, 1932) pp. 12,13.

[3] Leander E. Keck, *Mandate To Witness* (Valley Forge: Judson, 1964) p. 33.

[4] Jurgen Moltmann, *The Crucified God*, (New York: Harper, 1973) p. 71.

[5] Emil Brunner, *The Scandal Of Christianity*, (Richmond: John Knox, 1968) p. 79.

[6] Emil Brunner, *The Mediator* (Philadelphia: Westminster, 1947) p. 452.

[7] Moltmann, pp. 71,72.

[8] Helmut Thielicke, "Life And Death," Taped Lectures delivered at the Institute of Religion, Texas Medical Center, Houston, September, 1975.

[9] Leslie D. Weatherhead, *How Can I Find God* (London: Hodder and Stoughton, 1933).

Summary of Part 1

Many today wonder whether there is a power which can redeem life and make it whole and meaningful. The New Testament provides us the core gospel which has power to change lives and alter history itself. It continues the narrative of God with mankind and shows how the story ends. The Bible contains many stories within the great story. The greatest of all tells of the life, death, and resurrection of Jesus of Nazareth. In light of this story the stories of our lives come into focus and make sense.

Those who wrote the New Testament knew the story. They told it to evangelize, referred to it in defending the faith, and shared its meaning to edify individuals and communities of believers. They kept telling the story despite the fact that Jesus was himself a scandal while he lived, his cross was offensive, and the word of the cross was unacceptable. When Christians went out telling the story they offended everyone.

The core gospel narrative is not merely a matter of history. What God did on Golgotha remains today the nuclear secret of Christianity. The New Testament not only tells us what the core gospel was in the first century, it provides us means by which to appropriate the power for ourselves and for others. The gospel story lines tell us much about the meaning of Jesus' death. The epistles spell out implications for daily life. The whole New Testament contains pictures which illustrate the story. The book of Revelation tells us how the story ends.

A Quantitative Summary

The attached chart shows in a quantitative way how central the cross is in the New Testament. Not in form, but in purpose and content the New Testament is preaching. It preaches to evangelize, to defend the faith, and to edify believers. So one might ask: "If one divided the New Testament into sermon-sized portions, in what percentage of those 'sermons' is there some mention of the death, burial, and resurrection of Jesus or the 'word of the cross'?" I have analyzed the New Testament as a whole in that way to discover how it preached the word of the cross. (See Appendix A for assumptions and methodology.) The word of the cross was not all the New Testament writers had to say, but it was the basis of all they had to say. They preached it 100% of the time in every kind of situation to meet all kinds of needs. They told the grand old story, they painted pictures to portray the mystery of God's love and they spelled out the implications in the "word of the cross."

Explanation of The Chart, Fig. 1.

The chart reports in a quantitative way what we have described already regarding the word of the cross in the New Testament. Across the TOP OF THE CHART one finds listed the thirty-three portions of scripture which roughly approximate the New Testament divided into sermon-length portions, here called "units." (See Appendix A for assumptions and methodology.)

103   Summary of Part I

Working down the chart on the LEFT SIDE, one finds "frequency of mention." The numbers across the chart beside this designation indicate the number of references to the death, burial, and resurrection in each scripture unit. For example, "Unit No. 2" has four references to the core gospel. Next, one finds "Treatment - Substantial or Incidental" These figures indicate what number of the total references in each scripture portion contain some content ("substantial")and what number of reference are merely made in passing ("incidental.) For example, Unit no. 2 (Matthew 8:31-14:16) contains four references to the death, burial and resurrection. Two of those are substantial, two are incidental.

Next, one sees "Kinds and occurences of N.T. Materials." This simply reports the number and kinds of materials referring to the death, burial, and resurrection. For example, how often and in which units one finds the reconciliation metaphor or the scandal of the cross. These numbers do not necessarily add up to the total number of references in the unit because a single reference may include more than one metaphor. The "Gospel Story Line" item at the bottom of the chart indicates every time the story is either told or referred to. Consequently, every unit in the gospels is obviously part of the telling of the story and so each counts at least for one reference. However, in unit no. 23, the story is not told but referred to twice.

On the RIGHT SIDE of the chart are the totals. At the top one sees that, in the thirty-three sermon-sized units, there are 217 references to the core gospel. As one looks across the chart it is clear that every single unit contains some reference. So the total rate of mention for the New Testament as a collection of thirty-three "sermons" is 100%. Beneath that figure one discovers that 160 of those 217 references were substantial, or 73%. Fifty-eight were incidental or 27%. Below those numbers are the simple totals for the number of references for the various kinds of materials found referring to the core gospel. For example, the Victor over Satan metaphor is by far the most frequently used, appearing 84 times in all.

The results recorded on this chart will be used later as a yardstick by which to measure Restoration preaching of the core gospel.

We Restorationists should ask how well we have preached the core gospel. We are not trying to restore the church at Corinth or the church at Rome. We are trying to restore the New Testament gospel. The more I examine the New Testament doctrine of the atonement the more I am overwhelmed with its pervasiveness, versatility, richness, depth, and beauty and power. With this brief overview of the New Testament theology of the cross in hand we will attempt to measure our Restoration understanding and proclamation of the core gospel.

Figure No. 1

TABULATION OF REFERENCES TO THE DEATH, BURIAL AND RESURRECTION OF JESUS IN THE NEW TESTAMENT

Unit #	Thirty-Three Sermon Sized Units	Total	Sub.	Inc.	Priest/ Sacrifice	Redemption/ Ransom	Propitiation/ Expiation	Reconciliation	Victor over Satan/Death	Suffering Servant	Justification (law court)	Example (pattern)	Scandal of the cross	Gospel story line
1	Matt. 1:1 - 8:30	1		1					1				1	1
2	Matt. 8:31 - 14:16	4	2	2					1				3	1
3	Matt. 14:17 - 21:25	6	1	5				1	4	1			1	1
4	Matt. 21:26 - 26:28	5	1	4			1					2		1
5	Matt. 26:29 - Mk. 4:11	3		3			1	1					4	1
6	Mk. 4:12 - 9:46	3	1	2					2	1		1	2	1
7	Mk. 9:47 - 15:2	6	3	3			1		3			1	4	1
8	Mk. 15:3 - Lu. 4:17	3	1	2			1	1					2	1
9	Lu. 4:18 - 9:4	2		2				1					3	1
10	Lu. 9:5 - 13:19	5	1	4					2				1	1
11	Lu. 13:20 - 20:12	4	2	2				1					1	1
12	Lu. 20:13 - Jn. 1:17	10	4	6	1			1	3				3	1
13	Jn. 1:18 - 6:65	9	4	5	2				1				4	1
14	Jn. 6:66 - 12:21	16	9	7			1	2					5	1
15	Jn. 12:22 - 19:19	11		11				2	6	2		2	4	1
16	Jn. 19:20 - Acts 5:19	11	3	8				3	11		3			2
17	Acts 5:20 - 11:19	4	1	3	1			2					3	1
18	Acts 11:20 - 18:6	3	1	2				2					4	1
19	Acts 18:7 - 26:31	3	1	2	1			2						
20	Acts 26:32 - Rom 6:13	6	1	5		2		4		3				1
21	Rom. 6:14 - 15:3	6	1	5	2	1	1	1	6	1				
22	Rom. 15:4 - I Cor. 8:12	9	2	7	1	3							3	
23	I Cor. 8:13 - 16:21	4		4	2			2						2
24	II Cor. 1:1 - 12:13	5	1	4	1	1		2						
25	II Cor. 12:14 - Eph. 4:13	10	3	7	3			2		2		1	1	1
26	Eph. 4:14 - Col. 3:23	9	1	8	2		1	3	1		1	5		1
27	Col. 3:24 - I Tim. 6:1	5		5	2		1	2					1	
28	I Tim 6:2 - Heb. 6:11	10	1	9	4	2	1	3			4		1	1
29	Heb. 6:12 - Jas. 2:4	6		6	3	1		1					2	
30	Jas. 2:5 - II Pet. 3:5	10	4	6	3	1		6	1			5	2	1
31	II Pet. 3:6 - Rev. 2:14	7	2	5	1		2	2				2		
32	Rev. 2:15 - 14:1	13	6	7	1			3						1
33	Rev. 14:2 - 22:21	9		9	1			4						
TOTALS	218 or *100%* Appears in 33 of 33 "Sermons"		160 or *73%*	58 or *27%*	36	25	4	16	84	14	6	21	57	26

Part 2

Introduction
A Survey of Restoration Preaching, 1800-1950

We Restorationists do not want to reinvent the wheel. Our supreme joy is to rediscover it. It is our responsibility and opportunity to measure ourselves by the New Testament canon (yardstick) as a reminder of what the gospel is. Ours was not the only "Restoration Movement," many American traditions have had their versions of restorationism.[1] But our interest here is to look back over our own movement to see how well we have preached the New Testament core gospel.

Since this work includes an evaluation of our preaching the reader has a right to know from what vantage point the author writes. I was born into a family which was second generation in the Church of Christ. The Church of Christ is where I met Jesus Christ, made my confession of faith and was baptized into him. I regard that relationship to him as the most precious gift any human can ever receive. Consequently, my affection for the Church of Christ is enormous. My uncle Vern Love was a minister in Kansas and spent his life preaching in the mid-west. My father was a deacon and an elder at various times and places. My two older brothers, Robert L. Love and Max D. Love, are preachers. They were my boyhood heroes and today have my greatest love and respect. From grade four through the M.A.

program I attended Abilene Christian. My formative years were lived in the warm and supportive fellowship of the College Church in Abilene. I made my first "talk" as a fifth grader one Wednesday night at the College Church which met in old Sewell auditorium on campus. Among those who confirmed, instructed, and encouraged me over the years were: Jesse P. Sewell, E.W. McMillan, George Bailey, Fred Barton, Holbert Rideout, Lemoine Lewis, Carl Spain, Frank Pack and J.W. Roberts. The College Church supported us five years during our first ministry out of school in Winnipeg, Canada. The Church of Christ is my family; I love it and feel privileged to be a part of the Restoration tradition.

That is not to say that I see no problems. Loving one's family does not mean denying its problems. I suppose none of us would claim that our tradition has been trouble free. We have suffered sicknesses from time to time. Our unity movement has divided again and again. My own family was deeply affected by the "cooperation controversy" in the early fifties. Another symptom has been our tendency to believe in self-salvation. I have met scores of people over the years who have felt that the faith is a harsh, legalistic system. They wonder if God loves them and what they might do to win his favor. Sometimes the medicine for that disease has been as bad as the malady itself. Individuals and churches who have fought free of legalism have sometimes fallen into other traps of self-salvation: salvation by knowledge, salvation by feelings, salvation by social activism, salvation by religious experience, salvation by success. A third sign of pathology has been our fascination with the "latest things down the pike." Over the generations we have been enthralled by various issues and methods. Some of these preoccupations reflected a deep love of the truth and of lost souls. But as "first things" and substitutes for the core gospel they disappointed us, as our rapidly changing tastes have shown.

For diagnostic purposes, let us hold our tradition up to the New Testament to see how well we have proclaimed the core gospel. This section of the book examines our preaching over the generations from 1800 to 1950. The survey can be understood correctly only if we see clearly what we are not asking and what we are asking. We are not asking whether individual preachers preached grace or salvation by works. In every generation we have had both kinds of messages proclaimed. One can preach the cross legalistically, or one can preach a kind of grace that is not tied to the cross. We are not asking whether your church and mine back home were warm fellowships of honest, loving Christians. As I said above, I have been richly blessed by my early experiences. Thousands of others could say the same. We are not asking whether the preachers studied here were men of integrity, dedicated to their vision of God and to their God-given ministries of caring for souls to the glory of God. That is assumed.

What we are asking is a very specific question: Did the church hear from the pulpit the core gospel of the death, burial, and resurrection of Jesus Christ and the word of the cross "as of first importance"? In other words, was the "word of the cross" central in our proclamation as it is in the New Testament? To say it yet another way, did the event of Golgotha and the open tomb so capture the hearts and imaginations of our preachers that they drank deeply of the metaphors of atonement, relished telling the gospel story, and braved the disapproval which comes from holding up the scandal of the cross? Or again, was the cross of Christ for us the source of evangelism, the sure ground for defense of the faith and the fountainhead for edification?

Before proceeding to the study of our history another preliminary note must be struck. Preaching is not the only way the core gospel is traditioned from generation to generation.

The child at home hears the Bible story. Sunday School teachers have long told the Bible narrative in ways that captured young minds. Our worship services and revivals have included scores of songs which point to the meaning of Golgotha: "The Old Rugged Cross," "Victory In Jesus," "Rock Of Ages," "When I Survey The Wondrous Cross," "Tell Me The Story Of Jesus," "When We Meet In Sweet Communion," "Beneath The Cross Of Jesus," and many more. Some churches have a custom of communion meditations in which the meaning of the cross is regularly stated. The core gospel has been and always should be traditioned in many ways.

But it is still true that the pulpit sets the tone for the church. This has been true historically over the centuries and it has especially been true in our Restoration Movement. No single factor has so influenced grass roots faith, has so determined our direction as our preaching. For that reason the central question is: What have our people actually heard from the pulpit about the atonement? To answer the question I have restricted my study almost exclusively to books of sermons.

In the following four chapters I report the findings of a study of the four generations of Restoration preachers from 1800 to 1950. Analysis of the sermons of twenty preachers in all will be given. There is "method" in my "madness," and the assumptions of this study are several.[2] We turn now to survey four generations of Restoration preaching regarding the core gospel. We will spend a disproportionate amount of time with the first generation because the die was cast in the early years of our movement.

The First Generation

Stone and Campbell

What did our two most influential early leaders have to say about the atonement? They published no books of sermons. For that reason we must range farther afield to get an accurate picture of their preaching of the core gospel. We examine first their backgrounds, then their writings including their extended debate on the atonement, and then their preaching from the reports and manuscripts which remain.

Backgrounds

Barton W. Stone (1772-1844) was born in Maryland and received his religious orientation and training in the Episcopal Church. He became a Presbyterian and served in that fellowship for eight years. His worked centered in Kentucky and Ohio. He and five other Presbyterian ministers wrote "The Last Will And Testament Of The Springfield Presbytery." Their plea was for a return to the New Testament without creeds, party names, and church hierarchy. He came to a parting of the ways with the Presbyterians and became the major leader of a "Restoration" movement in the frontier of that time. A man of some education,

Stone's orientation was nevertheless to the frontier. In personality he was turned toward the warmth of Christian piety, and he promoted strongly an emphasis on Christian living and holiness. His movement predated the Campbells' by several years. Their movements united formally in 1832.

Alexander Campbell (1788-1866) was born in Ireland, the son of a Presbyterian minister. Thomas Campbell had the means to provide his bright young son the best education available. Alexander attended the University of Glasgow and early on distinguished himself as a scholar of the first rank. He joined the Presbyterian church and intended to follow his father into the ministry. Thomas, a man of independent mind, began to challenge some of the beliefs of his particular part of the Presbyterian church, and especially to decry the disunity among believers in Christ. He immigrated to the United States in 1807 and Alexander followed two years after. Father and son worked together for a return to the Scriptures as a method of producing unity among believers. Alexander came to believe the millennium would come when all believers were united on the Scriptures. Like Stone, he eventually parted ways with the Presbyterians. For a while he had a loose and tenuous association with the Baptist church. Eventually he began calling disciples from all churches to come out and unite on the Scriptures alone. He became nationally known as a scholar, lecturer, writer and editor. From his home in Virginia his influence spread far and wide, especially in Pennsylvania and Ohio.

Their Writings On The Atonement.

Our study of the writings of Stone and Campbell on the atonement should begin with Stone's publication, in 1805, of "Two Letters To A Friend."[3] In answer to the inquiry of the unnamed friend Stone confirmed that he had recently changed his views on important central matters of faith. He wrote his friend, warning him, "lest you be caught in the labyrinth of Calvinism where I have been myself." He then stated briefly the four basic doctrines contained in the Presbyterian Church of America's Confession of Faith: 1) God entered into a covenant with Adam, promising life or death depending on man's keeping of that covenant. 2) Adam broke the covenant and his posterity was bound over forever to wrath and death. 3) Christ Jesus became the surety (substitute) for mankind, providing salvation from death. 4) As surety he fulfilled the precepts of the law, suffered the curse, and paid the penalty of sin.

Stone explained his objections to this confession on four grounds. First, he found no mention of any such covenant in the Bible. Second, in Stone's words, "I am convinced that real wrath cannot exist in God...God is love." Third, Stone objected to the doctrine that Christ is the surety for mankind because he found nothing of it in the Bible. The word is only used once in Scripture, in Hebrews 7:22. He said this theory of substitution was the "nail" upon which the whole Calvinistic system of election, partial atonement, direct operation of the Holy Spirit hung. Fourth, Stone disagreed with the idea of imputed righteousness. What, he asked, is the meaning of saying that Jesus paid our debt of obedience and suffering? For example, did he save us from obeying God's call to love him first and our neighbors as ourselves?

In the second letter Stone wrote that Jesus came to make at-one-ment, to reconcile God and man. He came to be a propitiation, the same thing as atonement or reconciliation. Jesus came to redeem us from the devil, from sin, from the curse of the law by showing us God's grace. Stone saw all the New Testament metaphors of the atonement as essentially interchangeable with reconciliation.

In his autobiography Stone devoted half a chapter to his change of mind on the atonement. In addition to his objections to Calvinism outlined above, Stone protested the Presbyterians' understanding of God. To say that God changed in some way at Calvary or that he suffered was unacceptable to Stone. He believed God was perfect, could never change, and so could never suffer.[4]

It is clear that Stone's doctrine of the atonement was determined in reaction to what he saw as the harsh, cold Calvinism of the Presbyterian Church Of America. He rejected talk of the wrath of God, the suffering of God, elect and non-elect, and Jesus as man's substitute before the law. He believed Christianity was a religion of God's love expressed in the cross of Christ which, if taken internally, produces godliness in believers.

Campbell was fifteen or sixteen years Stone's junior. In 1829 he wrote in "The Christian Baptist" four articles, "sermons" to young preachers about the work they were to do as proclaimers of the gospel. In the fourth sermon he asked what the job of ministers should be in the current situation. His answer was clear. A great army of volunteers was teaching the fundamentals of the faith to children and new converts. These were mothers and fathers, Sunday school teachers, nurses, and others. An "army of volunteers" was much preferable to an expensive "standing army." Preacher and people alike already know the basic facts of the gospel. The young preachers could safely assume the basics and go to work retrieving the "ancient order" of things in the churches for the sake of unity among all believers.

> To begin to proclaim that all men will die, and to prove it by argument, would not be more unnecessary and superfluous, than to proclaim that there will be a

> judgment — that there is a Savior, and a future state of bliss and woe, to them who doubt not any of these fundamentals. It is necessary to proclaim reformation to such a people who, with all these acknowledgments, are serving diverse lusts and passions, living in malice and envy, hated and hating one another.[5]

Campbell went on to say that John the Baptist might be their model. He assumed basic Judaism and announced the coming of the Messiah. Further, he affirmed that, if the apostle Paul were present in nineteenth century America he would follow a similar methodology.

Campbell, himself, practiced what he preached. His book, *The Christian System*, written in 1835, contained his outline of Christian theology addressed to the religious world of his day. The subject of atonement claimed only thirteen of three hundred and thirteen pages or approximately four percent of the book. The reason was not that Campbell intended to de-emphasize the cross. It is clear that Campbell considered the atonement the doctrine of first importance.

> The 'doctrine of the cross' being the great central doctrine of the Bible, and the very essence of Christianity—which explains all the peculiarities of the Christian system, and of the relation of Father, Son, and Holy Spirit, as far as mortals can comprehend them, and as it has been, to skeptics and many professors 'a stone of stumbling, and a rock of offence, 'for the sake of some of the speculative and cavilling, who ask why are these things so?[6]

It is clear that Campbell considered the atonement supremely important. He assumed that most Christians and all preachers believed the same. His distress was over divisions among believers of various kinds. Since all believers agreed on the basics they should take the Bible to be their rule of faith and practice to correct matters of church order which divided them: entrance requirements, government, worship forms, nomenclature, etc.

Campbell held with Calvinism on most major doctrines of the atonement. He believed in substitutionary atonement and that Jesus died only for the elect. In contrast with Stone, he believed the metaphors of the New Testament were not interchangeable. However, the Priest/Sacrifice metaphor was dominant. His whole discussion of the atonement was under the heading, "Sin Offering."

For two years, 1840, 1841, Campbell and Stone debated the atonement in their papers.[7] The older Stone expressed reluctance at the outset. He feared such a discussion might prove divisive among their followers. Campbell reassured Stone that division need never occur when brethren seek the truth honestly. Perhaps he was also thinking of his father's distinction between "matters of faith" and "matters of opinion." The "fact" of the atonement was a matter of faith, while an interpretation was a matter of opinion and should never be bound on another. The discussion began in deference, each extending kindness to the other at every turn. Before the debate ended Stone was accusing Campbell of "New England theology," and Campbell was lecturing Stone on Greek and Hebrew words. Each leader had accused the other of "speculation." The exchange ended without either man moving from his position. Perhaps both came to see that Stone's initial fears were not unreasonable after all. Both men seemed to shy away from the subject thereafter. So far as I have been able to discover, there has never again been such an in-depth discussion of the atonement among our brethren.

Their Preaching Of The Core Gospel.

I have found only eleven of Stone's sermons and lectures for study. He mentioned some aspect of the death, burial, and resurrection in nine of these eleven, or eighty-two percent of the time in this sample. That rate of mention is higher than that of any other preacher studied in this volume. He made no mention of the core gospel in a sermon entitled, "Having A Form of Godliness" from II Timothy 3 or in one of his four lectures on Christian union.

In "The Family Of God On Earth," a sermon reported in Stone's "Christian Messenger," 1826, he pled for the union of believers in all traditions. "Because they are all reconciled to God, they should have the hearts and will to reconcile to one another. Not my will, but thine be done, is the language of the heart." Stone said.[8] A year later he printed another sermon against inter-denominational bitterness entitled: "A Humble Address To The Various Denominations Of Christians In America." He claimed that Jesus' command to "love one another" had been too long overlooked by "professed believers of the Lamb." He preached acceptance of one's fellow believer as the first order of business; discussion and debate could come later.

> This man is one of God's elect. And 'who shall lay any thing to the charge of God's elect? It is God that justifieth. Who is he that condemneth? It is Christ that died, yea, rather that is risen again' — shall any presume to reject such a Christian from the house of God — from communion with the saints — from union with the body of Christ?[9]

"An Orthodox Sermon" was a facetious rebuttal of the Calvinistic view of atonement and election. From Romans 8 he presented the "orthodox" Calvinist position as if it were his own, answering objections (which were truly his own) as a Calvinist might. By this method Stone wanted to show the absurdity of the orthodox beliefs. One of the objections was that the Scriptures present Jesus' death as for the whole world, not for the elect only. The "orthodox" preacher would answer that Jesus died for the whole world, the whole "elect" world. Another objection was that the whole system was based on speculation and that Christ had not died as a substitute for mankind. The "orthodox" preacher would answer that the objection was based on ignorance. Stone concluded by offering an invitation, commenting in irony that he did not know whether there were any elect in his audience. "Believe, repent and turn to the Lord, perhaps you may be saved..."[10]

Another sermon Stone preached in 1834 was based on Luke 22:19, "This Do In Remembrance of Me." He explained the meaning of communion in light of Israel's deliverance and the paschal lamb. Stone's warm heart comes through clearly. (Quoted here as it appears in Stone's own handwritten manuscript:)

> Our Savior also was crucified the same day of the same month in which the Israelites were delivered from Egyptian bondage, the 15th day of that month now called March. In the 25th of Matt we find where christ instituted this sacrament and that it was evidently intended to be a solemn commemoration of the ...(words illegible)..death of Jesus Christ to be substituted in the room of the Passover...O can you hear him from that upper chamber after the supper Can you hear him in his deepest agony in Gethsemane, can you hear him from that cross on which he groaned & died — can you hear him from the right hand of God in the highest heavens "Do this in remembrance of me"?[11]

In 1834 and again in 1838 Stone preached a sermon entitled "Be Not Deceived, God is Not Mocked" (Galatians 6:7). He asked his hearers how they spent their Sabbaths. Stone pleaded for his hearers' spiritual welfare like a lawyer pleads for the life of his client. This quote is taken from his handwritten outline:

> ... the Lord Jesus Christ the night before he was betrayed instituted the Sacrament of the Lord's Supper, as a standing, perpetual memorial of his dying love for man, and he says to his disciples, thro the successive ages of time, Do this in remembrance of me. Here now is a duty, a known duty, an acknowledged duty...

Stone said that gospel preachers lead their hearers past Mount Sinai with its lightning and thunder and Law to the cross of Golgotha.

> ...they lead us to Gethsemane, from thence to the Court of Pilate, and from its partial tribunal to the hill of Calvary and to the Cross and there suspended between heaven and earth, they shew us God's Son dying in the stead of Sinful man, they point us to his bleeding wounded side, they tell us to enter there, they point you to the table of the Lord.[12]

Stone's sermon is consistent with what he wrote on the atonement. The cross was, more than anything else, an expression of God's love which breaks open the sinner's heart and calls him home.

In 1841 Stone published four "lectures" delivered in Jacksonville, Illinois on "The Union Of Christians." For all four lectures he took the text, John 17:10-22, Jesus' prayer for unity among his followers. He began by saying that the union of all Christians was the "all engrossing subject" which occupied the tongues and pens of the Christian community at the time. His formula for union was a return to the mind of Christ, Christians should be filled with his Holy Spirit. While many denominations had hoisted their own flags, Jesus Christ was the only ensign under which all could unite. His cross could melt proud hearts and unite believers.

> It may be asked, How can faith in Jesus as the Son, and the anointed of the Father, produce such divine effects? I answer: In believing this we ascend to the Father in heaven, and see his boundless love to the world, bursting forth in the gift of his Son, to live, die, and raise again for our justification and salvation — we see the love of the Son in leaving the abodes of glory, and his matchless condescension in humbling himself for our good. Who in heart can believe these things and remain unaffected?[13]

The last sermon of Stone's studied here is marked: "1841—New Year's Sermon." Stone was sixty-nine and would survive only four years after this sermon was preached. The poignant statement which shows the ripe fruit of his long ministry is based on II Corinthians 12:15. "I will most gladly spend and be spent for your souls. If I love you the more, am I to be loved the less?" (As written in his own hand:)

> Take the bible and see where the ground of your salvation is the lamb, you are delivered in his blood you are redeemed 'not by corruptible things as gold and silver'...are you justified? if so it is by the blood of Christ. Are Christians permitted to enter into the Holy of Holies? It is all by the blood of Christ. Do they overcome all things? They overcome by the blood of the Lamb. Do they live? They have life through his blood.

> ...thus are we here to contemplate the two great leading doctrines in the gospel of Christ...the fall of man by sin...and his recovery by the blood of Christ...and these are the great truths in the enforcement of which the ministry should be willing to spend and be spent...[14]

How does Stone's preaching compare in form and content with the New Testament treatment of the atonement? He mentioned the core gospel in eighty-two percent of his sermons sampled here. That mark compares with one-hundred percent of the New Testament sermon length portions. Stone's rate of mention is higher than that of any other Restoration preacher in this study. Eight of these references were substantive and one was incidental. He used the priest/sacrifice metaphor four times, example three times, propitiation, reconciliation and justification twice each, ransom and victor over Satan once each. He made no references to the "Suffering Servant" or to the scandal of the cross. Once he pointed to the gospel story line.

Despite his warm-hearted appeals on the basis of the cross and the frequency with which the core gospel appeared in his preaching, Stone may have put a damper on further study of the atonement by others. Because of his strong aversion to the speculations of Calvinism about substitutionary atonement, satisfaction of the law's demands, the elect and non-elect, the suffering of God and because of his concern that discussion of the subject might lead his and Campbell's followers toward division Stone left a deposit of discouragement where the study of the atonement is concerned. It may seem ironic that this one who had such a developed "word of the cross," who preached it so extensively would fail to encourage younger preachers to explore this central doctrine of the faith.

As samples of Campbell's preaching we have, in various forms, twenty-six of his sermons and lectures. He mentioned the cross in thirteen of these or fifty percent of the time. Of the nineteen sermons reported in Richardson's *Memoirs* there were fourteen which contained no reference to the cross. Themes Campbell addressed without the "word of the cross" were: Christian unity, "gaining the whole world but losing one's own soul," judgment, the Christian's walk with God, great things from small beginnings, Restorationism — preparing the "highway" for the Lord, Jesus as the "Bread of life," externals in religion, ordination not necessary for ministers, the glory of God's Son, the purposes of the church, respect for other Christians' scruples, and entrance to the church or God's kingdom.

Before he was thirty Alexander Campbell preached the landmark "Sermon On The Law" to the Redstone Baptist Association in 1816.[15] He set out to prove that Christians are no longer under the Law of Moses but under Christ. Had he given the sermon a positive title it might have been, "Salvation At The Cross." The heart of his message was that the Law was deficient for man's salvation on several counts. First, it could not give righteousness and eternal life. This Jesus did in his life and death. Second, the Law was inadequate to show the seriousness and demerit of sin. Again, this was only to be seen in the cross of Christ. Third, the Law could not function as a suitable moral guide for all mankind since it was given only to the Jews. Campbell's sermon was centered in the cross as the center and source of God's new system in Christ.

In 1827 Campbell published in "The Christian Baptist" a sermon on the captivity of the churches to the creeds. He spoke from Nehemiah 4 and 6, from II Thessalonians 2, and from Revelation 17 and 18. He began by pointing up the many "types" of the Christian age found in the Old Testament: the immersion of the

Hebrews in the Red Sea was a type of baptism, and the Tabernacle sacrifices were types "of the sacrifice of our great High Priest," observed Campbell. He went on to speak of the main "type" in the Old Testament which spoke of the situation in nineteenth century American Christianity: the captivity of God's people in Babylon. Of creeds, sectarian systems and organizations Campbell called: "Come, out of her, my people, that you may not be partakers of her sins, and that you may not receive of her plagues."[16] He mentioned the cross of Christ only in passing.

In 1836 David S. Burnet asked Campbell to submit a sermon to his first volume of the paper, "The Christian Preacher". Campbell sent a sermon entitled: "The Riches Of Christ." He began by pointing to the riches of creation, the cosmos, and the good earth. All of this is under the lordship of Christ. He went on to say that the Redeemer's wealth in his ransomed people is beyond calculation. "The wealth of the Lord Jesus in the church, is, therefore far greater than his wealth in all material nature. The price paid for man's redemption is the best proof of the value set on him by his Redeemer." When one considers the riches of Christ as Lord of all, as head over the church he can only join the thousands who surround the throne of heaven in saying: "'Worthy is the Lamb that was slain to receive power, and riches, and wisdom, and might, and honor, and glory and blessing' — 'To the Lamb be blessing and honor, and glory, and strength, for ever and ever, Amen!'" With an eye to the readers of the new journal, Campbell added:

> How noble the enterprize of the Christian preacher, who devotes his life to the salvation of men! And is not this the true intent and meaning of that good work which is called the preaching of the gospel? Jesus died, not only as a martyr to attest the truth which he spoke, but as a

> sacrifice to expiate our sins, and to justify God in justifying man; 'to magnify the law of God and make it honorable,' and to open a way, 'new and living' by which a penitent sinner might return to God, and find acceptance. But it is not enough that Jesus died and rose again — that the original witnesses once published these glad tidings and confirmed their testimony by their blood; nor, that we have all of this in writing — it must be read to others, and their attention must be called to it, and its evidences, and arguments, and exhibitions, must be laid before mankind in order to their acceptance of this great salvation. Now he that does these things is called a Christian Preacher, and is engaged in the very enterprize which brought the Messiah into the world, to the cross, to the grave, to the skies, to the throne of the universe.[17]

We now turn to the sermon reports found in Richardson's *Memoirs*.[18] I have chosen sample sermons as representative of those which contain mention of the cross. From Galatians 1:4 Campbell preached on the one "who gave himself for our sins that he might deliver us from this present evil world." The evils, according to Campbell, were three forms of ignorance: of ourselves, of the gospel, and of man's glorious redemption. (Vol.I, p.371) Another sermon was based on Matthew 11:27. Campbell affirmed that "all things have been delivered" to Christ who, as Philippians 2 says: humbled himself, became a servant, even to death on the cross. He was hated and despised and yet he finished his work and the price of salvation has been exacted. (I, 375)

In a sermon for which no text was recorded Campbell discussed the nature of faith. He said the simple element in every religion is sacrifice for sin, in Christianity the sacrifice of the Lamb of

God. The reporter said Campbell kept two elements clearly before the audience; the perfection of Scripture and Jesus' sacrifice for man's redemption. (II,608-611)

Campbell's wife, Selina, preserved a full length sermon manuscript in her volume about their life together. She explained that the sermon was written for a collection of twenty-eight sermons preached by distinguished preachers of various denominations. Campbell entitled it: "On The Justification And Coronation Of The Messiah." His text was I Timothy 3:16: "Without controversy, great is the mystery of godliness. God was manifest in the flesh, justified by the spirit, seen of angels, preached to the Gentiles, believed on in the world, received up to glory." He worked his way through the text, asking what Paul meant by saying that Jesus was "justified." The answer, according to Campbell, was found in the narrative of Jesus' trial, crucifixion, resurrection, ascension and coronation. In ten pages he retold the story, showing that Jesus' crucifixion left him a convicted felon. Campbell told of the disciples waiting in Jerusalem as Jesus had instructed following his resurrection.

> And here we shall return to Jerusalem where he had been degraded and crucified as a felon. There we find the twelve Apostles in full assembly met;...and waiting too under the public reprobation consequent upon the condemnation and crucifixion of their leader. Under such a load of infamy how could they presume to say one word in his favor! They were therefore, both kindly and wisely commanded by the Leader 'to tarry in Jerusalem till they should receive power from on high.'

Nevertheless, Jesus was vindicated and justified by his resurrection and coronation. He was given all authority in heaven and on earth. Peter preached on Pentecost that God had made the crucified one both Lord and Christ. There was a new king in heaven and a new era on earth. Campbell tied the coronation of Christ in heaven to the birth of the church on Pentecost in Jerusalem. The central event of the drama was Pentecost, not Golgotha.

> This Christening, or anointing, of Jesus as autocrat of the universe was, indeed, the most grand, august and sublime event that ever transpired; and the proclamation of it the most thrilling and soul-subduing annunciation ever uttered on earth. This honor Peter had, and Jerusalem witnessed. It was indeed, the proper place. It was the capital of the only kingdom on earth especially related to God. It was 'the city of the Great King,' and the theatre of the temple of God. It was that Zion upon which Isaiah and Micah foretold the new law — the last message of Jehovah — should go forth; 'For out of Zion shall go forth the law, and the word of the Lord from Jerusalem.' Hence it was that the Lord, in giving His last directions to the apostles, commanded them to begin at Jerusalem. Christianity was never clearly understood by any man who did not begin at Jerusalem and fully learn the meaning of the events that transpired there at the time of the first annunciation of the coronation of the Lord Messiah. It was, indeed, 'the holy city,' the consecrated theatre of all the grand scheme of human redemption.[19]

Several lectures of Campbell's are preserved in the volume, *Popular Addresses And Lectures*. One speech was entitled, "Life and Death." It was against "Destructionalists," those who believed that death was the end of the human spirit. Campbell replied that Jesus said, "'I am the resurrection and the life'...so we can say with Paul 'I am crucified with Christ, nevertheless I live; yet not I but Christ liveth in me.'" Later he recalled also how Jesus said two sentences on the cross which indicated a life after death: "Today you will be with me in Paradise," and "Into Thy hands I commit my spirit."[20]

In that same volume is found Campbell's address to the American Bible Union in New York City, 1850. He noted that the inscription above Jesus' head on the cross was written in three languages. He concluded that the Bible should also be translated into many tongues.[21]

In 1860 Campbell addressed the American Christian Missionary Society. His subject was the "Divine Philanthropy" which made missions possible. He spoke of the "sin offering" as the most remarkable and generous display of love the world has ever known "though for a good man one would dare to die." On the basis of Jesus' atonement he appealed to unity in the mission outreach, saying: "We are met here, not as Episcopalians, Presbyterians, Congregationalists, Methodists, and Baptists, but as the Christian Missionary Society."[22]

Campbell mentioned the cross in thirteen of twenty-six sermons and lectures or fifty percent of the time. Nine references were substantive and four incidental. He mentioned the priest/sacrifice metaphor seven times, ransom five times, propitiation, justification and reconciliation twice each, victory over Satan and example once each. Once he mentioned the scandal of the cross in the single use he made of the gospel story line. There was no reference to the Suffering Servant.

These two leaders had such an enormous influence on our movement it is important to summarize the views of each on the atonement. Young Barton Stone's view was shaped by his reaction to the Calvinism of the Presbyterian church. He saw those views of God, elect and non-elect, limited, substitutionary atonement as unbiblical and harsh. Stone would not accept any doctrine of the wrath of God because God's very nature is love. He saw the New Testament metaphors of the cross as interchangeable with his favorite metaphor, reconciliation. His preaching was full of warm, pleading appeals to his hearers on the basis of the cross. In a Pauline way he took a practical concern like low church attendance to the cross. He saw man's whole relationship with God as determined by what Jesus did on Golgotha. On the other hand, Stone's aversion to Calvinism's speculations and his concern for unity among Campbell's followers and his own left a less than enthusiastic endorsement for the study of the atonement.

Campbell's writing and preaching took a more scholarly turn. His personality was clearly less warm than Stone's. He wrote that the atonement is the "essence of Christianity" and confirmed preachers in their high calling of proclaiming salvation in the cross. However, Campbell practiced what he preached to the young preachers. He told them to assume the basics and preach the reformation. In only half of the sermons and addresses one finds any mention of the cross. In different ways, for different reasons Campbell also shifted the focus away from the atonement as the central matter for preaching. He spoke most often to restore the ancient order of things, to remove hindrances to unity among believers. When the atonement does appear it is used most often as a "proof" of such "propositions" as: "God is Love," that there is life after death, and that all Christian traditions should join in mission outreach. Campbell proclaimed the coronation of Jesus and Pentecost the grandest event in history. He treasured the core gospel; but most often he preached restoration of the ancient order of the church.

Walter Scott (1796-1861)

Background and Writing

Born in Scotland, orphaned at a young age, Walter Scott desired to fulfill his parents' wishes that he become a Presbyterian minister. He immigrated to the States in 1818 and through associations in Pennsylvania began to examine his inherited faith according to the patterns of the Scripture. He met Campbell in 1821 and they became lifelong friends and fellow reformers. Scott moved from the Presbyterian church to the Baptists and then joined in the independent call for unity on the basis of Scripture only. He would become the first great evangelist and popularizer of the Restoration plea. His work centered in Pennsylvania and Ohio. From there he preached far and wide on the frontier.

From early reading of John Locke's *The Reasonableness Of Christianity* Scott had found a guide and kindred spirit. This was especially true in the assertion that the central article of the faith was acknowledgment of Christ as Messiah, as proved by: (1) his miracles, (2) his fulfillment of Old Testament prophecy, and (3) the testimony of Scripture. In other words, the faith rested on a "fact," an article of faith proved by Scripture. On these bases Scott came upon his famous "Golden Oracle," the single cardinal truth that Jesus is the Christ, the Messiah. Scott promoted that oracle as the creed of every Christian, the only bond of Christian union, and the way of personal salvation.[23]

Scott wrote in the preface of a book of essays, *The Gospel Restored*, his own summary of his association with Campbell and what they had achieved. Their work had accomplished three vital achievements: the Bible was adopted as sole authority in their assemblies, restoration of the "ancient order," and restoration of the "ancient gospel." Campbell had made a unique contribution to the history of Christianity by calling the churches back to the "ancient order." Scott's own gift to the Restoration was the restoration of the "ancient gospel."

> Presiding, at that time, over a church which had already attained the ancient order, or at least as much of it as seems even now to be attained, the gospel, or rather a uniform authoritative plan for preaching it, became more the object of my attention, as may be seen from a few essays published in the C. Baptist, cut short, however by the then limited knowledge of the extraordinary topic which had been selected; in 1827 the True Gospel was restored. For distinction's sake it was styled the Ancient Gospel.

Two paragraphs later Scott explained the content of the "Ancient Gospel" by a quote from Campbell.

> 'Brother Walter Scott, who in the fall of 1827, arranged the several items of faith, repentance, baptism, remission of sins, the Holy-Spirit, and eternal life, restored them in this order to the church under the title of ancient gospel, and preached it successfully to the world...'

Scott then explained how these six steps (which would later become his "five finger exercise," "eternal life" being deleted) actually saved the sinner from sin.

> In other words, brethren, to make us see the beauty and perfection of the gospel theory as devised by God; faith is to destroy the love of sin, repentance to destroy the practice of it, baptism the state of it, remission the guilt of it, the Spirit the power of it, and the resurrection to

> destroy the punishment of it; so that the last enemy, death will be destroyed.[24]

The central argument of Scott's book, *The Messiahship Or Great Demonstration,* was that everything in Christianity stands or falls with the messiahship of Jesus. He used the death, burial, and resurrection of Jesus among many other arguments as proof of Jesus' messiahship.[25]

In 1853 Scott published a small book he entitled, *He Necrosis, or The Death Of Christ.* The title page explained that it was written for the "recovery of the church from the sects." He addressed it mainly to preachers, urging them to lay aside creeds, systems and theories and simply to preach "Christ crucified." His aim in writing was the unity of all believers and the salvation of all the lost. His own theory of the atonement was clearly and succinctly set out.

> 1. God has attributed the sin of one to all;
> 2. And the sins of all to one.
>
> The facts in this basis are, that man has forfeited his life and blood, and that his redemption is not by truth, law, logic, or moral suasion, but by blood — the blood of the cross — the blood of the Son of God.[26]

Scott disagreed with Campbell on the scope of the atonement. He believed evangelism would be pointless and perhaps wrong had Jesus not died for all.[27]

Scott saw his belief, not as a theology of the atonement, but as "fact" based on scripture without interpretation. From Locke's views, he believed common sense reasoning could replace all creeds and all theologies of the atonement. His purpose was practical: the proclamation of a saving gospel.

> Are my propositions the basis of revealed religion, and practical guides to the preacher? If so, treat them as such... Philosophists, philologists, and theologizers, delight in words and speculations, and seek God's decrees and eternal purpose in reveries, metaphysics, and empty reasonings, but common sense will abide by facts, history, and the propositions of Scripture. My propositions embody facts; their systems, only empty generalities.[28]

In the final words of this treatise Scott stated clearly his distrust and disdain of any preachers who would attempt to understand the atonement.

> Theories and hypotheses about Adam's sin and Christ's death, and about the personal application of their respective merits and demerits with subtle disquisitions on faith and human nature, may be game for thelogists but they do not meet the necessities of the case — the soul longing for heaven.[29]

Scott's Preaching.

Only one full length sermon of Scott's remains. In addition we have outlines of thirteen others. He mentioned the cross in seven sermons, or fifty percent of the time. In "Moses And Christ," based on a comparison of the two as type and antitype, Scott spoke of Jesus as hero. He answered the Pantheist who considers the atonement a pernicious doctrine of punishing the innocent for the guilty.

> The gentleman evidently viewed the death of the Messiah under the delusive idea that all good and great actions necessarily turn on the maxims of ordinary morality; but history proves that the great mutations and ameliorations of society have turned rather on an extraordinary heroism. In both religion and politics, science and the arts, this held good. Adam, Noah, and Moses, Nimrod, Cyrus, Alexander, Caesar, Napoleon, were heroes; Socrates, Aristotle, Plato and Pythagoras were heroes; Newton, Bacon, Watt, Franklin and Morse were all heroes — all self-sacrificing men. Messiah, then, was a hero — a hero from heaven, to achieve what none but a hero from heaven could achieve, namely, the emancipation from Satan, sin and death of the race of man.[30]

In Scott's personal notebook one finds thirteen sermon outlines.[31] In six of these there is some reference to the cross of Christ. Ten treat some aspect of the person and work of Christ: missionary, teacher, messiah, ambassador, and as the Christian's creed. The seven lessons which had no reference to the cross had these titles: "Messiah Greater Than David," "Apostasy," "Faith On Evidence," "Christ Is God's Ambassador," "Christ A Missionary," "Confession Of Christ," "Christ Greater Than Angels." The outlines of these sermons follow the old Latin form: exordium, narration, proposition, confirmation, confutation, and peroration.

In a sermon entitled, "The Messiahship of Jesus, To Be Established As True And Provable" Scott argued inductively. Beside the outline heading, "Confirmation," is written - "By all Induction" and then seven points. (Reproduced here just as in his outline:)

1. Of the Types - Adam, Noah, Melch, Moses, Aaron,
2. Symbols - sacrifice, mercy seat, altar, etc.
3. The Ages - Antediluvian, Patriarch, Isaiah, John
4. Prophecy - Pedigree: Life, Death, Resurrection, Ascension, Glory
5. Institutions - the body of Christ
6. Church - foretold, new government and Gentiles
7. Nations were to wait for his law

The atonement was mentioned under "symbols" and "prophecy" as two of the seven proofs of Jesus' messiahship. These were two sub-points under seven major headings.[32]

On I Timothy 3:16 Scott preached "The Mystery of Godliness." He said the church was the guardian of a great mystery. That mystery is great, compared with many others which are not great. The church's secret is greater than that of any other society. As one of four points under "Narration" he concluded: "God on the cross, man on the throne; divinity or humanity — the throne of God —the throne of the Lamb. The Messiah was to be justified and condemned; acquitted, yet slain."[33] The church was based on a mystery. True to his own dictum about not engaging in theory and theology, he apparently offered no rationale for the death of Christ. It was mentioned simply as a proof of the mystery.

In "The Messiahship of Jesus Conforms To The Messiahship of the Prophets" he pictured Jesus as the divine teacher. Under "Proof" these points were used as inductive reasoning: (1) Jesus must be an Incarnation, (2) Inaugurated by God and the Spirit, (3) Transfigured, (4) Crucified and buried, (5) Raised from the dead, (6) Received up into heaven, and glorified.[34] This way of treating the cross seems to have been typical of Scott; he used the death, burial, and resurrection as proofs. In all these sermons only twice does he focus on the cross in itself. That main point was usually the proposition that Jesus is Messiah.

Scott's antipathy toward discussing the atonement as such was part of his anti-creed, anti-theology conviction. In the sermon, "The Creed Is A Person, Not A Doctrine" he makes that distinction clear beyond question. He stated his premise: "The divinity of Christ is among the other matters and things of Christianity as Christ personally is among the seven golden candlesticks — they are eclipsed — we see only him." In nine points he affirmed that the creed is a person, not a point of dogma. Notice how, in the process, he sublimates the death, burial, and resurrection of Christ to his person and office as Messiah.

1. Not his death
2. Not his resurrection
3. Not his ascension
4. Not his advent
5. But his messiahship and divinity
6. Not the person of men
7. Not the person of angels
8. Not the person of the Holy Spirit
9. Not the Father, but the Son[35]

One might summarize the writing and preaching of Scott on the atonement as follows. He said clearly and boldly that the cross was the center of New Testament faith. He encouraged other preachers to study his proofs for the "golden oracle" and discouraged their studying the atonement itself. In his own proclamation Scott gave himself to the reclamation of the "Ancient Gospel." He believed he had restored the New Testament gospel by outlining the "five steps" of salvation. The work was complete "in the fall of 1827."

Scott's main theme was the messiahship of Christ, the "golden oracle." The death, burial, and resurrection of Jesus were used mainly to prove the truth of that proposition. He believed in substitutionary atonement for all. He believed his "facts" and inductions should be suitable and biblical substitutes for divisive creeds and systems of theology. The message was clear, the faith was understandable. The only important question for Scott was what he called "the necessities of the case," the "soul's longing for heaven." Jesus' messiahship was a proposition clearly proved by Old Testament prophecy and the miracles, including the miracle of his resurrection. One must believe in Jesus' messiahship and respond to that truth to be saved. The death, burial, and resurrection are "proofs" of the "fact" which, if believed, will save. It is a subtle but important distinction: the "fact" does the saving, not the person of Christ crucified. Scott did not preach the cross as such, he preached the messiahship of Jesus.

One can compare Scott's treatment of the atonement with that of the New Testament as follows. He mentioned the cross in seven of fourteen sermons, or fifty percent of the time. Five references were substantive, two were incidental. Regarding the New Testament metaphors, he mentioned redemption/ransom four times, reconciliation three times, priest/sacrifice twice, and victor over Satan, propitiation and the law court picture once each. He made no mention of the Suffering Servant or of the scandal of the cross. He did not present the gospel stories as stories or the metaphors as pictures. All New Testament teaching on the cross was recast into the logical categories of John Locke. Like Campbell, he moved the focus just a degree or two away from the core gospel of Jesus' death, burial and resurrection. Campbell focused attention on his method of restoration. Scott shifted attention to the messiahship of Jesus, then to his own understandable plan of salvation, the "five finger exercise" which he called the "Ancient Gospel."

Jesse L. Sewell (1818-1890)

A younger contemporary of Stone, Campbell, and Scott's was Jesse L. Sewell. He was born in Tennessee and his family were faithful Baptists. From childhood he had great interest in studying the Scriptures. He would become a well-known and respected preacher in the Restoration movement. Some of his sermons, and much about his life, were preserved by David Lipscomb in the book, *Life And Sermons Of Jesse L. Sewell.* One of the current issues among the Baptists when Jesse was young was what, precisely, constituted a "call to preach." Not long after Sewell married Elizabeth Speer he gave his first sermon during a worship service at his father's house. When they returned home she said: "Well, there is no use to be silly about it, I suppose from tonight's work you intend to preach." He responded, "Yes, do you object to it?" She had made up her mind never to be a hindrance to him. Her reply was, "No, if you will make a preacher and not a mere gouger. We have plenty of gougers already."[36]

Sixteen full manuscripts of Sewell's sermons are found in the book. Lipscomb characterized the sermons on the title page: "Sixteen of His Best Sermons on Conditions of Forgiveness." Sewell mentioned the cross in twelve of those sixteen sermons or seventy-five percent of the time. The four sermons not containing any reference to the cross were: "What Must I Do To Be Saved?" "The Holy Spirit," "Moral and Positive Law," and "The Witness of the Spirit."

One of those sermons in which Sewell mentioned the cross was entitled, "The Atonement Or Reconciliation."[37] He agreed to use the word "atonement" despite the fact that it was used only once in the New Testament in Romans 5:11 according to the King James. He chose as his text II Corinthians 5:18-21. The sermon was preached to correct a popular misconception that people might pray their way to salvation. From passages in Romans and Colossians and the text Sewell contended that God did not have to be persuaded to forgive man. Reconciliation had already been provided in the cross. It did not remain for God to be reconciled, but for man. God had already sent Jesus, the perfect mediator who had removed the obstacles to man's forgiveness. Sewell discussed three of these barriers: sin, the power of Satan, and the Law. In the cross Jesus had overcome all these hindrances. Regarding the Law, Jesus had removed the penalty by removing the Law altogether. "And he 'took it out of the way, nailing it to his cross.' Colossians 2:14." Sewell explained that Jesus took down the wall of division by the blood of his cross. (Ephesians 2). The Gentiles as well as the Jews were now ransomed from their judgment under the Law. He concluded that both God and man were changed, moved by what happened on Golgotha.

While man's reconciliation had been settled in the courts of heaven, it was still to be arranged with human beings on earth. Jesus sent his disciples out to proclaim the reconciliation and to call men to obey the gospel. The gospels contained the proof that Jesus was the Son of God. That fact was his authorization to issue the great commission. Notice the terms in which Sewell reported the earliest disciples' response.

> And when we look at the record of the preaching of the apostles under this commission, as recorded in the Acts of apostles, beginning with the 2nd chapter, we find that

> they preached the facts concerning the life, and miracles, death, resurrection, ascension, and coronation of Christ. And when the people believed these facts they commanded them to repent, and be baptized in the name of Jesus Christ for the remission of sins, and they promised them that they should receive the gift of the Holy Spirit.

Sewell said the original apostles were the only designated ambassadors of this gospel so there were currently no ambassadors left on earth. It is then the work of preachers of the gospel to proclaim that the reconciliation has taken place, that it was proclaimed in the first century as is recorded in the Scripture. He explained how the gospel should be proclaimed in contrast with the way many preachers of the day presented it. Whereas the earliest gospel preachers told people to be baptized, many in Sewell's day told people to pray for salvation.[38]

In another sermon entitled, "The Bible," Sewell explained that the gospels were written as a narrative or history of Jesus' life, including the key events: birth, baptism, temptation, teaching, miracles, crucifixion, resurrection and ascension. The purpose of the gospels was to convince the reader that Jesus is the Messiah. But salvation is not found in the gospels.

> These books constitute the first division of the new Testament and are in every way sufficient to accomplish the object for which they are written. But we do not find everything that is necessary for us to know in regard to the salvation of sinners in these Books, and hence we must look for another division.[39]

By "another division" Sewell meant the book of Acts.

In view of the mystery of the atonement in New Testament theology, the second sermon in this volume is especially interesting. "Is The Bible A Mystery?" was the title. He began with an observation about the significance of the Restoration plea regarding the subject.

> Forty-five years ago almost if not all the ministers of various denominations taught that the Scriptures are a profound mystery to the common people, and that none but those who were divinely called and qualified and sent to preach, could understand them.

He said Catholic and Protestant clergy alike had insisted that the book was so full of mystery only the ordained could understand and interpret it. Others said only a special enlightenment of the Spirit made a passage of Scripture understandable. Many in society saw the Bible as a "dead letter," incomprehensible to the average reader. Sewell was holding up the claim that, due to the Restoration plea and plan, the Bible was now understandable by the average reader in all matters of salvation. He admitted that he didn't understand all its mysteries; but that the only matters of real practical importance were those relating to man's responsibilities in salvation and they could be clear to all. In commending the Bible to the average reader Sewell left the door open to the idea that whatever mystery the Bible contained was not very important after all.[40]

The mystery of the atonement was not inviting to Sewell. He went on to say that salvation was only in preaching "Christ crucified," not the wisdom of man. He contrasted the plain facts of Jesus' crucifixion with any theology or understanding of what happened on Golgotha. The latter came under the heading of "human wisdom." Like Scott, he set the gospel forth as faith, repentance, and baptism. He affirmed that one must believe the facts, obey the commands, and trust in the promises if he would enter the kingdom.

In the sermon, "What Must I Do To Be Saved?" Sewell contended that the only really important question to be considered was man's part of salvation. He said that, in Acts 2, the people were told what God had done and then called to do their part. The implications, according to Sewell, were that the gospels contained facts to be believed, Acts and the epistles commands and examples to be obeyed.

In summary, one notices that Sewell thought of the atonement and preached about it as over against the Methodists' prayer bench as a means of salvation. Salvation was not something waiting to be negotiated with God, it was achieved on Golgotha and had only to be proclaimed, believed, and obeyed. The cross not only reconciled God and man, but made salvation possible for Jew and Gentile alike. He said the gospels were written to prove that Jesus was God's Son, to establish his authority, and to record his commission to preach the gospel. He believed the atonement was a mystery which could never be understood, all that was really important for salvation had now been made abundantly clear. He took Paul's words about not preaching human wisdom as a reference to any interpretation of the facts of the death, burial, and resurrection. Only the facts should be proclaimed, without interpretation. These facts he considered to be the heart of the gospel.

When one compares Sewell's preaching with the New Testament treatment significant features emerge. He referred to the cross in twelve out of sixteen sermons, or seventy-five percent of the time. Three references were substantial and nine were incidental. He referred to the victor over Satan metaphor three times, to priest/sacrifice, propitiation/expiation, reconciliation, and the law court metaphors one time each. No mention was found of the Suffering Servant picture, the scandal of the cross, or the gospel story line. He referred to the gospels as proofs, not as narratives which carried their own meaning.

It is somewhat misleading to report that Sewell mentioned the cross seventy-five percent of the time. While that is true statistically, there was far less content in his preaching of the cross than that figure might indicate. His use of the death, burial, and resurrection was mostly as proofs. He argued for a God's completed reconciliation with mankind and against salvation by prayer and modern day apostles. He took preachers in other churches to task for not preaching baptism. In recovering the Bible for the common people he denied the mystery in anything of vital, practical importance to salvation. Sewell believed one's main concern should be what man should do for salvation. Like the other three leaders, he shifted the attention away from the cross to important but secondary matters.

Benjamin Franklin (1812-1878)

The fourth-generation descendent of a brother of his Revolutionary War namesake, Benjamin Franklin was born in Belmont County, Ohio. His family moved to Indiana in 1833 and in the next year responded to the Restoration gospel of Samuel Rogers and were baptized. He and four brothers became ministers. He was devoted to evangelistic work in many states and Canada and was also a noted debater. He founded and edited "The American Christian Review" which he produced for the last twenty-two years of his life.

Few preachers in our history have had such a far-reaching influence as Benjamin Franklin. In 1868 W.T. Moore wrote that Franklin's tract, "Sincerely Seeking The Way To Heaven" had sold more copies than any ever published by the Disciples.[41] His two volumes of sermons, *The Gospel Preacher*, went to multiple printings and were widely read well down into the twentieth century. For example, the two volumes found at the Abilene Christian library, each in their sixteenth editions, were gifts from the library of C.R. Nichol.[42] By the time he published the second volume Franklin, himself, saw the possibility of influencing preaching by his sermons. In the introduction he reported that the first volume had benefitted members of the church and young preachers alike.[43]

The two volumes contain forty-one full length sermon manuscripts. Another sermon, "On The Eternal Purpose of God" is found in John F. Rowe's *Biographical Sketch And Writings Of Elder Benjamin Franklin.*[44] Franklin mentioned the cross in twenty of these forty-two sermons or forty-nine percent of the time. Themes he treated without reference to the cross were: predestination, regeneration, the "safe course" in religion, the second coming, man's destiny, baptism, judgment, prayer, dancing, and the Restoration movement. In addition there were five sermons on the plan of salvation, one on the gospel and three on the church which contained no mention of the atonement.

The sixteenth sermon of volume one was entitled, "The Love Of God To Man," John 3:16. Jesus demonstrated in his life the power and compassion of God. For ten pages Franklin described in detail the passion from Gethsemane to the resurrection. He then said that these events, followed by the ascension and Pentecost comprise God's final appeal to mankind.

He has made a full and perfect atonement for sin. In the end of the ages, he has made one sin-offering to purge us forever from our sins. He bore our sins in his own body on the tree. He suffered, the just for the unjust, that he might bring us to God. He is the propitiation for our sins; and not for our sins only, but also for the sins of the whole world. He now makes his last appeal to our affections. Can we not, and will we not love him, who first loved us? Shall any man be found so hardened and abandoned that he can not love him who withheld not his own Son, but gave him up freely for us all? Can any man, who has the heart of a man in him, look at this last appeal to the affections of man as he hung, suspended between the heavens and the earth on that ignominious tree of the cross, crowned with thorns and robed in purple, till he breathed his last breath, gave the last struggle, and expired, and not love him? Can any human being, not perfectly chalice and under the influence of total apathy — any one not wholly past feeling — view him, as the Roman spear pierces his side, and his warm heart's blood streams down like water on the ground, and not love him? How can any human being turn away from our Lord and refuse to love him?[45]

In his second volume of sermons Franklin included a topical sermon without a stated text entitled, "Mediation of Christ, and Man's Reconciliation To God." It was intended as an answer to those who were teaching an immediate power from God apart from Scripture that converts sinners and reconciles them to God. Franklin set about correcting false doctrines. The Calvinists who, fifty years before, spoke only of man's depravity were wrong. The Universalists who talked of salvation for all really had no salvation for anybody. The Bible teaches that all men are under sin, that all have "sinned and come short of the glory of God."

When alienation occurs the first thing that happens is that the offending party can not meet the offended face to face. Franklin observed that a mediator, a go-between is needed. God provided that mediator in Jesus Christ. He explained that Jesus alone was qualified for that work.

As we saw above, Franklin could issue fervent appeals by describing the crucifixion. But here the process of reconciliation was described almost without reference to the cross. The only mention of the cross in the sermon pictured Golgotha as the possible undoing of the mission of Jesus. Not as the basis of the faith, but as a threat to the saving proposition by which sinners are saved!

> Christ is the foundation, and the truth that 'Jesus is the Christ, the Son of the living God,' is the truth concerning the foundation, on which the whole rests. Overthrow this one truth and the whole is gone forever. The Lord recognized this when he said, 'On this rock will I build my Church.' The clause that follows shows that he saw the crucifixion, and that he would enter Hades; but the gates or power of Hades should not prevail against him, or against the rock, or foundation; that he would rise and triumph over the powers of Hades. The great struggle was over his rising. 'Will he rise?' His declaration is the triumphant language of victory. He will rise and vanquish all his enemies.

Franklin pulled his lesson together in a single sentence, adding his main point of contention.

> The reconciliation, then, is from God, through Christ the Mediator, through his ambassadors, through the Holy Spirit that spoke in them, and through the word of

reconciliation. This is set aside by the modern idea of an immediate, or direct power from God that converts sinners, and reconciles, and makes them Christians.[46]

What seems significant to me is that the whole process of mediation could be explained without recognition that the cross is the means of reconciliation. The cross is mentioned only as a threat which is overcome in the resurrection.

Several sermons from volume two show how Franklin typically treated the atonement. In "Things to Which Salvation Is Ascribed" Franklin listed seven items to which salvation is ascribed. He spent one paragraph on "the blood of Jesus" and four pages on baptism. "The blood" was one of seven things which save.[47] His sermon "Remission Of Sins" contended that everything in the Bible from Abraham on was done for man's salvation. Jesus' whole life, everything he did, ending with his crucifixion was for man's salvation. The apostles were shattered until the resurrected Jesus appeared and gave them the Great Commission. They went out and preached repentance in response to the gospel as proof. They preached the cross in the wisdom and power of God and called men to faith, repentance, and baptism. Franklin saw it as strange that all of the other items of proclamation were commonly accepted but that baptism was rejected. He then spent the rest of the sermon on baptism, arguing from the cases and verses in Acts. However, he did not argue the necessity of baptism because of its connection with the cross of Christ.[48]

Two of Franklin's sermons showed agreement with Campbell's admonition to the young preachers to assume the basics and stress matters of Reformation. Corresponding to Campbell's "Sermons To Young Preachers" two of Franklin's sermons were entitled, "Matters Of Agreement" and "Matters of

Disagreement."⁴⁹ He said that everyone agreed on the person and work of Jesus, that he was the only Mediator between God and man, "that God lifted him up to draw all men to him." These were twenty-one matters of almost unanimous agreement. Franklin explained his meaning in "item 2." regarding "Lord Jesus, the Christ, the Son of the living God." All believers believed that Jesus was man's only Mediator and Savior. They might "speculate" in different ways about exactly how the work was done. That was unimportant. All should unite on the plain fact and forsake all speculations as to the method and meaning of the atonement. Notice also that the person and work of Jesus including his work on Golgotha could be listed with twenty other items without indicating that it was any more important than the rest.

"Why Was The Primitive Church Persecuted?" was the name of a sermon asking why the "true church" was still persecuted in Franklin's day. According To Franklin, Jesus was offensive because he pointed up the hypocrisy of the Scribes and Pharisees, he showed the shallowness of their religion, and he confronted their leaders. Franklin said the Reformation of which he was part was offensive because it preached the "Gospel itself" as found in the Bible, was exclusive as the only true religion, took the Bible as its only creed, adopted only biblical terminology, called for unity on the Bible alone, set out clearly the biblical plan of salvation, bypassed apostolic succession for obedience to the primitive gospel, and followed the Bible alone in faith and practice.⁵⁰ For him the first century drama was being played out again.

The influence of Benjamin Franklin's sermons reached far down into the twentieth century, farther than any other first generation restorationist. Regarding the cross, Franklin had a firm grip on the core gospel. He clearly and succinctly set out what was "of first importance" to Paul and Peter. He included at least one lengthy narrative of the crucifixion and called the cross God's final appeal to mankind. Several of his sermons which included references to the cross were polemical. He was especially in conflict with those who taught direct and immediate salvation through prayer and experiences. Franklin's emphasis was not on the cross itself, but on the cross and resurrection as part of the data or facts to be believed and obeyed in order to be saved. Atonement meant reconciliation and all of the New Testament metaphors he used were interchangeable with that picture.

A review of Franklin's preaching reveals that he referred to the cross in twenty of forty-two sermons or forty-eight percent of the time. Of those seven were substantive and thirteen incidental. He mentioned the priest/sacrifice metaphor four times, the redemption/ransom, propitiation/expiation, and reconciliation metaphors once each. In one sermon he recognized the gospel story line as a source of meaning for the atonement. No sermon mentioned of the Suffering Servant. In one sermon he treated the scandal of the cross as the drama by which he interpreted opposition to the restorationists' program.

His real emphasis was on the authority of Jesus, handed down to the apostles, received by the church in the Bible as a system or plan of salvation. The cross, and especially the resurrection proved and supported Jesus' claim of authority. In several sermons Franklin used the cross as emotional proof to urge baptism. On one occasion he listed seven items to which salvation were ascribed, devoting one paragraph to the blood of Christ and four pages to baptism. On another occasion he presented the cross as a threat to Jesus' mission which was overcome in the resurrection. The death, burial, and resurrection were used most of the time in polemics.

Summary of Chapter I

In contrast with the New Testament, one finds in these sermons no mention of the Suffering Servant. This is a glaring omission in light of the fact that Jesus characterized himself as the Suffering Servant. As disturbing is the fact that only three times in sixty-one sermons is there reference to the scandal of the cross. None of these early leaders drew deeply on the narrative aspects of the gospel stories, they seldom referred to the gospels at all. Campbell included one lengthy retelling of the trial, crucifixion, resurrection, and coronation of Jesus.

The most significant finding in the study of our first generation preachers is the paradox of their practice. Every one of our first preachers set forth the atonement as of primary importance and then took it back in some way. Stone believed it was the essential gospel, the cross was the greatest overture of God's love to man. He preached it with fervor from his heart to evangelize and to meet a variety of needs in the church. He referred in some way to the core gospel in eighty-two percent of his sermons. On the other hand, his strong negative reaction to Calvinistic "speculation," his penchant for reducing the metaphors to one, and his fear of division over the atonement may have had the effect of discouraging serious thought on the "logos" of the cross.

Campbell said clearly that the cross was the "great central doctrine" of the faith. He defined saving faith as hearty reliance on what Jesus did at the cross. His sermons and writings show that he had inherited and studied through a developed theology of the atonement. But Campbell believed these basics could be assumed, that his job and the work of the young preachers should be to preach the Reformation. We also saw that when he discussed the atonement it was not in terms of New Testament forms (letters, narratives and metaphors,) but as propositions and proofs. Faith was belief in facts as proved by the events of Jesus' life as set forth by credible witnesses. In the sermon on the coronation of Christ he called that event and its earthly counterpart on Pentecost the most important event in history. Paul and the other New Testament writers set out the death, burial, and resurrection as the key event. That subtle shift of attention from cross to crown, from the crucified to his kingdom would have profound implications. There is no doubt that Campbell would object to any suggestion that he in any way diminished the core doctrine of the faith. But he assumed that central core and gave himself to finetuning the church for unity among believers. He encouraged the next generation of young preachers to do the same.

Jesse L. Sewell mentioned the cross in seventy-five percent of his sermons. He understood that salvation was not something yet to be negotiated by each believer with God, the work had been finished at Golgotha. His message was that one must believe and obey the gospel to receive the gift already provided. On the other hand, his preaching of the atonement was not for its own sake. It was a weapon used in his battle against mourner's bench religion, and against Roman Catholic "mystery." In working out that polemic he left the impression that salvation is a cut-and-dried business transaction between God and man, a proposition offered and accepted. He had no use for any mystery in the faith. Mystery about the Bible had existed until forty-five years before when the restorationists opened the Scriptures for all to understand. Since that time all that was really important was clear to all who would hear. Whatever other mysteries remained were of no great importance.

Walter Scott wrote and preached the proposition that Jesus was the Messiah. That "golden oracle" was the center of the faith.

Doubtless, one of the reasons for his enormous success as an evangelist was his focus on the person of Christ. This proposition was proved by fulfillment of prophecy in the events of Golgotha and the open tomb. All of that was done, God's part was finished. It was now up to man to respond. Consequently, it was neither profitable nor necessary to talk about the meaning of what God did on Golgotha. The only practical question was man's part in salvation. He was against "theologizing" about the atonement. As an alternative to theology and experience, Scott set out a plan of salvation in five steps. Referring to his "five finger exercise," he believed he had restored the "true gospel" in 1827. Scott called attention from the cross to the person of Christ, from the person of Christ to the proposition that he was the Messiah, from that proposition to the proofs, and from the proofs to a "five finger exercise" of human response which he called the "true gospel." All of it was connected with the cross, but only remotely.

Benjamin Franklin had a firm grip on the core gospel. In one sermon he set out a moving narrative of the crucifixion. He made the connection of the cross to baptism and the Lord's Supper. But his real emphasis was on the authority of Jesus handed down to the apostles, written into Scripture, transmitted to modern readers. The death, burial and resurrection served as authorization for who Jesus was and his right to set out a plan of salvation. He saw little reason to explore the meaning of the cross in itself. At one point he said the cross was a threat to God's great plan which was overcome in the resurrection. While he set out the connection between the cross and baptism, he taught the meaning of baptism from verses and examples found in Acts and the epistles without reference to the cross. His emphasis was demonstrated in the sermon which had two paragraphs on the blood of Christ and four pages on baptism. Like Campbell, he assumed the cross and preached other important matters.

All five of these were ten-talent men of large hearts and bold vision. Each was true to his understanding of God, willing to stand against the tide and face the brunt of the storm's fury. Each spoke to the situation and issues of his world. There is much here to admire, much in which we should take pride as their heirs. But so far as the "word of the cross" is concerned, one discovers that they mentioned the death, burial, and resurrection and the word of the cross in only sixty-two of one hundred nine sermons. This is a composite percentage of only fifty-six percent in comparison with one-hundred percent in the New Testament. From the very first something of the core gospel was missing in our Restoration preaching. For the purposes of our unfolding story, the most significant finding is that each of our first forefathers gave us the atonement with one hand and took it back with the other.

NOTES

[1] See Richard T. Hughes and C. Leonard Allen, *Illusions Of Innocence, Protestant Primitivism In America, 1630 - 1875.* (Chicago: University of Chicago Press, 1988).

[2] See APPENDIX B.

[3] Barton W. Stone, Atonement, The Substance of Two Letters Written To A Friend (Lexington, Ky.: Joseph Carless, 1805).

[4] *The Biography Of Elder Barton W. Stone with additions by John Rogers* (Cincinnati: J.A. and U.P. James, 1847) pp. 56-59.

[5] Campbell, "Sermons To Young Preachers — "Sermon No. IV" "The Christian Baptist," Vol. VII, pp.639,640.

[6] Alexander Campbell, *The Christian System*, (Nashville: Gospel Advocate - Reprint - 1956), p.26,27.

[7] Barton W. Stone (Ed.) "The Christian Messenger," Jacksonville, Ill.: Vol. X: pp. 2-28,37,42-58, 72-82, 87-96, 109-118; Vol. XI: pp. 145-154, 147-169, 181-189, 219-232, 261-279, 325-329. 181-189. Alexander Campbell, (Ed.) "The Millennial

Harbinger," Bethany, Va.: Vol. IV: pp. 243-250, 289-298, 291-296, 464-273, Vol. V: pp. 12-34, 59-68, 113-122, 156-163, 234-237, 248-258, 295-304, 369-373, 389-402.

[8] "The Christian Messenger," Vol. I, Nov. 25, 1826, p.8.

[9] "The Christian Messenger," Vol. II, Nov. 1927, p. 6.

[10] "The Christian Messenger," Vol. VII, Jan. 1833, p. 97ff.

[11] Unpublished manuscripts held at the Disciples' of Christ Historical Society, Nashville. All quotations include spelling, capitalization, abbreviations just as they appear in Stone's own hand.

[12] Manuscript Sermon On II Corinthians. Disciples' Historical Society.

[13] "The Christian Messenger," Vol. XI, Mar. 1841, p.238. (The four lectures are to be found on pages: 232-241, 253-258, 312-317, 330-334).

[14] Manuscript sermon, Disciples' Historical Society.

[15] B.C. Goodpasture and W.T. Moore (Arrangers and Editors) *Biographies And Sermons of Pioneer Preachers*, (Nashville: B. C. Goodpasture, 1954) pp. 1-46.

[16] "The Christian Baptist," Vol. 4, No. 7, Feb. 5, 1827, p. 310.

[17] "The Christian Preacher," Vol. I, Jan., 1836, p. 15.

[18] Robert Richardson, *Memoirs Of Alexander Campbell*, (Cincinnati: Standard Publishing, 1897)

[19] Salina Huntington Campbell, *Home Life and Reminiscences of Alexander Campbell.* (St. Louis: John Burns, 1882) p. 160.

[20] Alexander Campbell, *Popular Addresses And Lectures*, (St. Louis: Christian Publishing, 1853), pp. 418,442.

[21] *Popular Addresses*, p. 602.

[22] *Popular Addresses*, pp. 562,563.

[23] Dwight E. Stevenson, *Walter Scott, Voice Of The Golden Oracle* (Joplin, Mo.: College Press, 1946) pp. 34-36.

[24] Walter Scott, *The Gospel Restored*, (Cincinnati: O.H. Donough, 1836) pp. v,vi. Dwight E. Stevenson relates from William Baxter's Life Of Walter Scott the story of how Scott taught children to remember the steps by using the fingers of one hand. p. 74.

[25] Walter Scott, *The Messiahship Or Great Demonstration*, (Kansas City: Old Paths, n.d.) p. 182.

[26] Walter Scott, *He Necrosis Or The Death Of Christ*, (Cincinnati: Walter Scott, 1853), p. 82.

[27] *He Necrosis*, pp.24,25.

[28] *He Necrosis*, p. 55.

[29] *He Necrosis*, p. 87.

[30] F. L. Rowe, (Compiler) *Pioneer Sermons And Addresses* (Cincinnati: F.L. Row, 1925) p. 167.

[31] Walter Scott, Unpublished Personal Notebook, Library of Lexington Theological Seminary.

[32] Scott's Notebook, p. 274.

[33] Scott's Notebook, p. 286.

[34] Scott's Notebook, p. 290.

[35] Scott's Notebook, p. 292.

[36] David Lipscomb, *Life And Sermons Of Jesse L. Sewell* (Nashville: Gospel Advocate, 1954. A reprint of the original, 1891.) (This copy a reprint of the Gospel Advocate, 1954) pp. 54.

[37] Lipscomb, *Sewell's Sermons*, ave 294-307.

[38] Lipscomb, *Sewell's Sermons*, p. 304-307.

[39] Lipscomb, *Sewell's Sermons*, pp.128,129.

[40] Lipscomb, Sewell's Sermons, pp. 131-139.

[41] W.T. Moore, *The Living Pulpit*, (Cincinnati: R. W. Caroll, 1868) p. 340.

[42] Benjamin Franklin, *The Gospel Preacher* (Richmond, Ohio: Daniel Sommer, Vol. I, 1891, twenty-eighth edition, Vol. II, 1899, sixteenth edition.)

[43] Franklin, Volume II, p. v.

[44] John F. Rowe, Ed. *Biographical Sketch And Writings of Elder Benjamin Franklin*, (Cincinnati: G.W. Rice, 1880), pp. 74-92.

[45] Franklin, Volume I, pp. 405,406.

[46] Franklin, Volume II, pp. 315-336.

[47] Franklin, Volume I, pp. 81-102.

[48] Franklin, Volume II, pp. 132-134.

[49] Franklin, Volume II, pp. 219-268.

[50] Franklin, Volume II, pp. 278,279.

The Second Generation 2

T. W. Brents (1823-1905)

Brents was unique among Restoration preachers in that he was a medical doctor for whom preaching and writing were favorite avocations. He was born in Tennessee, never located as the preacher of a local church, was widely known as a debater, writer, and preacher. For a while he was President of Burritt College at Spencer, Tennessee. His book, *The Gospel Plan Of Salvation*, was one of the most influential books ever published in our movement.[1] H. Leo Boles claimed that the book contained "all the principles of the gospel." For our purposes it is significant to note that Brents mentioned the cross on only eighteen of six hundred sixty-two pages, or in a little less than three percent of the total work.[2] Boles also commented that Brent's book, *Gospel Sermons*, contained "many of his strongest sermons."[3] So to that volume we now turn to taste a sample of second generation Restoration preaching.[4]

The volume contains twenty-one sermons. Nine contain some reference to the death, burial, and resurrection of Jesus at the rate of forty-six percent. It is significant to ask what topics were treated in the eleven sermons not mentioning the cross. Five of the sermons dealt with conversion. These included studies of the following: the Great Commission, the conversion of the Philippian jailor, the exodus of the Hebrews as a type of Christian salvation, and a lesson from Titus 3:4-7 on regeneration. Other sermons included studies of the mission of John the Baptist, Jesus' transfiguration, Paul's charge to Timothy, angels, the millennium, church organization, and Paul's "natural man" from I Corinthians 2:14.

Brents spoke from Matthew 22:42 on the sonship of Christ. It was a sermon against Unitarians and Trinitarians. Jesus was neither just a man on the one hand or God's equal on the other, but the "Son of God." Brents called his listeners to confession on the basis of Jesus' love expressed on the cross and ended the sermons with verses from the song, "When I Survey The Wondrous Cross."

Discussing Romans 6:17 in a sermon entitled "Freedom From Sin" Brents emphasized Paul's admonition to "obey that form of doctrine" he had delivered to them. Some were preaching belief in the death, burial and resurrection apart from baptism. Brents emphasized the connection, but in a way that put distance between the two. If the gospel is something that human beings can do to be saved then one cannot obey a fact, i.e. the fact of the cross. The gospel must, then, be something other than the "word of the cross." It must be a command.

> ...That Christ died for our sins according to the Scriptures—can we obey this? No, there is nothing in it to obey. And that he was buried—can we obey this? We can see nothing here to obey. And that he rose again the third day according to the Scriptures—can we obey this? We cannot see how. Mould these items as we may, or arrange them in any way we can there is no way by which

> to obey them. This doctrine consisted of facts and could not be obeyed. We may obey something symbolizing, or resembling it, but the facts themselves we cannot obey. Then the apostle did not mean that the Romans obeyed some special arrangement of the doctrine itself. This is not the thought exactly. We have the gospel in facts, commands and promises. The facts may be believed, the commands may be obeyed, the promises may be enjoyed; but neither facts nor promises can be obeyed.[5]

Brents was arguing for baptism as the only appropriate response to the death, burial, and resurrection of Jesus. He was taking issue with "faith only" salvation; i.e. salvation without baptism. He was also addressing a common belief that the only baptism necessary was baptism of the Holy Spirit. But in so doing he defined the gospel as what the *believer* can do to accept God's salvation.

In another sermon, "Justification," the doctor was arguing against what he understood to be Luther's "faith only" doctrine. To show that people are not saved by faith only, he cited a long list of things which save, the blood of Christ was mentioned as one among many. Nothing was "of first importance," everything was considered of equal weight.

> Now, friendly sinner, when Jesus says: 'He that believeth and is baptized shall be saved;' and Peter, to whom this commission was given, commanded believers to repent and be baptized for the remission of sins, and said to the saints scattered abroad, baptism now saves us; and James says we are justified by works and not by faith only, is it safe to adopt and act upon a theory of faith only? Is it not infinitely more safe to let the word of God be the guiding star of our lives? When the Bible says we are justified by

grace, believe it, for it is true. When it says we are justified by Christ, believe it. When it says we are justified by his blood, believe it. When it says we are justified in the name of Christ, believe it. When it says we are justified by the Spirit, believe it. When it says we are justified by faith, believe it; but add not the word only, or any thing else, to it, for it is dangerous to add to the word of the Lord. When the Bible says we are justified by works, believe this also, for the bible is the same inspired book when it says that, that it is when it says we are justified by faith...[6]

Brents was most of all a polemicist. He was confronting false teaching on more than one front. From time to time he showed Old Testament "types" of the cross to demonstrate the importance of Jesus' death. He sometimes made appeals on the basis of God's love shown on Calvary. Brents preached the cross in answer to a "faith only" stance which refused baptism. He called attention away from the death, burial, and resurrection of Jesus because there was nothing to be obeyed in these facts. In another lesson he would list the cross among all the things which save in order to demonstrate that one is not saved by "faith only."

To sum up Brent's use of the cross, we note that in four cases his mention was substantial, in five incidental. He mentioned the cross in nine of twenty-one sermons or forty-three percent of the time. He pointed to the priest/sacrifice, redemption/ransom and propitiation/expiation metaphors once each. There was no mention of reconciliation, victor over Satan, the Suffering Servant, example, or the law court pictures. There is no mention of the scandal of the cross and no recognition of the gospel story line.

T. B. Larimore (1843-1929)

Few preachers in our history have been so loved as T.B. Larimore. Born in Tennessee, he became known far and wide as a preacher of the gospel. The name of one of the books written about his ministry was *Maine To Mexico And Canada To Cuba*. He was also an educator, founder of Mars Hill College. Twenty-seven of his sermons and sermon extracts are preserved in a volume edited by F.D. Srygley, *Letters And Sermons Of T. B. Larimore*.[7]

Larimore mentioned the cross in fourteen of twenty-seven sermons, or fifty-two percent of the time. Sermons without mention of the cross were: "Reasons for Not Preaching On Baptism," "The Iron, the Silver, and the Golden Rule," "A Mother's Love," "Manliness in Boys," "Origin of Man," "The Spirit of Christ," "The Faith of Moses," "Union and Unity," "The Salt Of The Earth," "Pure In Speech," "Race Not To the Swift," and "Times That Try Men's Souls". It may be noteworthy that the last eleven of these are only sermon "extracts" and that all but two of the full length sermon manuscripts contained some mention of the cross.

In a sermon on Ecclesiastes 12 Larimore concluded that there is no salvation in wealth. Typical of his warm invitations was this one:

> 'Take my yoke upon you, and learn of me; for I am meek and lowly in heart: and ye shall find rest unto your souls. For my yoke is easy, and my burden is light.' Jesus practically says: 'Poor dying sons and daughters of men, I am your Savior; I by the grace of God am your only Savior. I came from the courts of glory to these low grounds of sorrow, lived a life of poverty and pain, and died on the cross, and now I call you to me...If you

believe these things; if you believe the Bible; if you believe the Savior tells you the truth; if you believe the Savior does actually say to you, 'Come unto me, all ye that labor and are heavy laden, and I will give you rest;' that he says, 'I, Jesus have sent mine angels to declare unto you that I am the root and offspring of David, the bright and morning star' — if so, may the Lord bless every one of you in rising and coming to Jesus to be saved, while we wait to lovingly welcome you and pray that you come.[8]

In "Rest For The Soul" Larimore told of a monument erected by Queen Victoria to the memory of a beautiful daughter of Charles I. She was shown lying down with her face against a Bible. The inscription read: "Come unto me, all ye that labor and are heavy laden, and I will give you rest." Larimore went on to show how all mankind is weary and in need of rest. He pictured Christians as sailors on a storm-swept sea, anxious to make port. "Then we shall be conveyed to the shore and be permitted to walk the streets of the New Jerusalem rejoicing in that peace and rest purchased by the blood of Jesus."[9]

In a sermon, "Sin And Righteousness," he told of the mother of a robber whose love facilitated his actions. What should she have done at the grave of her son? "She ought to rise and rush to Jesus, grasp the cross, and hold it until she dies."[10] In his sermon, "The Prayer Of The Cross" Larimore studied Jesus' agony of Gethsemane. He held Jesus up as an example of prayer, that one should pray for his enemies, that anything important should be prayed about, that prayer may not be answered immediately but that God has his times. Larimore based this on Jesus' participation with us in our human condition. "He was no intruder on earth. He had been sent by the Father in mercy to save a lost and ruined, wrecked and recreant race."[11] In a sermon based on Jude 3, "Contending For The Faith," Larimore refused to be characterized as contending for "Campbellism."

> We must contend for what? Not for Campbellism, not for Mormonism; for it was seventeen hundred years after Jude wrote this before Campbellism and Mormonism was known in the world or had an existence. Not for Judaism, for Judaism had already been abolished. Jesus took it out of the way, nailing it to the cross.[12]

In the sermon, "Communion," Larimore stressed the importance of taking the Lord's Supper in the appropriate frame of mind. He explained what the Table means.

> The loaf represents the body broken for the sins of a lost and ruined and wrecked race; the fruit of the vine—if the Bible calls it 'wine' in that connection, I am not aware of it; it does call it 'the fruit of the vine' — the fruit of the vine represents the blood of Jesus that was shed on Calvary that we who love him might live with him in glory forever. This institution is the institution that represents his death, just as baptism represents his burial and resurrection. In the Lord's Supper and in baptism we have the death, burial, and resurrection of the Lord Jesus Christ clearly represented and memorialized, and we are led to remember all these things.[13]

With the story of Mary Magdalene coming to the tomb of Jesus Larimore began the sermon, "The Great Commission." Jesus was risen, she and the others were told to go tell the good news to the brethren. They went out quickly and said nothing for they were afraid. The preacher compared his own commission to Mary's.

> But if I simply preach the gospel, do my very best to lead the lost to the Lamb of God that taketh away the sins of the world teaching them what God says they must do to be saved, then I can lay my hand on this blessed Book and claim that this commission is my authority for preaching.[14]

In that same sermon Larimore reviewed Peter's sermon on Pentecost. Jesus had given him the keys of the kingdom, the Holy Spirit had descended full of power, and Peter preached the first gospel sermon.

> He preached the birth, the life, the death, and incidentally the burial, and directly and specially the resurrection, of the Lord Jesus Christ, his ascension to glory, his coronation as King of kings and Lord of lords, and his sending the Holy Spirit to the earth to bless and save a lost and ruined world...When they heard that he had been raised from the dead,...They realized then that their souls were stained with the innocent blood of the Son of God, whom they with wicked hands had slain, and that unless something could be done to relieve them from the pressure of that dreadful sin they must be eternally lost; and though they had ignored the tears and sighs and prayers of the Savior as they nailed him to the cross, and cursed him as he died, they remembered that he was loving, tender, merciful, and kind; that as he hung upon the cross, quivering and trembling, every muscle writhing in agony, every feature distorted with pain, he prayed from the depths of his stricken soul: 'Father, forgive them; for they know not what they do.' This thought would naturally bring the light of hope to their hearts...Then they that gladly received his word were baptized: and the same day they were added unto them

> about three thousand souls.' (Acts 2:37-41). What did Peter understand to be the conditions of pardon that he was to proclaim to a lost and ruined world? Faith, repentance, and baptism, the divine record being true. Certainly all of us can see this.[15]

We notice at the end of this quote the familiar Restoration emphasis on human obedience as "conditions of pardon." Unlike most Restoration preachers, Larimore set his call for obedience to Christ in the context of what God had done on Golgotha. Most of these preachers called for obedience as a response to the authority of Christ and the Scriptures.

Larimore referred to the core gospel in fifty-two percent of his sermons. He treated the cross eleven times in passing and three times with substantial comment. He mentioned the priest/sacrifice and reconciliation metaphors once each, and redemption/ransom twice. There was no use of the scandal of the cross or of the Suffering Servant metaphor. As noted above, he once recognized the narrative nature of the gospel and told his story in that form.

One cannot read the sermons of T.B. Larimore without feeling his warm heart and sincere concern for souls. The cross was obviously of great importance to him. It was connected with Jesus' gracious invitation, "Come unto me..." Jesus' atonement was the only hope of sinners, proof of Jesus' love for and identification with mankind, the meaning of baptism and the Lord's Supper, the message and mandate for preaching, and proof of who Jesus was — the central truth of the Bible. In Larimore's preaching the kingdom was directly connected with the cross. The reader may fairly conclude that Larimore had a deep appreciation for and a considered theology about what happened on Golgotha and used it extensively in his preaching.

Only when one compares Larimore with the frequency, breadth, depth and richness of New Testament preaching of the cross, only when one looks for the scandal of the cross and the Suffering Servant themes does Larimore come up short.

W. D. Frazee (1822-1902)

A second generation Restoration preacher who lived and worked in southern California was W.D. Frazee. He was not supported full-time by the churches. Benjamin Franklin Coulter was a wealthy and powerful personality on the conservative side of the California brotherhood before the split with the Disciples. He sponsored Frazee in preaching assignments and underwrote the publication of his book of sermons. The heart of Frazee can be seen to some extent in a sermon in his book entitled, "Advice To A Young Preacher." He advised the young minister to treat all members of the church alike, not to be a ladies' man, never to take an active role in politics and civil affairs since no one can serve two masters, to dress plainly and neatly, and never to aim at eloquence. Regarding the last matter, he suggested expository preaching through books of the Bible. Frazee carried on a tradition from the first generation regarding humor in the pulpit and in the preacher's life generally. The view was that one pleading for the souls of men and women should not be found speaking in a humorous way.

> Never try to be witty. Men may enjoy wit, but they will lose respect for the preacher, a man whose vocation it is to win souls from eternal death should always be solemn. If a young preacher is noted for trifling, frivolous, witty conversation, he is apt to have a light chaffy mind...[16]

In his own preaching as represented in this book of sermons Frazee mentioned the cross in ten of twenty-five sermons, or forty percent of the time. Those sermons not mentioning the cross treated the following themes: the Holy Spirit in conversion, stewardship, "faith only," advice to young preachers, prophecies fulfilled as proof of the inspiration of the Bible, unreliability of feelings for salvation, prayer, personal purity, the church as the true tabernacle of God with the laver at the door, spiritual growth, the value of the soul, where the church is going today, David and Solomon compared, the importance of small kindnesses, and "What must I do to be saved?"

Frazee gave substantial treatment to the atonement theme in three sermons. In "Reconciliation" he discussed God's endless love for the sinner. He began: "Christ died to reconcile man to God, so taught the great apostle to the Gentiles; but the Christian world at present paraphrases it, Christ died to reconcile God to man." Frazee was dealing with a current debate on the atonement, whether something happened in the heart of God which led to Golgotha ("objective" atonement) or just in the heart of the person who sees God's love in the cross ("subjective" atonement). Some suggested that God's willingness to forgive the sinner is an undecided, case by case matter. Each person must plead for forgiveness. Prayer for salvation was advised, implying that the whole matter was still unsettled. Frazee stressed the fact that God had already moved, that something had happened in the heart of God which led to the cross, that there was no doubt about the standing offer of God's forgiveness. To demonstrate the graciousness of God's love he retold the story of the Prodigal with his own ironic and imaginative twist at the end:

> 'And he arose and came to his father. But when he was yet a great way off his father saw him, but without much

compassion. He told the elder brother to bar the door. The young son pleaded in vain to be admitted, his elder brother said, "Plead on, my brother, and take no denial, our father will after a while relent and speak peace to your soul." But the door remained barred, and the boy was left in the cold for six months.'[17]

In "The Lord's Supper" based on Luke 22:19 Frazee said that, had there been no death and resurrection, mankind would still be in their sins. He remarked what an interesting event the Last Supper must have been: the leader celebrating his own death. Those attending would be given a world revolutionizing commission in three words: "Go, said he, proclaim my death." Because Jesus died Christians can come boldly before the throne of grace in the name of their great High Priest. No other Restoration preacher studied here spoke so movingly of the godforsakenness of Jesus on the cross.

> The prophet says, 'All we like sheep have gone astray; and have turned everyone to his own way, and the Lord hath laid on him the iniquity of us all.' It was not the suffering from his lacerated back nor mangled limbs, that suffering was as but a drop to the ocean compared to the indescribable anguish of God withdrawing his presence from him. 'The Lord laid on him the iniquity of us all' and God would withdraw in holy indignation against sin; although sin was only imputed to him, the punishment was real. He felt not the horrors that are experienced by perishing sinners. The extreme torture heaped upon him by his enemies, he bore with serenity, without a groan. But when God withdrew his presence from him, he had to tread 'the wine press alone, and of the people none with me.' For an instant the Son of God seemed to be sinking with despair. When his Father withdrew from

> him, then was wrenched from his bleeding heart, 'My God! My God, why hast thou forsaken me?' At this dreadful cry the earth shook, and graves gave up their dead. Sinner, when you come to die and God withdraws his presence from you, and you are left alone to sink forever in outer darkness, then you will know what suffering is, all other suffering will seem as sport.[18]

When one considers that godforsakenness was perhaps the ultimate scandal of the cross Frazee's comments mean even more. This understanding is rare among Restoration preachers. He concluded by calling all Christians to surround the Table in thanksgiving and joy over the benefits given them by God in Jesus' death and resurrection.

In his sermon, "Sufferings of Christ," Frazee read five verses from Matthew's description of the crucifixion and then added from I Peter 1 "which things the angels desired to look into." It was an appeal addressed to the unconverted. His imagination led him to see that angels have always been baffled at the death of Jesus. Man's sin should have brought God's judgment. Instead it moved him to this incredible love! He said again that sinners will never know suffering until God withdraws from them. And what a tragedy since Christ died that man might live forever. He concluded by referring to the sweet love of mother and father, surpassed only by the love of the heavenly Father for each of his children.[19]

Frazee mentioned the cross in forty percent of his sermons. Three of Frazee's ten references to the cross were substantial, the other seven were made in passing. He mentioned the priest/sacrifice metaphor four times, the redemption/ransom and reconciliation metaphors one time each. There was no mention of the Suffering Servant. In recalling Jesus' godforsakenness he presented one aspect of the scandal of the cross. He was the only second generation preacher to mention it even once. In another place he tied baptism directly to the death, burial, and resurrection of Jesus. He said salvation was in the blood of no other. Since Jesus bought Christians with his blood they should be known by no other name than his. He made significant statements showing a well-considered theology of the atonement in treating reconciliation, the Lord's Supper, and God's love for mankind.

However, these quotes do not represent the great bulk of Frazee's sermons. What one does find appears strong and biblical; there is just not much of it. Only four in ten of his sermons contain any reference at all, most of those were incidental in nature. One might also ask how subjects like spiritual growth, the value of the soul, and "What must I do to be saved?" could be addressed without reference to the cross. Despite notable passages on the cross here and there, Frazee falls somewhat short of the New Testament preaching of the atonement.

John S. Sweeney (1834-1908)

Born in Kentucky, John Sweeney spent the largest portion of his preaching life at one church in Paris, Kentucky. He was widely known as a preacher, evangelist, and debater. Sweeney trained for the law and was a young practicing attorney when Alexander Campbell came through his part of Illinois. Campbell's preaching stirred up a great controversy. Sweeney had heard Campbell and would not allow misrepresentations of his views to go unchallenged. Before long he became the area "champion of Campbellism" and soon left the practice of law to preach. A study of Sweeney's hermeneutic may prove helpful to one who wants to see how our second generation preachers interpreted Scripture.[20]

Sweeney mentioned the cross in seven of seventeen sermons, or forty-one percent of the time.[21] The ten sermons containing no reference to the atonement were: "The Simplicity That Is The Gospel," "The Word Of Truth," "Our Aim," "Acts Of Apostles," "The More Excellent Way," "Paul's Answer To King Agrippa," "Action of Baptism," "Infant Baptism," "A Plea For The Church Of God," and "Baptism, Its Action, Subject, and Design."

Sweeney had an aversion to talk of the atonement. The sermon which states this most clearly was "The Three Sides of Christianity." It was based on John 3:16, the three sides were God's, Christ's, and man's. God's love was the prime cause, Jesus' death was the meritorious cause, and man's faith was the instrumental cause of salvation. In his discussion of Jesus' work on Golgotha Sweeney expressed himself about the current controversies over theories of the atonement. He was impatient with debate over whether "propitiation" meant that the cross of Christ appeased God's wrath in some way. Speculations over the Calvinistic doctrine of limited atonement, over the precise meaning of atonement, of God's wrath and atonement and a host of other questions held no interest for Sweeney.

> What is the atonement? Well, that's a pretty hard question to answer to the satisfaction of almost anybody, to say nothing of satisfying everybody. But what I mean is, that Jesus died for sinners; died that sinners might be saved; died that whosoever believes in him might not perish, but have everlasting life; died that God might be just and the justifier of him that believes in Jesus. About the truth of all this there can be no question among people who believe the Bible. Among such believers

> there can be no question about the fact or the necessity of the sufferings and death of Jesus in order to the salvation of sinners. But over different explanations of the fact there have been bitter controversies from the second century down to the closing decade of the nineteenth. Of course, one has not time in a single discourse to discuss the various and conflicting explanation of the atonement. But we may spend a moment with them.

He then proceeded to discuss two main theories of the atonement: the objective theory in which the death of Jesus somehow changed the heart of God and the subjective view which said that the cross was an exhibition of God's love intended to break the hardened heart and bring the sinner to God. For our purposes, the most revealing comment was what he said next:

> But what I wish to say, and to say with emphasis, is that it is safest to follow no explanation of the matter, but to stop with and rest in the simple scripture statements upon the subject. Unbelievers and doubters have waged their war chiefly upon the explanations uninspired men have made of the atonement, rather than upon the simple statements of Scriptures. No man has ever been able fully to explain the sufferings and death of Jesus; and possibly, the mystery may remain unsolved for all time. Then let it be called a mystery. That the just should have to suffer and die for the salvation of the unjust, is a mystery, turn it any way you will. It is better to allow that it is beyond human comprehension, than by attempted explanations to make it only more incomprehensible and objectionable. But is the doctrine to be rejected simply because it is a mystery? Is the fact that it is

> incomprehensible sufficient proof that it is false? Are we to reject as false everything that is to us mysterious? This will hardly be affirmed by the most rationalistic among us. For there is a great deal in nature as well as in grace that is full of mystery. Whoever attempts to bring all the ways of God within the comprehension of the human mind will ultimately find his attempt futile.

Sweeney went on to point up vicarious suffering in nature, all life comes out of death. Somehow Jesus died to save sinners, it was God's plan. Is that not enough? We can never understand the atonement as relates to God. We can see how it affects the lives of believers. "Who will willingly suffer for the good of others like those who believe the story of Gethsemane and the cross?" He concluded that attempts to understand the mystery are unnecessary and destructive. "If we can be content and satisfied with the simple New Testament statements on this subject, we shall avoid a great deal of unnecessary and bitter internal controversy, and have less external opposition."[22]

There was yet another concern in Sweeney's mind about theological discussion of the atonement: it might divert the preacher from his main mission and the sinner from his salvation. In the sermon, "What Must I Do To Be Saved" Sweeney said:

> This is a practical question. It is the practical question, and, in fact, the only really practical question in the whole matter of salvation. Of course, God saves us. His love is the prime moving cause of our salvation. But all questions as to the divine attributes are theoretical, and all deduction as to the action of these attributes are more or less speculative.

> God saves us through Jesus Christ. The death of Jesus is the sole meritorious, or compensative cause of our salvation. But even the atonement is not a practical question. Just how God can, in virtue of the sacrifice of Christ, be just and the justifier of the believer, we may not understand. How the death of Christ met the demands of justice and satisfied the claims of the law against us, is not a practical question. It is enough for us to accept the facts as stated in the Word of God.
>
> All we do or can do is merely appropriative. But what God has required of us must be done. This is, therefore, the practical question: 'What must I do to be saved?' It is not what must God, or Christ, or the Holy Spirit do, but what must I do? That's the practical question with us in the whole matter.[23]

Sweeney mentioned the core gospel in forty-one percent of his sermons. Four references to the cross were substantive, three were incidental. He referred to the priest/sacrifice metaphors twice, the reconciliation picture once. There was no recognition of the story line of the gospels, of the Suffering Servant theme, or the scandal of the cross.

Here we see a much-loved preacher and debater of the second generation. Early on he came under the direct and formative influence of Alexander Campbell. Sweeney had a theology of the atonement, a "word of the cross" which he set forth in his preaching upon occasion. As the quotes indicate, Sweeney's only concern about the atonement was that it not be preached *per se.* He discouraged study and discussion of the subject because it was full of mystery, not man's practical concern for salvation, because it was divisive among brethren and was disruptive of the unity program of the Restoration movement.

J. W. McGarvey (1829-1911)

Another second generation Restoration preacher influenced immediately by Alexander Campbell was J.W. McGarvey. He was born in Kentucky, and was not a Christian when he went to Bethany College. After becoming a Christian he set his mind to the study of Scriptures and became our premier Bible scholar of the second generation. McGarvey was preaching in Lexington in 1865 when the University of Kentucky moved there and he accepted a chair in the College of the Bible. For many years he was a professor of Bible and preached for the church. He became widely known as a scholar, writer, preacher, and defender of the faith against the destructive higher criticism of the time.

In their commentary McGarvey and Philip Y. Pendleton wrote the following on I Corinthians 2:2 ("For I decided to know nothing among you except Jesus Christ and him crucified."):

> Paul here asserts that the subject-matter of his preaching was selected from choice, or fixed design. He does not mean to say that every sermon was a description of the crucifixion of our Lord, but that all his teaching and preaching related to the atonement wrought by Christ upon the cross. This atonement, through the sacrifice of our Lord, was recognized by Paul as the foundation of the Christian system, and he here means to say that he handled no doctrine or theme at Corinth without remembering and recognizing its relation to that foundation.[24]

McGarvey mentioned the cross in thirteen of twenty-four sermons or in fifty-four percent of his lessons. That frequency is greater than any other second generation preacher studied here.

In the introduction to "The Remission Of Sins" McGarvey quoted from Matthew 26: "This is my blood of the covenant which is shed for many for the remission of sins." At the end he offered the invitation: "Then come to Jesus according to those conditions by which he offers you that which he purchased with his own blood, free and complete and perfect and eternal forgiveness and you will be happy."[25]

In the sermon, "Conditions of Forgiveness," McGarvey told the story of Jesus' death, resurrection, and ascension. After a lengthy discussion he concluded: "Christ has died for you, my dear friends. He has made it possible for God to be just in justifying you; but then, there are conditions laid down for you to comply with, in order that you may receive the benefit of that shed blood."[26] Here McGarvey attached meaning to the cross: it allows a holy God to forgive unholy sinners.

In a sermon from Hebrews 11 on faith McGarvey pointed up the ethical implications of faith in the crucified.

> Do we believe in Him as having laid down His life to redeem us from sin, and make it possible for God to forgive us? Do we believe that? Then, to act in harmony with that, is to love Him, and to show by every day's walk in life that we are grateful to our Redeemer. And thus our faith will cause us to live a life of love, of devotion, of service, to Him who is our Redeemer, our Savior, our Friend. And if that faith dwells in any man's soul, and he is not living thus, he feels every day that there is an antagonism between his faith and his life.[27]

In another sermon, "Cases of Conversion, The Eunuch," McGarvey defended his frequent emphasis on baptism. I quote his response here because the criticism against him was couched in language of the atonement. If he stressed "Christ crucified" in his preaching at least some of his hearers missed it. He defended his emphasis on baptism without affirming the cross as of supreme importance.

> I have had people say, 'Brother McGarvey, I would like your preaching better if you would just preach Christ crucified and not of baptism so often.' Well, I like to gratify my friends, but I can't get along that way. When Philip was preaching Christ to the man, it seems that baptism was a part of the sermon. Indeed, it is impossible to preach Christ fully to a sinner and leave baptism out of the sermon. You have to mention baptism early in the story of Jesus; for he was baptized by John; and at the end of the story; for then he commanded the disciples to go and baptize men in every nation. You have to leave out both these chapters in the history of Christ if you leave out baptism. It is a mutilated gospel that leaves baptism out of the sermons addressed to sinners.[28]

In another study of conversion, the story of Lydia from Acts 16, he presented the passion and resurrection of Jesus as that legal and technical point at which the dispensations were changed, it was the line of demarcation between old and new covenant.

> The question might be raised, What need had she of being changed at all? Would not she go to heaven if she died as she was? Perhaps she would, if Christ had not been crucified and ascended into heaven, and if the law had not gone forth that men should believe in Him and obey Him, in order to obtain the forgiveness of sins and life everlasting; but that had been the established law of heaven for quite a number of years, and it was necessary, if Lydia, under the Christian dispensation, should be

> saved, that she should hear of Christ, that she should believe in Him, and that she should come to Him as the mediator between God and men, to obtain the forgiveness of her sins. This she did at once — as soon as she heard the Gospel message.[29]

The point is not to question McGarvey's ruling on Lydia or his understanding of baptism. The point is to show a typical reference to the cross in his preaching. Most often, as in this case, McGarvey mentioned the cross in connection with another topic, not as the matter under discussion.

The fullest discussion of the atonement is found in the sermon, "Redemption In Christ," Ephesians 1:7,8. Even with all of his theology of the atonement obvious in the sermons mentioned above, McGarvey was against theologizing about the subject. He said one could study the atonement for a thousand years without understanding on what basis God acted. At one point in the sermon McGarvey confessed that neither he nor anyone else understood the atonement. The clear implication was that efforts to understand it are useless at best and harmful at worst.

> What is, then, the explanation? Well, I don't know. I don't know. I don't believe any other man knows what the reasoning of God was on this subject, by which he felt compelled, according to His own infinite nature, to refuse to pardon a single sin except through the blood of His Son. I don't know. I don't know how many sermons I have heard, trying to explain it. I don't know how many pages — heavy pages — in many books, I have read, from some of the ablest men in the world, trying to set it forth; but I have never yet been able to see it; and if any of you have, I congratulate you.

> God's thoughts are not as our thoughts on many things. His ways are far above our ways, as heaven above the earth, and we may not expect to understand the reasons in His mind for the wondrous works of His prudence and mercy. I think on all such themes, we are prone to look at the subject from the wrong point of view. We try to get at God's ideas about it. It is enough for us to see the part which addresses itself to man...[30]

McGarvey was our ablest scholar among second generation of restorationists. As writer and preacher his influence extended far beyond his home in Lexington and his period in our history. He mentioned the atonement in fifty-four percent of his sermons. Six references to the cross were of substantial content and seven were incidental. McGarvey mentioned the redemption/ransom metaphor twice, the priest/sacrifice and propitiation/expiation pictures once each. He did recognize and employ the narrative nature of the gospels twice in these sermons. There was no mention of the Suffering Servant or the scandal of the cross.

In our study it is instructive to bring into focus what McGarvey said about the atonement. He either wrote or endorsed the statement in the commentary on I Corinthians that "Christ crucified" was the core gospel and the foundational truth of all Christian preaching. He made it clear that salvation was only in the blood of Christ. There were conditions to salvation, but salvation was provided by God at Golgotha. He affirmed that what Jesus did on Golgotha made it possible for the holy God to be both just and justifier of the ungodly. It was the crucified and resurrected Lord who appeared to Saul of Tarsus and turned him around. McGarvey tied baptism to the cross. He showed how the Christian's stewardship and ethical behavior are rooted in gratitude for what Jesus did on Calvary.

On the other hand, there is ambivalence in his sermons. His statement of loyalty to baptism almost emphasized the ordinance more than that which it signifies. He said that baptism itself "imparts hope." He made a technical, legal point that Lydia might have been saved on her own merits had the kingdom not come under new management since the cross. Most negative of all were the scholar's words about the futility of studying the atonement. Taken as a whole, his statements about the centrality of the cross are almost offset by his aversion to discussing the subject, his emphasis on the cross as the precise point at which the new system of salvation came into effect, and his stress on man's side of salvation. The rather full quotations from his sermons may leave with the reader the impression that McGarvey had a lot to say about the cross. Actually, all he had to say in all twenty-four sermons is reported here. The atonement was decidedly a minor note in his preaching. All things considered, McGarvey trumpeted an uncertain sound on the atonement.

Summary Of Chapter II

When we compare the first and second generations of Restoration preachers we see a decline in mention of the core gospel from 56 to 46 percent. Other patterns regarding treatment, purpose, and use of the gospel story line and metaphors of the atonement hold constant at a level well below that of New Testament preaching. In the one-hundred and fourteen sermons there is no mention of the Suffering Servant and only one reference to the scandal of the cross.

It cannot be claimed as with the first generation preachers that all of these preachers had a developed theology of the atonement which appeared in their preaching. In the case of T.W. Brents the theme is present hardly at all. He seemed more concerned to debate and defend the inherited system of thought than to proclaim the crucified and risen Lord. While W.D. Frazee produced a few gems on the subject of Jesus' death, he could also speak of the plan of salvation, spiritual growth, and the value of the soul without mentioning the cross. T.B. Larimore was often found pleading with his listeners to accept the gospel. The cross was obviously important to him as the only hope of sinners, as Jesus' identification with man, the meaning of baptism and the Lord's Supper, and message and mandate of preaching. He saw the death, burial, and resurrection as proof of the central truth of the Bible: Jesus is the Son of God, the one who brought in the kingdom. And, yet, Larimore referred to the core gospel in just over half of his sermons. He gave almost no attention to the metaphors of the atonement, none to the scandal of the cross or the Suffering Servant.

Especially important for our study are John Sweeney and J.W. McGarvey. Both had a considered theology or "logos" of the cross. They preached it for salvation, sanctification, ethics and hope. On the other hand, both the preacher and the scholar discouraged study and preaching of the subject. They saw it beset on all sides with controversies which might defeat the Restoration program of unity and discourage sinners from doing their part for salvation. They saw mystery in it which could not and should not be explored.

This second generation preaching shows a measurable decline in both the quantity and quality of references to the cross. What the first generation considered obvious and took for granted seemed less obvious to the second generation.

NOTES

[1] T.W. Brents, *The Gospel Plan Of Salvation*, (Nashville: Gospel Advocate, 1875).

[2] In one way this paucity of references to the cross may be understandable. Brent's book was a polemic against Calvinism on the one hand and easy salvation by "faith only" on the other hand. My point is that Boles saw in it "all the principles of the gospel," the book had enormous influence in our movement as it evidenced by its republication after seventy-five years, and the title claimed to deal with the essential substance of the faith.

[3] H. L. Boles, *Biographical Sketches Of Gospel Preachers*. (Nashville: Gospel Advocate, 1932), p.

[4] T.W. Brents, *Gospel Sermons*, (Nashville: McQuiddy, 1918).

[5] *Gospel Sermons*, p.140

[6] *Gospel Sermons*, 176.

[7] F.D. Srygley, *Letters And Sermons Of T. B. Larimore*, (Hollywood: Old Paths: 1950).

[8] Srygley, p. 33.

[9] Srygley, p. 58.

[10] Srygley, p. 93.

[11] Srygley, p. 233.

[12] Srygley, pp. 269,270.

[13] Srygley, pp. 297,298.

[14] Srygley, p. 305.

[15] Srygley, pp. 310-312.

[16] W.D. Frazee, *Reminiscences And Sermons*, (Nashville: Gospel Advocate, 1892), pp. 265-269.

[17] Frazee, p. 312.

[18] Frazee, pp. 261,262.

[19] Frazee, pp. 322-327.

[20] See my article, "The Preaching Of John Sweeney, A Case Study In Restoration Hermeneutic," Restoration Quarterly, First Quarter, 1989, pp. 26-37.

[21] Fourteen of these are in *Sweeney's Sermons* (Nashville: Gospel Advocate, 1897). Two are found in Z.T. Sweeney's *New Testament Christianity*, Vol. I. (Columbus,

Ind.: Z.T. Sweeney, 1923.) pp.141-157. and one is found in W.T. Moore's *The Living Pulpit Of The Christian Church*, (Cincinnati: R. W. Caroll,1868) pp. 255-278.

[22] John Sweeney, pp.83-88.

[23] John Sweeney, pp. 252,253.

[24] J.W. McGarvey and Phillip Y. Pendleton, *Thessalonians, Corinthians, Galatians, And Romans* (Cincinnatti: Standard, n.d.), pp. 58,59.

[25] J.W. McGarvey, *Sermons*, (Cincinnati: Standard, 1894), p.68.

[26] McGarvey, p. 81.

[27] McGarvey, p. 93.

[28] McGarvey, p. 129.

[29] McGarvey, p. 152.

[30] McGarvey, p. 51.

The Third Generation 3

E. M. Borden (1874-1951)

One of the most colorful of the Texas preachers over the turn of the century was E.M. Borden. Born in Shelby County, he worked as a preacher, debater, and editor in the Texas and Oklahoma areas. He related his call to preach, emphasizing that "we do not believe men are called in a miraculous way." As a boy preacher he heard one infidel express his opinion on the subject. "I have no objection to any man who makes a claim of Christianity, but I do detest men who take gall for godliness, bile for benevolence, and chronic laziness for a call to preach."[1] In his book of sermons Borden told of his first gospel meeting, listed the twenty-four tracts and booklets he had written, chronicled his editorial work with two papers, described debates and other colorful episodes. In the last category he told how, after the elders closed one meeting he reopened it, how three saloons were put out of business, and of a couple of incidents when dogs disrupted his preaching.

Borden mentioned the cross in nine of the twenty-five sermons or thirty-six percent of the time. The fifteen sermons with no mention of the atonement dealt with the following themes: what conversion is and is not, whether people go to heaven as soon as they die, Old Testament prophecy and fulfillment, how one knows he is saved, righteous living, the call to preach, the human and the divine, Jesus' second coming, the incarnate Word, and resisting the Holy Spirit.

In "Time Shall Be No More" he pointed to the Day of Judgment and the certainty of the resurrection. Hearers were urged to "show forth his death until he comes." In the sermon, "How I Became A Member Of The Church of Christ" he said: "I understood that Jesus died for all, and that I was also included. So, naturally, in my own mind, I asked what to do."[2]

Borden used the burial of Jesus as proof of the truth of Christianity in the sermon "The Shepherd, The Sheep, and the Sheepfold." Taking his text from John 10 he quoted from Isaiah 53. "He made his grave with the wicked, and the rich in his death." He took that passage to be a prophesy of roles played by Joseph of Arimathea and Nicodemus. "No one but Jesus could be the Christ foretold by the prophets."

In "Stand Still And See The Salvation Of The Lord" he compared the experience of the Hebrews recorded in Exodus 14 to salvation for all sinners. Borden emphasized that human beings cannot raise themselves, as Jesus promised to do in John 5:28. "We cannot raise ourselves from the dead, but we do what the Lord has told us in order that we may be raised to eternal happiness."

In the sermon, "Jacob's Ladder" Borden's point was that Jesus is our ladder by whose death, burial, and resurrection we come into the Body of Christ. Faith, repentance, and baptism are also rounds on the ladder. Many, however, do not keep climbing the ladder: after baptism "adding faith, virtue, etc."

The most extensive statement on the atonement is found in the sermon, "What Is Christ To Me?" Here Borden relates the death and resurrection of Jesus to forgiveness of sins, baptism, the Lord's Supper, sanctification, the fellowship of the church, and the Christian's hope.

> Jesus shed his blood to save us from our sins. 'But if we walk in the light as he is in the light, we have fellowship one with another, and the blood of Jesus Christ his son cleanseth us from all sin' (I John 1:7) Then we are cleansed by his blood. He shed his blood that we might be saved. When Jesus instituted the Lord's Supper, he said: "This is my blood of the New Testament, which is shed for many for the remission of sins.' (Matt. 26:28) Just think what he did for us. He died for us. He shed his blood for us. It is by his blood that we are saved. 'In whom we have redemption through his blood, even the forgiveness of sins' (Col. 1:14) Yes we are saved by his blood. Ananias told Saul to arise and be baptized and wash away his sins. His sins were washed away by the blood of Christ, but after baptism. We are saved by his blood, but we must go to where the blood is. Paul tells us that we are baptized into the death of Christ and that is where he shed his blood. Do we appreciate what Christ has done for us? 'Take heed therefore unto yourselves, and to all the flock, over the which the Holy Spirit hath made you overseers, to feed the church of God, which he has purchased with his own blood' (Acts 20:28) If we are saved we are purchased, for the church is made up of a purchased people. The Lord adds to the church such as should be saved.
>
> One of the sad things of time is when we die, yet there is consolation in the fact that we will be raised from the

> dead. What did his resurrection do for us? He tasted
> death for us. He went into the regions of death. His body
> was buried in Joseph's new tomb, and his spirit was in
> hades. The man who took upon himself the seed of
> Abraham, left that body while he was in hades. He came
> out of that state, and in so doing he purchased a
> resurrection for all. 'For as in Adam all die, even so in
> Christ shall all be made alive.'³

E.M. Borden was one of the most colorful characters among his generation of preachers. We see in him a further decline in the mention of the cross. The last lengthy reference shows that Borden had a theology of the atonement. It was an understanding which ran in several directions and gave meaning to distinct facets of the Christian life. What is important to see here is that his whole theology of the atonement is found in only two sermons. Generally speaking, his preaching of the cross is thinner in content than that of the second generation preachers. More and more the cross is mentioned only in support of other themes, especially baptism and church membership.

Borden mentioned the cross in nine of twenty-five sermons, just over one third of the time. Seven of these references were incidental and two were substantive. He mentioned the reconciliation metaphor twice and the redemption/ransom picture once. There was no recognition of the gospel story line, the scandal of the cross, the Suffering Servant or the other metaphors of atonement found in the New Testament.

A. G. Freed (1863-1931)

The opposite of E.M. Borden in personality and bearing, A.G. Freed's picture in the front of his volume of sermons reminds me of Clifton Webb in the movie, "Cheaper By The Dozen." Erect, the pince nez precisely placed on his nose, a nappy dresser, mustache perfectly trimmed, he is the picture of a cultured gentleman for his time and place. Born in Indiana during the Civil War, reared and educated in that state, he made his contribution mainly in Tennessee. From there his influence radiated as a preacher, debater and especially as an educator. He spent fifty years of his life in school work. His first love was training young men and women for Christian service. With N. B. Hardeman, he was the founder of the school which later became Freed-Hardeman College. He finished his teaching career at David Lipscomb College.

Freed mentioned the cross in nine of twenty-seven sermons contained in his book, or thirty-three percent of the time. Titles of sermons not containing any reference to the cross were: "It's Better Further On," "Wise Readings," "Our Thinking," "The Bible," "Faith," "Victories of Faith," "Opportunity," "The Beginning," "The Shepherd Hymn," "A Solemn Charge," "A Message from the Dead," "The Doctrine Vrs. Doctrines," "Upon This Rock," "Apostasy," "Reminiscence," and "Infant Baptism."

In a sermon called, "Ingratitude," Freed told how Jesus' own people betrayed him and chose a murderer to go free rather than release him. In another lesson entitled, "God and His Word" the educator spoke of the many mysteries of the faith. He explained that the resurrection, though a mystery, was the fact which undercut the godless theory of evolution.

> ...The central fact of his word is, 'He is not here; he is risen.' The resurrection of Christ is an historical fact, just as much as the reign of the Pharaohs in Egypt or the discovery of America. The most massive, magnificent fact of all history is the resurrection of our Lord. This is the

weapon that still inflicts the mortal wounds in all parts of the theory of evolution.[4]

In another sermon comparing the old and new covenants Freed outlined twenty points of contrast. Fifteenth in the list was the "blood of animals" versus "the blood of Christ." As others had done before him, he could list the cross along with other agents of salvation without indicating its premier importance.

In a sermon, "The Millennium" based on Revelation 20:1-7 Freed spoke of God's victory over Satan and "the chain of evidence" too strong for Satan to break, by which he is bound. That chain is composed of the death, burial, and resurrection of Jesus. He spoke of the twelve sitting on the twelve thrones, apostles of "the Lamb." The "souls of martyrs" will reign with Christ because "in Christ" they will have had resurrection and victory. That victory was secured when they obeyed that "form of doctrine," that symbol of Jesus' passion, baptism. (Romans 6) All Christians will be there because his blood "cleanses them from all sin." (I John 1).

In "A Solemn Charge" based on II Timothy 4:1-2 Freed gave examples of the preaching recorded in Acts. He then asked the question: what does man need? What is necessary for salvation? He answered with a list of twenty-five items man needs for salvation. His long list of items vital for salvation contained no mention of the cross. In "How To Read The Bible, New Testament" he made the usual distinction of Old and New Testaments divided by the cross of Christ. He then treated the cross under the metaphor of victory. The cross was God's love for man, Jesus' resurrection was God's victory.

> Loving hands take the body down, wrap it in a clean linen cloth, lay it in a new tomb. 'He made his grave with

> the wicked, and with the rich in his death.' The tomb is made 'sure as ye can.' But after three days he comes out a mighty conqueror. He had said, 'Destroy this temple, and after three days I will rear it again.'

Freed then cited Peter's sermon on Pentecost, registering his own emotional response to those convicting words.

> 'Ye have taken and by wicked hands have crucified and slain.' But 'God raised him up...' '...Therefore let all the house of Israel know assuredly, that God has made that same Jesus whom ye have crucified, both Lord and Christ,' — enough to pierce them in their hearts. No wonder they say unto Peter and to the rest of the apostles, 'Men and brethren, what shall we do?' How personal! How Vital!

He then asked why preachers of his day preached all that Peter preached up to the point of baptism.[5] This was Freed's fullest statement of the atonement and its implications. Notice the meaning he saw in it: the line of demarcation between old and new covenants, the key for reading and understanding the Bible correctly, Jesus had tasted death for every man as evidenced in his godforsakenness, he won victory for every man in the resurrection, the story became the core gospel and the seed of God's church.

In "The Grace of God" Freed invited his hearers to accept God's gift. God had done his part, man must now do his. The contract was clear. God does for man what man cannot do for himself. Included in what man cannot do for himself is the incarnation and death of Jesus. Why then are not all saved? Because all will not obey. They will not do their part. If the children of Israel had refused to march around the walls of Jericho those fortifications would not have fallen. "God has lovingly done his part, will you not do yours?"[6]

A.G. Freed had a large impact on our tradition. His influence was felt as a preacher, debater, and especially as an educator. If one compares his preaching with New Testament preaching the findings are meaningful. He mentioned the cross in nine of twenty-seven or exactly one-third of his sermons. Two references were substantial in content, the other seven were made in passing. He mentioned the priest/sacrifice and the victor over Satan metaphors twice each. There was one instance when he recognized and used the gospel story line. No mention was made of the scandal of the cross, the Suffering Servant or the other six metaphors of the cross.

In the few references Freed made to the cross he taught lessons on ingratitude, stated his case against evolution, argued his view of the millennium, affirmed victory over death, and argued for the necessity of baptism over against the thief on the cross episode. He described grace as God doing for man what man could not do for himself, including the incarnation and death of Christ.

There appears a paradox in Freed's preaching. On the one hand he could hold up the cross as central to the faith. On the other hand, he could list man's twenty-five necessities for salvation without mentioning the cross. As was the case with E.M. Borden, Freed had one sermon into which he poured his whole theology of the atonement. We notice again that the "word of the cross" seems to become more and more a separate topic, not the core gospel it was in New Testament preaching.

J. D. Tant (1861-1941)

In the last sermon of his book J.D. Tant reviewed his life and work.[7] He was born to "well-to-do" parents in Paulding county, Georgia in 1861. His father had owned four farms before the Civil War. Between Sherman's march to the sea, unscrupulous lawyers, and hard times he lost everything. Young Tant was so poor he had no books for his schooling. At one point the teacher left a window of the schoolhouse unlocked at night so he could get in and study his lessons for the next day. He joined the Methodist church at age fifteen and passed his examination to preach at nineteen. With his family he moved to Texas. He heard the gospel from Church of Christ preachers and was immersed. The young preacher found himself with no money, sporadic preaching assignments, and an increasing responsibility for supporting his parents and family. By hard experience he learned that many "brethren pay cash for their tobacco, and get their preaching on credit." He preached from place to place, started churches, and held debates. It gave him pain that he established several churches who would not have him back later to preach for them. On one occasion a church hired him, agreed to pay him 1000 for a year's work. The large sum would have paid his debts and made his parents livelihood secure. Tant was shattered when the church reneged, "for I thought all brethren were true to their word...But experience has taught me that when in trouble, trust only yourself." He lost his wife and all three of their children in death. His second wife had six children and she was his faithful help mate in preaching. He said he told his story so younger preachers would not think preaching was "all flowers and sunshine."

In his volume of sermons J.D. Tant mentioned the cross in seven of sixty sermons or twelve percent of the time. The fifty-three sermons containing no reference to the cross treated the following themes: the Bible as God's word, the church, the three dispensations of Bible history, lessons on the Holy Spirit, baptism, a comparison of Moses and Christ, "old time religion," the "five states of man," "Why I Am A Christian," "Campbellism," the nature of man, salvation, heaven, the Christian's warfare, repentance, the need to go onward, why he could not "Preach The Gospel But Let Other People Alone," the gospel, fellowship, worship, distinctiveness of Churches of Christ, the Christian's hope, and prayer.

In a sermon called "Three Kinds of Righteousness" from I Corinthians 10 Tant spoke of the Seventh Day Adventists.

> Another class of good and religious people who claim to have no confidence in the flesh, who do not believe in the righteousness of man come one step this side and take up the law of Moses, and spend three fourths of their time preaching 'Remember the Sabbath day to keep it holy.' They forget this Sabbath day was kept in memory on account of the children of Israel being delivered from Egyptian bondage (Deut.5:15). They also forget that Paul teaches that the law was blotted out and nailed to the cross (Col. 2:13-14).[8]

In "The One Body," Tant lists six identifying marks of the true church. The "blood of Christ" was one of these six. He referred to the priest/sacrifice and law court metaphors in his explanation.

> At this time it was proclaimed to the world that Christ had been crucified, had shed His blood for our sins. As we expect forgiveness only in the shed blood of the Son of God, no one can go further back than the time when He shed His blood and established His church without

> introducing the blood of bulls and goats, for they were the only shed blood then; and by them we can never claim to be justified.[9]

Tant was arguing against religious practices which looked for their authority to the Old Testament. The cross is used here, not so much to proclaim our salvation on Golgotha, as to nail down the fact that life in the Christian dispensation is to be conducted only under the New Testament. In other words, the way one can tell the true church is to listen to hear that we are no longer under the Old Testament, no longer saved by the blood of bulls and goats. The other side of that truth, that we are saved by the blood of Christ, is not explored.

At the top of the lesson, "What Benefit Is Your Church?" Tant included the chart he used in preaching the sermon. Two large boxes were drawn. At the top of the box on the left were written the words: "Church Of Christ." At the top of the box on the right side were the words: "Your Church." In these boxes, side by side, he listed benefits to be found in the Church of Christ while the opposite deficiencies were shown in other churches. Consistent with the sermon mentioned above, one of the items to be found only in the Church of Christ was salvation in the blood of Christ. So, in the "Church of Christ" box: "Inside The Blood Of Christ," and under "Your Church": "Outside The Blood of Christ."

An indication of Tant's view of preaching is found in his sermon: "Preach The Gospel, But Let Other People Alone." He was responding to the criticism that he was too harsh on other religious groups. In reply he chastised the "ecumenical movement" in the Church of Christ. The sermon must have first been preached during World War I because Tant chose an analogy from that conflict to express his feelings about his critics.

> "The desire of some of my brethren. Parallel: Wilson to the army: 'Boys, be sure to fight and shoot, but be careful to try not to hit the Germans.'"[10]

In summary, J.D. Tant referred to the death, burial, and resurrection in only seven of sixty sermons. Those references which do appear were not made to explore the meaning of the atonement itself. They were used as proofs for church membership, the superiority of the Church of Christ over other churches, to prove that Christians are no longer under the Old Testament. One reference was substantial and six were incidental. He mentioned the priest/sacrifice metaphor twice, victor over Satan and justification once each. There was one sermon in which he recognized the story line of the gospel. There was no mention of the scandal of the cross or the Suffering Servant theme.

With Tant the faith had become a sword with which to slay opponents in other religious groups and those in the Church of Christ who took views different from his own. The church of his understanding was to be promoted and defended at all costs against all comers. The gospel was less about a person and what he did on Golgotha than a doctrine. The propositional language Alexander Campbell and Walter Scott had adopted from John Locke found its extreme expression in Tant's sermon "The Peculiar Sect." Jesus had now been reduced to "a proposition."

> As Christ was recognized as a proposition through faith for remission of sins that are past (Rom. 3:25) they then became citizens of the kingdom, children of God, spiritual, governed by the Spirit of the life of Christ walking by faith, not by sight.[11]

Neither for himself nor for his listeners could Tant see the goodness of God in the cross. As I leave Tant to move on in this survey, the last statement in his book haunts me. What torment any Christian must suffer who approaches death without knowing the sure salvation won for us at Golgotha, and as Paul said in Romans 5, that "we have peace with God through our Lord Jesus Christ"! These were Tant's final words:

> As I come nearer the river's brink, I am fighting harder and trying to do more that God may welcome me, than ever before. Only a few more miles and I shall rejoice to see the other side. If God accepts me, all will be well with me. If not, I know he doeth all things well and I shall humbly submit to his will.[12]

R. C. White (1872-1961)

Born in Bedford County Tennessee, R.C. White became a member of the first graduating class of the Nashville Bible School in 1896. The school would later become David Lipscomb College. He studied under both David Lipscomb and James A. Harding. White preached in Tennessee and Alabama, his ministry extending almost sixty-nine years. Well-known and much loved, White pledged himself to preach wherever he was asked. His plan was to work in destitute and weak places. "With a home and some means besides, I am able to work at whatever place needed, hoping always to help destitute places." It was said that he never turned down a call from a poor congregation.

White's book of sermons contains one hundred and three short outlines of sermons. For this study there are both advantages and disadvantages of studying mere outlines.[13]

He referred to the cross in fifteen of one hundred and three sermons, or approximately fifteen percent of the time. In broad categories, the themes White treated without reference to the cross were judgment, worship, the church (salvation in, identity of, organization), steadfastness, repentance, baptism, the Christian's influence, salvation, warnings about apostasy, the Bible, spirituality, great Bible questions, heaven, the marks of a Christian, church leadership, giving, excellent things, proofs of pardon, the worthy woman, Christian living, bearing trials, sanctification, faith, hope, fellowship and brotherly love. He also included a funeral sermon and a wedding ceremony.

"The Gospel" was a sermon based on Romans 1:16 and I Corinthians 15:1-4. It had five major points: I. Its Beginning, II. Time of Beginning of the Gospel, III. Full Gospel Has Record of Five Points: 1. Death of Christ, 2. Burial of Christ, 3. Resurrection of Christ, 4. Christ's Blood shed on Calvary, and 5. Faith, repentance and baptism for remission of sins—all to be preached and accepted. IV. Where? When? By Whom Was Such Teaching and Obeying Done? V. Study the Five P's: Purposes of God; Promises; Prophecies; Preparation; the Cross; Perfection.[14]

In two sermons one finds the fullest treatment of the atonement. The first entitled, "Reconciliation," was taken from II Corinthian 5:17,18. It was a problem/solution sermon. The problem was the barrier which stood between mankind and God: the power of sin, the power of Satan, and the power of the Law (no mercy). The solution was stated: "Only Christ can reconcile. He shed his blood to do it." White quoted Matthew 26:28 and Hebrews 9:24 in exposition of this theme. However, he did not explain further his text from II Corinthians 5.

The other sermon was "Blood and Remission of Sins." In the introduction White said that sin is the most terrible reality known on earth. He then made three main points. I. Sin and Blood from the Beginning. (Three sub-points:) 1. Sin before any law concerning sin. 2. Blood the life, sin to shed or eat. 3. Blood of animals in sacrifices. II. Christ's Blood Alone Can Bring Remission. (Subpoints:) 1. Remits sin under both old and new covenants. 2. Blood of animals and Christ's suffering contrasted. 3. Efficacy of Christ blood two-fold: (Under that:) (1) Cleanses completely, blood of animals could not. (2) Brings a new song to saved. III. How The Blood Brings Remission of Sins. (Subpoints:) 1. Must walk in humble obedience to God's will. 2. Fellowship is on condition we keep His commands; else God brands us as a liar. 3. The cleansing by the blood is assured if from a pure heart we are fully obedient. The conclusion urged the listener to accept the Savior's invitation.[15]

In these two sermons White shows considerable thought about the death of Christ under the reconciliation and priest/sacrifice metaphors. One might only wish for more than two sermons like these in this collection of one hundred and three lessons. To me the most difficult sermon to understand is "The Foolishness And Weakness of God." It was based on Paul's statement in I Corinthians 1:25, which is "ground zero" for the apostle's preaching of the cross as God's scandalous power to save. White preached the whole sermon without mentioning the scandal of the cross, without referring to the cross at all. He had three main points about the "foolishness of God." I. Basis On Which the Gospel Rests. (Not human logic or reason). II. Lord's Work Done by Church Without Human Societies, and III. Examples Further Illustrating Text. (Jericho, Joshua 6; Gideon vs. Midianites; etc.; "the Lord's Supper as monument. Silly to the world.")[16]

R.C. White was obviously much loved in Tennessee as a good and unselfish minister who was willing to serve wherever needed without regard for fame or fortune. He used the cross to prescribe what should be preached, but did not preach the cross much himself. The cross appears in his preaching about the church, obedience to baptism, and as an argument against mere sincerity in religion. He called Christians to live as if they had been "bought with a price." But the cross was typically a subpoint for illustration or proof. It was not an important matter in and of itself, not the fountainhead from which all else flowed. He used the cross sometimes in issuing an invitation, offering God's salvation to the sinner. Most remarkable of all to me, he was able to preach on a key text on the scandal of the cross without mentioning either.

If one compares White's preaching in quantitative terms with the New Testament preaching of the cross it does not fare well. He mentioned the atonement only fifteen percent of the time. Five references seemed to be substantial in content while ten appeared to be incidental. He did not use the story line of the gospels at all. He refers to the priest/sacrifice and reconciliation metaphors twice each and to the redemption/ransom once. There was no mention of the Suffering Servant or the scandal of the cross.

N. B. Hardeman (1874-1965)

Few Restoration preachers have had such wide influence as N.B. Hardeman. None has had a greater impact on twentieth century Church of Christ preaching. He was born in Tennessee and that state was his base of operations all of his life. He enjoyed a notable career as an educator, beginning in the rural schools of West Tennessee, continuing on the faculty of Georgie Robertson Christian college, then with A.G. Freed establishing the National Teachers' Normal and Business College in 1908. The school was renamed Freed-Hardeman College in 1919. He served as Vice President for twelve years and as President for twenty-five years, retiring in 1950. His best known preaching efforts were the "Tabernacle Sermons" delivered in Nashville and published in five volumes between 1922 and 1943.

In the five volumes there are one hundred messages. In forty-one of these Hardeman mentioned the cross, obviously forty-one percent of the time. The other fifty-nine sermons which contained no mention of the death, burial, resurrection of Jesus or the "word of the cross" treated the following themes and sub-themes: the Bible (as the church's constitution, its history, as Word of God, hearing it, teaching it), conversion and salvation (what is required, repentance, the truth necessary, the "way," essentials and non-essentials), man's accountability, Christ (as "vine" and disciples the branches, as living within Christians), materialism, prayer, the church (establishment, unity, identity, work, worship, instrumental music, relation to Christ, in the first century, the falling away, reforms), vowing, cost of discipleship, premillennialism, ethical living as witness, missions and evangelism, and the Restoration Movement. And, Hardeman preached one sermon on the church containing no mention of the cross entitled, "The Blood Bought Institution."

Most of the sermon, "The Great Commission," from Matthew 28:19-20 was devoted to a discussion of faith, repentance, and baptism as the appropriate response to the gospel. However, early on Hardeman gave a rather full statement of what he considered Golgotha and the open tomb to mean.

> When at last the Savior died on the cross, he blotted out the handwriting of ordinances that was contrary and against them and took it out of the way. He tore down the middle wall of partition between Jew and Gentile,

> having abolished in his flesh the enmity, even the law of the commandments contained in ordinances, that he might make thereby in himself of the twain — Jew and Gentile — one new man, so making peace, and that he might reconcile both unto God in one body by the cross, having slain the enmity thereby.
>
> Having spent three days and nights in Joseph's new tomb, he burst the doors thereof on the third day and came forth triumphant over the powers of the Hadean world, disclosing his identity to those round about, until at the end of forty days he led his apostles out to the heights of Galilee and there announced unto them a system of religion that was not narrowed down to a family nor even limited by national ties, but that was world-wide, that was heaven-born, that had been bought by the precious blood of the Son of God himself. The twelve having been selected, he gave them the most sacred charge ever couched in human words or delivered to mortal man. The salvation of the souls of men is the objective toward which all things are bound and toward which everything is converging. The one supreme object to be accomplished is the remission of sins, the saving of men and women, and the increasing of the kingdom of God and his Son, Jesus Christ.[17]

One notices in this quote Hardeman's beliefs that the cross provided justification for the believer, supplied the basis for fellowship among all kinds of people, and had a broadening effect on the mission of God's people.

From I Corinthians 1:25 Hardeman preached "God's Foolishness Vs. Man's Wisdom." He showed how all through the Bible God asked men to do what they considered foolish in order to be saved: Naaman the leper, the brass serpent in the wilderness, the blind man in John 9. A single paragraph appears on the cross after which the rest of the sermon demonstrated that baptism might seem foolish but is still required of God. He set his brief statement on the cross within Paul's meaning in I Corinthians, the scandal involved. But his main point was that, however foolish baptism seemed to some, it was God's ordained means of salvation. He focused on the scandal of baptism not on the scandal of the cross.

From Hebrews 11:11 he preached "The Terror Of The Lord," calling the cross "the greatest exhibition of the love of Heaven" and spoke of Jesus as an example for all who would please God. One might notice how he related the cross to Jesus' mission. "At last, his work on earth being finished, he yielded to the demands of a bloodthirsty mob and was crucified upon the rugged cross for the salvation of the race."[18] There seems to be ambiguity here in Hardeman's thought. On the one hand, he considered the death, burial, and resurrection the foundation of Christian doctrine. On the other hand, he considered the cross as something that happened "his work on earth being finished." The second statement implies that Jesus' teaching, miracles and commissioning of the disciples were his main work.

In "The Spirit of Christ" based on Roman 8:9, Philippians 2, and Hebrews 5 he spoke of the spirit of submission. The sermon was his own defense against criticism that he was pugnacious. He said he was proud to be a "scrapper" since that is what the Lord was and that was the reason for his death. Hardeman went on to make a distinction between merely preaching the truth and exposing error. Some brethren believed that the second was not a Christian preacher's task. He countered that it was precisely for condemning error that Jesus died. Hardeman saw a scandal in the cross and a similar scandal in his own conflicts.

> If Jesus had but preached the truth, he would have been living till this very hour, all other things being equal. Let me tell you the fact: because Jesus Christ condemned error and exposed the wrong, those very chief priests, scribes and Pharisees whom he had denounced went to old Caiaphas and said: 'That man must be killed.' Jesus Christ suffered on the tree of the cross, not for preaching the truth, but for exposing and condemning error.[19]

Given the enormous influence the sermons had on subsequent generations, especially among preachers, the study of Hardeman's sermon, "The First Sermon Under The Commission" is important. He held up Peter's sermon in Acts 2 as an example of how one should preach the gospel. Peter's four main points were: 1. Jesus of Nazareth was approved by miracles, wonders, and signs done among you. 2. He was delivered up by the determinate counsel and foreknowledge of God. 3. You by the hands of wicked men have crucified and slain. 4. God has raised him from the dead. "Here we have a model sermon outline," asserted Hardeman. Then he claimed that Peter gave no real attention to the cross because the crucifixion was obvious. Preachers should assume the obvious and prove that which is in question.

> Well, what's the next point? You have crucified him by the hands of lawless men. Now, why talk five minutes on that? Anybody doubt it? Nobody knew it better than did that crowd. Therefore, Peter passed it by and he said, God has raised him from the dead. Now, that's the only point among the four that Peter's crowd denied. They were bound to accept three of the propositions, and hence, he spent no time in arguing matters of that story,

> but he devoted his time to the proposition that needed
> support, and that was the resurrection from the dead.[20]

One can hardly argue with Hardeman's observation that the resurrection was the point at issue. It was because Jesus was raised that he was being proclaimed Messiah. No one doubted the crucifixion, it is true. But, on the other hand, how many saw its meaning? One might ask if the crowd on Pentecost believed that Jesus was crucified "by the determinate council and foreknowledge of God." As we indicated in Section I, there is considerable content about the cross of Christ in Peter's Pentecost sermon.

Hardeman mentioned the cross in four of every ten sermons. Thirty-four of these references were incidental, seven contained substantial comment. Once Hardeman used the gospel story line to carry his point. He mentioned the reconciliation metaphor three times, the priest/sacrifice, redemption/ransom, propitiation/expiation, victor over Satan, the law court, and the example metaphors once each. Hardeman referred to seven of eight New Testament metaphors. He mentioned the scandal of the cross once, the Suffering Servant metaphor not at all.

When one reads these five volumes of sermons it is not difficult to see why they have had such appeal and influence over the years. Hardeman was widely travelled, well-read, articulate, bordering sometimes on the eloquent, clear and reasonable in thought, in possession of a sense of humor. He was, no doubt, quite persuasive. Regarding the "word of the cross" there are several strong points we have seen. He tied baptism to the death, burial, and resurrection of Jesus. He gave exposition to his favorite metaphor for the atonement, reconciliation. He called for all to come together upon the Word of God since Jesus died for the church. Hardeman often said that the death, burial, and resurrection of Jesus were the facts of the gospel. Several times he vowed to preach nothing else. More than once he mentioned the cross as proof of God's love and Jesus' spirit as an example for all his followers. He also underscored the cost of discipleship in relation to Jesus' death.

On the other hand, there were weaknesses in Hardeman's preaching of the cross. It is my judgment that in several ways Hardeman's great influence may have actually discouraged further study of the atonement. Most significant is the fact that in only three of a hundred sermons is there any real focus on the cross. Other sermons contained references which seem problematic. In a sermon on I Corinthians 1:25 the emphasis was not on the foolishness of preaching the cross but on what some considered the foolishness of baptism. In another place he held out Peter's sermon on Pentecost as a model in such a way that the cross and its meaning are just assumed in favor of the resurrection. In a third sermon Hardeman stated that Jesus submitted to the cross "after he had finished his work." Symptomatic of the defective theology he inherited was his sermon, "The Blood-Bought Institution" in which the cross is never mentioned in a lengthy discussion of the church.

In truth, to say that Hardeman preached the cross in forty-one percent of his sermons is misleading. By reading the sermon titles one can discover Hardeman's real emphasis. Twenty-six sermons dealt with the church, seventeen with conversion, fifteen with the Bible, and nine with the Restoration plea. Taken together these sermons comprise sixty-seven percent of the sermons in these five volumes.

For all that can be said about the quality of Hardeman's sermons, they do not clearly define the atonement as that matter "of first importance" (I Corinthians 15:1-4). His preaching centered in the Church of Christ, its: nature, mission, worship, requirements for membership, unity, relation to other traditions, and issues. The atonement was, in theory, the center of his preaching. But in fact, the church was his main message.

Summary Of Chapter III

One notices sharp contrasts among these third generation preachers in personality, background, style, and field of ministry. Borden was a colorful, free-wheeling frontier evangelist. Freed was an educated, cultured, buttoned-up scholar, educator, and preacher. Tant was hard-bitten by life and his preaching reflected his own bitter experiences. He was at war with the denominations, the world, the church, and perhaps sometimes with himself. White dedicated himself to ministry among the disadvantaged churches. Hardeman was the standard bearer for a generation.

In this third generation we see a further decline in the pecentages of sermons with references to the core gospel. The rate of mention declined from 56 in the first generation to 46 in the second to 26 in the third. Even that low figure does not truly indicate the poverty of their preaching regarding the cross. One notices a continuing lack of reference to the metaphors of the atonement. Only three times was there any reference to the story line of Jesus' life leading to the cross. There was no mention of the Suffering Servant and a single reference to the scandal of the cross.

The slippage from the first generation preaching is most remarkable in preaching emphasis. The first generation endorsed and preached the cross as the core gospel, even though they moved the attention of our movement away from that center to secondary matters. The second generation did not want to explore the atonement because such study tended toward mystery, speculation and divisiveness. They saw no reason to study God's side of salvation, the only practical question was man's part in salvation. But by the third generation the cross was neither consistently held out as the center of the faith nor preached as such. These men made no case for or against study of the atonement. It was simply not a current issue. They had inherited almost nothing regarding the atonement. A.G. Freed could preach on twenty-five necessities of salvation without mentioning the cross. J.D. Tant used the cross only as proofs to make his case on other matters, never treating the atonement in itself. R.C. White could preach a sermon on the "foolishness of preaching" from I Corinthians 1 without mentioning the cross. Hardeman gave exposition to the atonement in only three of one-hundred sermons. The second generation had received a "cut flower" theology of the atonement. Some of its beauty and fragrance remained. By the third generation the bouquet had wilted and appeared ready to be thrown out altogether.

NOTES

[1] E.M. Borden, *Life, Incidents, And Sermons of Eli Monroe Borden*, (Delight, Ark.: Gospel Light, 1948). p. 131.

[2] Borden, p. 104.

[3] Borden, pp. 148, 149.

[4] A.G. Freed, Sermons, *Chapel Talks And Debates*, (Nashville: Gospel Advocate, 1930), p. 27.

[5] Freed, pp, 56-60.

[6] Freed, p. 162.

[7] J.D. Tant, *The X-Ray Gospel*, (Austin: Firm Foundation, 1933) pp. 238:291.

[8] Tant, p. 103.

[9] Tant, p. 148.

[10] Tant, p. 136.

[11] Tant, p. 176.

[12] Tant, p. 291.

[13] Perhaps the single advantage is that the reader is presented a larger than usual sample of the preacher's sermons from which to draw conclusions. The greatest disadvantage may be in the category we are calling "incidental references." For example, if the preacher often mentioned the cross in offering the invitation that might not appear in this kind of outline. However, in White's case his conclusions are well outlined and appear rather complete. If our study proposed to examine the style and language of the preaching these short outlines would produce an insurmountable barrier. But since this is a study of a theme, the "word of the cross," we can have a high degree of confidence that the substance of sermons is well preserved in these outlines.

[14] R.C. White, *The Sermons Of R. C. White*, (Murfreesboro, Tenn.: Dehoff, 1945.), pp. 40,41.

[15] White, p. 85.

[16] White, pp. 55,56.

[17] N. B. Hardeman, *Hardeman's Tabernacle Sermons* Vol. I (Nashville: McQuiddy, 1924.) pp. 102,103.

[18] Hardeman, Vol. I, p. 248.

[19] Hardeman, Vol. IV, (Nashville: Gospel Advocate, 1938), pp. 117,119.

[20] Hardeman, Vol. IV, p. 185.

The Fourth Generation   4

The last five men studied in our survey of Restoration preaching were all born before the turn of the century. Their influence extended to the middle of this century and well beyond. By studying these five men we can see the tradition regarding the atonement which was handed on to us.

G. C. Brewer (1884-1956)

G.C. Brewer was born in Tennessee. He served churches in his home state and in Texas, held several debates and wrote a number of books and pamphlets. In Brewer's book of sermons the seventeenth chapter is entitled "In Memoriam." Friends had suggested that he write a biographical sketch. He chose instead to relate the sorrow of his family, including three pieces he wrote upon the deaths of his sister Lillie and brother William. At the time of writing Brewer had known much grief and loss. Of a family with ten children five and the father had died. He lost four sisters, one brother, and his father between the years 1894 and 1918. Three years in a row he buried a loved one. All of these losses were endured before he was forty years old.

In the preface of his book Brewer commented: "I claim nothing original for these sermons. They tell the old, old story in as simple a way as I could put it. 'Christ crucified' is always my theme and I am determined never to preach anything else."[1] Brewer mentioned the cross in eleven of sixteen sermons in his book, or sixty-nine percent of the time. Those sermons in which he did not mention the atonement were: "Christ the Christian's Creed," "Christ Saves The Believer, Or What Does It Mean To Believe in Christ?", "The Immovable Kingdom," and "Heaven: What Will It Be to Be There?"

In a sermon on John 3:16 Brewer called for obedience to the gospel. He described the trial of Jesus and the crucifixion, how Jesus was our substitute in his death. He imagined Gethsemane and what had gone on in the heart of God to deny Jesus' plea, "If possible, let this cup pass."

> The Father looks again and there arises before him another scene. He looks down over the ages and sees the teeming and toiling millions of men as they stagger across the stage of life neath their burdens of sin. He hears them crying for mercy. He sees them standing by the open tomb with broken and bleeding hearts, yearning for light. He saw me and he saw you with our eyes swollen with weeping and souls stained with sin. He saw us all traveling down the brink of eternal woe, and he loved us, blessed by his name; he loved us so that he redeemed us. I see him dispatch an angel to the earth with the message:
>
> 'My Son, it is not possible. If you do not drink this cup then all my poor children of earth are lost forever.'[2]

Brewer spoke of the scandal of the cross in his message, "Christ, The Friend of Sinners" based on I Timothy 1:15-17.

> If we were called upon to name tonight the one thing the present day world needs more than anything else, we should say, a sense of sin. The reason that people do not come to the Lord is because that they do not feel that they are sinners and therefore they do not believe that they need the Lord. When we present to the people of today the story of the cross it becomes a stumbling block to them, because it is not complimentary to men. It does not compliment man to say that he had gone down into the depths of depravity to the extent that God had to send Jesus Christ from the heavenly world to save him; that Jesus must shed his innocent blood upon the cruel cross for man's redemption.[3]

In another lesson Brewer mentioned the scandal of the cross in contrast with the modernist view that vicarious atonement was offensive. He said that educators are depending on education, scientists on science, philosophers on their speculations. But none of these disciplines could transform lives and help people live ethically.

> Wisdom could not save Solomon from idolatry and polygamy. Philosophy could not save Bacon from bribery. Poetry could not save Byron from immorality. Education could not save Leopold and Loeb from crimes of the most shocking, brutal and atrocious nature.[4]

In the sermon, "Christ's Blood And How It Saves Us" he spoke again of the scandal of the cross and the essence of the faith.

> My friends, this is the whole substance of the Christian religion. This was the gospel preached by the apostles. This was the doctrine that produced the martyrs and this was the hope that sustained them when they felt the flames. This was the faith of our fathers and this is the faith that will give you the victory over doubt and fear and sin and death and hell.

Brewer concluded this message again claiming to preach only Christ crucified.

> We only ask you to come to Christ; to enthrone him in your heart as Lord of your life; to become a Christian by obedience to his will — as that has been clearly pointed out in this sermon. There is only one plea you need to make and that is that his blood was shed for you. Come relying upon that alone. Just as you are—waiting for nothing. Come saying: "Just As I Am..."[5]

The preacher explained yet another aspect of the scandal of the cross in the sermon "Christ On Trial or What Shall I Do With Jesus?" Some Modernists said that Jesus never called himself the Son of God. But before the ruler Caiaphas Jesus made the claim. Brewer told the story of Peter's denial of Jesus and how Pilate washed his hands of the matter. Peter had denied his Lord, Pilate had side-stepped responsibility.

> May God help us all to bear his cross after him. He is on trial in this age of the world — right now. Some are denying him, others are trying to wash their hands of him and others are bearing his cross. They are suffering the ridicule of an unbelieving world, but what is that? Think of what he endured for us. Behold, the man! What will you do with him? May the Lord help you right now to

decide to acknowledge him as the Son of God and your Savior.[6]

For the interests of our study Brewer's sermon, "The Gospel Paul Preached" is the most significant. He began by quoting Galatians 1:6-12. He explained that "anathema" was a strong word, meaning "irrevocably cut off." So it is important to ask what the gospel was Paul preached. Brewer proposed an hypothetical situation in which a young man felt called to preach, encountered Paul's stern warning, and set out on a quest to find the true gospel. He found in I Corinthians 15 that, for Paul, the matter "of first importance" was the death, burial, and resurrection of Jesus.

> 'Well,' says the young man, 'I have found it and that ought not to be hard to preach. There is no need for any one to pervert that. It is just the facts of the old, old story of Jesus and his love. How that Christ died for our sins, was buried and rose again the third day. Then the rest of the chapter is taken up on that third point — that Jesus was raised from the dead and was seen by witnesses. No wonder Paul had said to these Corinthians, 'I determined to know nothing among you, save Jesus Christ and him crucified,' for that is the gospel and if he had preached anything else — or anything contrary to this, or that violated that, he would have been anathema. Also it is no wonder that Paul said to the Galatians, 'God forbid that I should glory save in the cross of our Lord Jesus Christ.' That is the gospel and he who leads men to believe that they can be saved without the vicarious atonement of Christ's death is anathema, and he deserves to be. After Christ has suffered that most shameful death to save men, if I should go out and presumptuously set that sacrifice at naught, make it void, and tell men to trust

> their own strength and wisdom or their morality, their lodges or anything else for salvation, I would deserve to be anathema. I see Paul's viewpoint now. That is what it means to pervert the gospel: to direct the minds of men away from the grace of Christ to the works, wisdom or schemes of men.[7]

As indicated above, Brewer's view of baptism was determined by his understanding of the atonement. He asked his audience if they had obeyed the death, burial, and resurrection. If they knew how to obey it. Brewer was unique among our preachers in calling for obedience to the cross itself. Typically they asserted that there was nothing in the "facts" of the gospel to obey.

Like J.D. Tant, G.C. Brewer's preaching arose out of painful life experiences as well as his Bible study. He sustained great personal loss, knew by experience what it was to cry out, "My God, why...?" Brewer mentioned the cross in eleven of sixteen sermons or sixty-nine percent of the time. That high rate is explained partially by the fact that this series of sermons was focused on the cross. The other part of the explanation is that Brewer was focused on the cross enough to build a series of sermons on the theme and publish a book with "Christ Crucified" in the title. Ten of the eleven references were substantial. Three times Brewer revealed the gospel story line, more than any other preacher in this study. He used the law court and victor over Satan metaphors twice each. Priest/sacrifice, redemption/ransom and the reconciliation metaphors were mentioned once each. The Suffering Servant picture did not appear. Perhaps most significant of all, Brewer explored the scandal of the cross three times in these sermons.

Brewer showed a carefully considered "word of the cross" in various ways. Several times he spoke of the substitutionary and vicarious nature of the atonement. Jesus' death for all mankind meant that preaching must not be the mere promotion of any denomination or sect. He saw the scandal of the cross in several of its aspects: its statement about man's sin, its indictment of man's pride and self-righteousness, its connection with the cost of confession. He had thought through the connection between the atonement and other vital New Testament doctrines. From his understanding of the core gospel he pleaded with his listeners to respond to the cross.

Frank L. Cox (1895-1978)

Frank Lucious Cox was born in Texas just before the turn of the century. He preached in Oklahoma and Texas and published several books, including three books of sermons. He was active in evangelistic work in several states and was closely associated as a writer with both the "Gospel Advocate" and "Firm Foundation" periodicals. He was the first editor of the "Minister's Monthly," published by the "Gospel Advocate."

In his book, *101 Sermon Outlines*, Cox mentioned the cross in twenty-one of one hundred one lessons or twenty-one percent of the time.[8] The themes Cox treated without the "word of the cross" were: discipleship, God's Law, materialism, the problem of evil, Christ's invitation to sinners, the Christian and the world, the home, judgment, Jesus' miracles, the Holy Spirit, Jesus' baptism, the restoration of an erring brother, worship, the resurrection, grace, the abundant life, conversion, gossip, stewardship, fellowship, church discipline, service, faith, forgiveness, ministry of song, the nearness and nature of God, salvation, evil speech, values, church attendance, Jesus our advocate, the work of Christ, regeneration, the book of Jude, the second coming, the Lord's Day, and heaven.

More than any other preacher studied here, Cox highlighted the example metaphor when he mentioned the cross. In the sermon, "Christ's Universal Salvation," from Matthew 11:25-30 he commented on Jesus' promise: "and I will give you rest." He said that Jesus was never free of trials, temptations, persecutions and sorrows. Christians must endure life's heartaches, taking him as their model.

In the sermon, "Gethsemane" from Mark 14:32 Cox did treat the ordeal as he imagined it felt from God's side. He used the garden setting as the framework of his lesson. The garden was a place of: solitude, sorrow and shame, prayer, and victory. From his discussion he derived three points, two regarding God's part and one on man's side of salvation. The three points were: 1) The enormity of sin made the cup bitter, 2) The struggle showed the depth of divine compassion, and 3) This ordeal shows the power of prayer.

In "On the Mountain And In The Valley," from Luke 9:28-42 Cox made the provocative observation that the transfiguration and healing of the demoniac were meant to prepare Jesus for his death and the disciples for life. The insight seems intriguing but is not expanded on in any way.

A psychological treatment of witnesses to "The Empty Tomb" was based on Luke 24:1-12. Cox imagined what the emotions of the disciples must have been during the whole ordeal of the passion and the open tomb: love, disappointment, perplexity, hope, joy, wonder. He concluded the sermon:

> Let us learn: 1. That the empty tomb is eloquent with meaning. 2. That the resurrection assures us of Jesus' divine nature and oneness with God (Rom. 1:4). 3. That the resurrection is heaven's endorsement of all that Jesus

> did and said. It is in harmony with the voice that spake at the beginning of his ministry (Matt. 3:17). 4. That the empty tomb is a prophecy and an assurance of the day when all tombs shall be emptied (John 11:25; Rom. 8:29; I Cor. 15:20).[9]

From the story of Philip and Nathanael in John 1 Cox preached what might be called a novelty sermon, a lesson for which the main attraction is the uniqueness of its title or treatment. He entitled the sermon, "Eureka! Eureka!" and used an acrostic on the word, "Messiah" as his outline. For the second "s" in Messiah he listed "Suffering Servant" and mentioned Isaiah 53 and Acts 8. He affirmed that, "though Jesus did no sin, he suffered for sin, for sinful man that he might redeem and lead us upward."

Another sermon entitled, "The Cross of Christ" based on John 19:17,18 affirms that "the cross of Christ is the central figure of the ages." It is "our peace, our glory." Again in an appeal to novelty, Cox set forth six aspects from which the cross might be viewed. I. Under the cross, Jesus the weary pilgrim. II. Upon the cross, Jesus the sacrificial victim. III. Above the cross, a title nailed to be read by all. IV. Over the cross, darkness, Jesus forsaken by heaven and earth. V. Beneath the cross, the soldiers. and VI. By the cross, those who loved Jesus, the women.

In one sermon especially Cox pointed out the ethical implications of the cross. "Your Body Is God's Temple" from I Corinthians 6:18-20 was Paul's admonition about fornication. The preacher expounded the text in two main points. I. A wonderful fact: "You are bought with a price." II. Consequences: "You are not your own." You belong to the Purchaser. Your body is not yours to injure, abuse, divide and waste.

We should especially notice Cox's treatment of the atonement in his sermon, "The Church," from Matthew 16:13-18. He said that safety and security are in the church because Jesus promised that "the gates of hell will not prevail against it." But there is something odd about this building and builder, Cox said. Ordinarily the construction of a building is interrupted if the builder dies.

> But the crucifixion of Jesus did not thwart the plan of God. After the death of Jesus, the church was firmly established...Nor does the death of its members threaten. The church lives on...the dead shall live again.[10]

Here the cross was pictured, not as the foundation of God's plan and the church, but as a possible threat which was overcome. Cox leaves the impression that, despite the cross, the church was established. Then he placed the death of Jesus and the death of Christians on the same plane. In neither case could death overcome the triumphant institution. The church seems to be the hero of the piece, it survives no matter what.

When one compares Cox's treatment of the cross to the New Testament preaching there is much that commends it. Ten of the twenty-one references were substantive, had real content and teaching for his listeners. He referred to six of the eight New Testament metaphors of the atonement, more than most preachers studied here. He referred to redemption/ransom and reconciliation twice each, to example three times, and to priest/sacrifice, victor over Satan once each. Once he used the gospel story line. Most remarkable considering what we have seen in other preachers up to this point, Cox mentioned the Suffering Servant twice and with substantial comment. He made no reference to the scandal of the cross.

On the other hand, only one in five of his sermons makes any mention of the cross. He referred to the core gospel only nineteen percent of the time. For all the excellent insight shown in the references which do appear, he obviously felt able to handle most topics without any reference to the core gospel. That is to say, although he had a well developed theology of the atonement, it did not spring up naturally in all situations as it does in the New Testament. Equally as significant, the cross in one place was pictured as a threat to God's plan overcome in the resurrection. The church is pictured as conqueror over all.

Leslie G. Thomas (1895-1988)

Leslie G. Thomas was born in Tennessee and preached as a located minister in Texas, North Carolina, Alabama and Tennessee. He did evangelistic preaching in twenty states. Thomas was also a staff writer for both the "Gospel Advocate" and "The Minister's Monthly." The volume of his sermons studied here was the first of seven he published, the last was published when he was seventy-three and was entitled, *The Valedictory Sermons Of Leslie G. Thomas*.

Thomas mentioned the cross in twelve of one hundred sermons, obviously twelve percent of the time.[11] Themes he treated without mention of the atonement were many: the art of getting along with people, authority in Christianity, the unfulfilling life, farewells of Bible heroes, a summary of Paul's gospel, discipleship, hidden faults, evil, joy, the Law, gratitude, how to have successful gospel meetings, the philosophy of life, Christian polemics, materialism, and worship. He treated other topics repeatedly without mentioning the cross: faith seven times, character twice, choices four times, the advanced Christian life twice, Christ six times, the church seven times, on mocking God twice, Christian unity four times, conversion eleven times, Christian living seven times, truth and error three times, hope twice, the gospel three times, grace twice, God three times, the Bible three times, prayer twice, salvation four times, and sin seven times. Both from percentages and this overview of his themes it becomes clear that the cross did not play a large part in Thomas's thinking.

A sidelight on these sermons which makes them unique is Thomas's citation of religious leaders outside the Restoration tradition. At the end of sermons he often listed those to whom he was indebted for ideas and insights. Among these were: James Hastings, Henry Drummond, Clovis Chappell, Ralph Waldo Emerson, and John Henry Newman.

The references to the cross in these sermons were mostly incidental and relatively minor in emphasis. From John 6 Thomas preached the sermon, "If Not To Jesus, Then To Whom?" In only four lines out of a three page sermon he mentioned the atonement. He asked who can lift us above guilt and the power of sin, man's deepest need. Not ethics, science, philosophy, but the blood of Christ.

Thomas credited Benjamin Franklin's second volume of sermons in his lesson, "Different Things To Which Salvation Is Ascribed." He listed four things responsible for our salvation. He devoted one paragraph to faith, one paragraph to the blood of Christ, two paragraphs to grace and four paragraphs to baptism. In "the Gospel Paul Preached" from Galatians 1, Thomas spoke of the general characteristics of the gospel and its principles. Under principles there were four: it is of God, of Christ, of Christ and his church, and of the plan of salvation. As pertains to the gospel of Christ he spoke against "modernism," saying that the gospel rests on the virgin birth, vicarious death, victorious resurrection, triumphant ascension, and glorious coronation of Jesus. In a sermon based on the resurrection of Lazarus, Thomas said that God often does not do for man what man can do for himself. God gives the rain and the sun, man must work for the crops to see the harvest. God gave his love, his son, his son's blood and the plan of salvation. Man must obey that plan. In the last sermon in the book, "At the End Of The Way," he affirmed that death has become more of a friend to the Christian than an enemy because of Jesus' victory over the grave.

In three sermons Thomas made substantial mention of the cross. From the Garden of Eden story Thomas preached the "Conflict Of The Ages." He spoke of its origin, its history, and its end. Marking the end of the great conflict was Jesus' temptation to self preservation and his willingness to become the "Lamb of God," to drink the cup until he could say, "It is finished." In "The Cost of Discipleship" from Matthew 16, Thomas presented Jesus' death as an example for Christians. Jesus' announcement of his passion was prompted by the divine idea of self-sacrifice. Because Jesus gave of himself, Christians must give of themselves. "No one can be a disciple of Christ and not possess the spirit of self-sacrifice, hence the need for this lesson."

For another sermon Thomas used the story from Acts 17, the mob aroused against Paul, the beating of Jason, and the accusation: "they are all acting against the decrees of Caesar, saying that there is another king, Jesus." He asked three questions of the text. First, did Jesus really desire to be a king? Second, did he deserve to be a king? Third, is it possible for him to be king? Under the last point Thomas made the following comments:

> 1. By this it is meant: Is it possible for him to be the kind of king that he wanted to be — viz.: the ruler over all mankind?

> 2. It did not look like it when Pilate delivered him up and when the rulers of the world turned to slay his followers. It has looked dark for his cause a great many times.
>
> 3. In answering the question now before us, we must consider another question—viz.: Is it possible for all men to have the same religion? We cannot think of a nation that would make Mohammed, Buddha, or Confucius supreme, for men have seen the error of their teaching. But is it possible for Christ to be universally accepted? That is what he asked for and set his disciples to work to accomplish. (Cf. Matt. 28:19; Mark 16:15) Is there anything in the Christian religion that does not apply to any race, or that any people cannot accept?[12]

Perhaps the most significant feature of Thomas's sermons for our purposes is the way he could treat key themes and passages relating to the death, burial, and resurrection without mentioning the core gospel. From John 20:30,31 he preached "The Design of the Gospel Records." He contended that Jesus' work as recorded in the gospels was preparatory for the real mission of Christianity. From the text there was no mention of the sign of signs which prompted Thomas's confession: the prints of the nails. The real mission begins in Acts 2 when thousands were baptized and the church was born. The disciples had the main mission, Jesus' work and the coming of the Spirit were only preparatory.[13] Thomas preached "The Spirit of Christ" from Philippians 2:5. There was no treatment of Christ's self-emptying in the incarnation and the cross. The spirit of Christ was to be seen in his teaching, his spirit of self-denial (the text was listed among others), in his lack of sympathy with presumption, and in the characters he loved.[14] In the sermon, "The New Testament, Its Message To Man" there was no mention of the cross. He also preached a sermon summarizing

Paul's gospel, three lessons on the gospel and four on salvation without including the cross.

When one compares the preaching of Thomas with the New Testament the results are not positive. He mentioned the cross in only twelve percent of his sermons. Only three of those references held any content, nine were made in passing. The priest/sacrifice and victor over Satan metaphors were used twice each, the example picture once. Once he referred to the story line of the gospels. There was no acknowledgment of the scandal of the cross or the Suffering Servant metaphor.

Leslie G. Thomas was a man who, through his preaching and books of sermons, wielded considerable influence in the first half of the twentieth century. He read beyond the boundaries of the Church of Christ and quoted other authors. The vast majority of his sermons contained no reference to the core gospel at all. The references which did appear were very sketchy in content, with three notable exceptions. The most disturbing factor is the way he could treat key passages and themes relating to the atonement without mentioning the cross. His focus of attention centered in two areas. The first was Christian living: character, maturity in Christ, discipleship, and stewardship. The second and more pronounced emphasis was the church: its entrance requirements, standards of behavior, needs, mission and methods.

Fred E. Dennis (1894-1983)

Dennis was born in Ohio and that state was his base of operations throughout his ministry. Part of his education was earned at Ohio University. He published another book of sermons besides the one studied here, and yet another book on preaching. Dennis was never a located preacher but worked for thirty years as an evangelist. He was active in radio work and as a public school teacher. In the introduction to his book, *Fifty Short Sermons*, Volume II, the Gospel Advocate was quoted as saying that Volume I had a "phenomenal reception." Unique among all the books of sermons studied here, this was the only volume not published by a company in the Restoration tradition.[15]

Dennis mentioned the cross in fourteen of fifty sermons, or twenty-eight percent of the time. Those topics he could treat without mentioning the cross were: Bible study, salvation, judgment, mysteries of the faith, moral admonition, prayer, man's situation, faithfulness to God, hope, treasure of the faith, sectarianism, the church, death, primary and secondary things. Several of the sermon titles were provocative. It was observed in my statement of assumptions that our tradition in preaching seldom acknowledged current situations within society. Dennis provides a rare exception to that rule in his sermon, "To Our Boys in the Armed Forces." From World War II he also took a title for teaching Satan as the Christian's enemy, "The Devil's U-Boats." Neither of these sermons spoke to the world situation but were statements about personal discipleship within that situation.

Sermons containing a paragraph or two on the atonement furnish a better understanding of Dennis's preaching of the cross. In "The Gospel Of Christ" he set out the plan of salvation in what are now to us familiar restorationist terms.

> There are three fundamental facts of the gospel of Christ.(I Cor. 15:1-4) First, Christ died for our sins according to the Scriptures; second, he was buried; third, he rose again the third day according to the Scriptures. Facts cannot be obeyed, but they can be, and must be, believed. We believe the facts of the gospel. These basic

> facts were proclaimed for the first time on the first Pentecost after the death, burial, resurrection, and ascension of Jesus Christ. This took place in the city of Jerusalem. 'Out of Zion shall go forth the law, and the word of the Lord from Jerusalem.' (Isa. 2:3)[16]

Dennis went on to show that one of the ways of finding the true church was to ask which one had its beginning place in Jerusalem. This reference to the cross was to establish the facts of the gospel and to commend the Church of Christ as the one established on Pentecost. The atonement was not a subject in itself, it served to preach the church. "The Making Of A Christian" was an evangelistic sermon using as the text Paul's encounter with King Agrippa. Dennis stressed the connection between obedience to Christ and the name Christian. He set out squarely the fact that taking the name Christian meant and means paying a price. He quoted I Peter 4:16 to that effect. He then assured his hearers that God would underwrite the venture as he had in the resurrection and exaltation of Christ.

> To be a humble follower of the humble Christ and to wear no other name but his really means something. The name is above every other name. 'Wherefore God also hath highly exalted him, and given him a name which is above every name: that at the name of Jesus every knee should bow, of things in heaven, and things on earth, and things under the earth; and that every tongue should confess that Jesus Christ is Lord, to the glory of God the Father.' (Phil. 2:9-11)[17]

In "The Great Salvation" Dennis used the death, burial, and resurrection of Jesus to argue what salvation is not. It is not something "better felt than told." He reasoned that Jesus promised before his crucifixion to send a Comforter. The Lord restated the promise after the resurrection and before the ascension. The critical moment was not the coming of the Comforter, but the death of the one who made the testament. He quoted I Peter 1:18-21 to show that salvation has been bought by the blood of Christ.[18]

In a defensive sermon about "Calling Names" Dennis used Peter's sermon on Pentecost to show that the preacher must call names to make clear the sinners' peril. In proving his point he includes an exposition of the scandal of the cross. He cited Peter's accusations of the Jews on Pentecost.

> That kind of preaching brought results. They could see that the innocent blood of God's Son was upon their souls; it was dripping from their hands. What were the results? 'Now when they heard this, they were pricked in their hearts, and said unto Peter and to the rest of the apostles, Men and brethren, what shall we do?' (Acts 2:37) What brought them to a sense of their lost condition? The truth had been preached and the application made. Peter let them know that he was preaching to them. So many today preach 'pretty' little sermons, and folks go to sleep and do not know of whom the preacher is preaching. And the preachers seem just a little timid for fear some might find out![19]

In another sermon entitled "Worldliness" he spoke again of the scandal of the cross. This time it was a call to those in the pew to take up an unpopular and holy lifestyle.

> Paul said something about the world being crucified unto him and something about him being crucified unto the world. (Gal. 6:14) Many members of the church today are not crucified unto the world; rather, they are married

> unto the world. They want to participate in about every
> worldly thing that the world participates in. They go to
> about the same places, read about the same literature,
> talk about the same. If we want to go to heaven, we must
> crucify the world. Those worldly instincts must be put to
> death. I suppose very few worldly church members will
> read these lines. Most of them are not sufficiently
> interested in their souls to read religious books.[20]

Dennis treated a wide range of topics without any reference to the cross. Most often he used the death, burial, and resurrection of Jesus as proof and illustration of other agendas. He especially wanted to prove that salvation was only in the church. So much so that the church is presented as the place of salvation rather than Golgotha. Another issue with Dennis was his polemic against "better felt than told" religion. To meet that error he presented the cross as a "fact" that could and should be taught and learned.

His theology of the atonement set out in positive terms contained three facets. First, he use the example metaphor to teach Christian ethics. Second, the cross was set out as an incentive for evangelism in that God's love was demonstrated there. Third, and most remarkable, he twice presented the scandal of the cross, once as it applied to preachers who might be timid in calling for repentance and again for members who would avoid the call to holiness.

Dennis preached the cross in twenty-eight percent of his sermons. Twice one finds the passion receiving a substantive statement, twelve times it is mentioned in passing. He used the courtroom metaphor twice and the example metaphor once. He mentioned the scandal of the cross twice. Dennis focused mostly upon the church, the plan of salvation, and the call to holy living. The cross was barely visible, certainly not center stage.

Foy E. Wallace Jr. (1897-1979)

The son of Foy Wallace Jr. wrote a tribute upon the occasion of his father's death. Pointing up a side of the well-known preacher most people never knew, Wilson Wallace told how his father had cared tenderly for his invalid mother all the twenty-eight years since her stroke. He said he would like the epitaph on his father's grave to read: "Soldier of The Cross."[21] Foy Wallace Jr. preached sixty-eight years. He was known the width and breadth of the land as a preacher and debater.

Wallace mentioned the cross in ten of twenty-four sermons or forty-two percent of the time. *The Gospel For Today*[22] was an extended and amplified version of an earlier book, *The Certified Gospel.* The original sermons, most of which were preached before 1950, were expanded to full-blown essays of thirty to forty pages each.

The fourteen sermons without mention of the cross covered a wide range of topics: the Bible, the gospel, conversion, repentance, the "Ancient Order," sectarianism, and the church. The last five sermons in the book were arguments against various movements, practices and doctrines Wallace detested: "The Boll Millennial Movement," "Premillenialism," "The Music Question," "The Party Spirit And Pseudo-Issues," and "The Everlasting Gospel." The last sermon presented arguments against the "neo-orthodox" movement and new versions of the scriptures. Wallace was a polemicist. He made his statements, almost invariably, over against someone else's view.

For our study it is significant to see Wallace's view of preaching. In a sermon, "What It Means To Preach Christ" he reviewed the story from Acts 8 of Philip and the Ethiopian Eunuch.

> What then was the task of the preacher? And, 'he preached unto him Jesus' — that's God's only plan — preaching. It pleased God by the foolishness of preaching to save them that believe.' By man the gospel shall be preached to man — that is the divine plan. But what did it mean to preach Jesus? It meant just what preaching Christ meant in Samaria where Philip had closed his other meeting. Did he preach baptism? The answer is plain, in view of the fact that in the case of the Samaritans 'when they believed Philip's preaching...they were baptized' and in the case of the Eunuch, the man wanted to be baptized in the first water he saw. When the man heard the preaching, he believed it, and announced his faith in the simple confession: 'I believe that Jesus Christ is the Son of God.' The chariot was stopped. They went into the water. He was baptized.[23]

We should mark that, for Wallace, preaching the gospel meant preaching baptism. He gave "preaching Jesus" no other content, there was no reference to the Suffering Servant passage the Ethiopian was reading. The next to last sermon of the book was "The Mission And Medium of the Holy Spirit." At the end of the sermon Wallace addressed what he considered to be "first principles" and called his preaching brothers to task for not preaching them. What he meant by "first principles" will become clear as we study Wallace's preaching.

We now turn to the specific content of his preaching of the cross. In only one sermon does Wallace give an exposition of the cross itself. In the first sermon of the volume, "The Certified Gospel," under the heading, "It Is A Glorious Gospel" he quotes from Paul. Using the apostle's words in I Corinthians 2, Wallace said he was determined to preach nothing but "Christ crucified." He explained that the cardinal facts of the gospel support the death of Jesus Christ, his resurrection from the dead and his ascension. Wallace then said, "the redeeming element in all of the gospel facts is that in Jesus Christ we have a representative." He pointed to the cross and resurrection as proofs of that proposition. Jesus was our representative in death, burial, resurrection and ascension. Then Wallace turned away from these truths as too mysterious for discussion and spoke of more understandable and practical matters.

> The majesty of these truths is far beyond finite contemplation, and their range exceed the limitation of time and space for their further discussion now, so we shall proceed to the next element of the certified gospel.[24]

He moved on to a discussion of the Church of Christ and the "plan of salvation," man's part in the transaction.

The rest of the references to the cross in these sermons were of an incidental nature, used to support what were for Wallace more important issues. In "How and When The Church Began" he explained that the cross ended the Sabbath and the Law and made the establishment of the church possible. In fact, the cross was God's final act in the "remedial system" which lasted from Adam to Jesus' words, "It is finished." "There the remedial system was finished, the scheme of human redemption effected, and the law, having been fulfilled, ended." He then went on to explain what the real center of the Bible is.

> The second chapter of Acts is the hub of the Bible. The contents of the whole Bible center in this chapter. Everything in the Old Testament points forward, and everything in the New Testament points backward to the second chapter of Acts. In it Old Testament prophecy and prediction are fulfilled and New Testament blessing and promises are enjoyed.[25]

He explained why Acts 2 was the hub of the Bible. On Pentecost the church was established. Christianity is mainly about the church. The gospel could not be preached before the resurrection of Jesus from the dead. The first gospel sermon and the establishment of the church were the most important events of biblical history. Jesus had promised to build his church. On Pentecost that promise was honored.

Wallace strongly emphasized the relationship between baptism and new life in Christ. This passage from "The Bible Baptism" based on Romans 6 indicates his understanding.

> Still not satisfied with the emphasis, the apostle further says that we are baptized 'into his death.' Baptism stands between the sinner and the death of Christ — it stands between the sinner and the blood of Christ, the merits and benefits of his atoning death. Baptism is the recapitulation of the death of Christ; there the sinner being buried with Christ into death is made in the likeness of his death, his burial and his resurrection; there in death with Christ, and in Christ, he loses his sins, for 'the old man is crucified with him' and 'he that is dead is freed from sin.' No stronger figure could be employed by which to set forth the design, form and benefits of baptism. It is the reenactment of Calvary.

> But the capstone of the argument is yet found in the clause, 'like as Christ was raised up from the dead by the glory of the Father, even so we also should walk in newness of life.' Baptism stands between the sinner and newness of life.[26]

In this large volume Wallace spelled out clearly what he believed the gospel to be and what the church's mission is. In the last sermon, "The Everlasting Gospel," he attacked "Neo Orthodox" theology and new versions of the Bible. He then stated "the substance of the everlasting gospel" in four points: 1. Integrity of the Bible as the verbally inspired Word of God. 2. The creation of man in the image of God. 3. The virgin-birth of Jesus Christ as the 'only begotten Son of God.' 4. The organic and spiritual unity of the church of Christ.[27]

This summary of the gospel also reflected clearly Wallace's war of former years in the Modernist/Fundamentalist controversy. One notices that the core gospel of Jesus' death, burial, and resurrection is not listed as a part of the everlasting gospel.

In "The Party Issues And Pseudo-Issues" Wallace set out the ten propositions of the Restoration movement as he had known it and to which he had given his life.

> The principles consist in a set of ten scriptural propositions: (1) The all-sufficiency of the Bible as the rule of faith and practice as the basic truth; (2) the deity of Jesus as the only begotten, virgin-born, Son of God; (3) that the faith in Christ, as the Messiah of the Old Testament and Savior of the New Testament, together with obedience to all gospel commands, constitute the full conditions of pardon or salvation from sin; (4) that baptism, or immersion in water, of penitent believers in

(into) the name of the Father and of the Son and of the Holy Spirit is for (in order to) the remission of sins; (5) that in conversion the Holy Spirit operates only through the truth, the Word of God, never without it — a proposition sustained by every recorded case of conversion; (6) that the formation and government of the church must be in accordance with the divine pattern set forth in the inspired models; (7) the proper observance of the Lord's Supper on the first day of the week assembly of the church; (8) the refusal of any element of worship, such as incense, candles, organs, mechanical instruments — that every element of worship is specified in the New Testament and has not been left to human judgment or uninspired expediency; (9) the rejection of all sectarian names on the scriptural ground that the Bible only makes Christians only, (10) the repudiation of all denomination and party creeds, accepting the New Testament alone as the only divine creed. To these principles we steadfastly adhere without exception or deviation, deferring to no man, conceding to no set of men a greater degree of devotion, allowing none a higher claim of allegiance, fealty or fidelity to these inherent and distinctive truths of the real restoration movement.[28]

One notices that the cross was not included. Item number three states faith in Jesus as the Messiah of the Old Testament and Savior of the New Testament. He did not find it necessary to detail the central work by which Jesus fulfilled these roles. The spotlight here was not on Jesus but on the Restoration plea. In "Restoring The Ancient Order" he explained what he believed the first generation restorationists had in mind.

> So the task of those men committed to the principle of 'restoring the ancient order' and 'speaking where the Scriptures speak' was to rescue the Bible from the Protestant clergy and creed and to restore the New Testament church in its primitive perfection. Briefly summed up, the aim of the restoration movement was simply this: first, to abolish every human creed for the Bible, and the Bible alone; second, to abandon every party name for the name of Christ; third, to require of sinners the same acts of obedience as condition of their salvation as were required by Jesus Christ and the apostles; fourth, to practice in the worship only those things for which we have Scriptural precept, command and example. And that is yet the spirit and genius of the restoration plea.[29]

Whether or not Wallace accurately summarized the essential plea of the first generation, one notices there is no reference to the atonement. Wallace provides the reader with three summaries: of his own platform and message in preaching, of the Restoration program, and of the first reformers' intent. In none of these summaries is there any reference to the death, burial and resurrection of Jesus Christ.

Wallace mentioned the cross in forty-two percent of these sermons. One time he gave the atonement itself substantial treatment, the other nine times he mentioned the death, burial, and resurrection incidentally to establish other points. The only metaphor he mentioned was redemption/ransom and that only once. There was no recognition of the story line of the gospels, no mention of the Suffering Servant, no reference to the scandal of the cross.

He was able to treat a wide range of topics without reference to the cross. In the one sermon where he defined what it means to "preach Christ" the main emphasis was on baptism. One must preach the Church of Christ against all others. Preaching is "doing battle for the truth."

In the first sermon of the book, "The Certified Gospel," Wallace treated I Corinthians 15 and the core gospel. He affirmed that the resurrection and ascension of Jesus were central to the faith. Jesus died for the sins of mankind, was our representative in his death, resurrection, and ascension. Consequently, he is the pioneer and forerunner of all believers. The cross showed God's hatred of sin and love of the sinner. The "mighty arch" of the faith is the resurrection of Jesus which proves him to be the Son of God. After briefly stating the core gospel, Wallace declared these matters too "majestic" to be contemplated and turned to man's part in redemption, the "plan of salvation," and the church.

After this one sermon all of the other references used the cross to support propositions more important to Wallace: that salvation is only in the church, that the old covenant was nailed to the cross (the cross was part of the "remedial system" in effect from Adam to Golgotha), that Acts 2 and the birth of the church is the "hub of the Bible," that baptism is the content of "preaching Christ," that man's side of salvation is the main concern, and that various other churches held erroneous views on assorted topics.

The cross appeared in none of the summaries Wallace supplied of his own message, of the Restoration plea, and of the earliest leaders' purposes. In Wallace we see the church preached as the core gospel. Acts 2, the establishment of the church was the key event and hub of the Bible, not the death, burial, and resurrection of Jesus. That which was "of first importance" to Paul was not of first importance to Wallace.

Summary of Chapter IV

When one surveys the five preachers in the fourth generation each man's uniqueness is apparent. G.C. Brewer spoke of the core gospel more often than any other preacher after the first generation. In terms of content, he preached the most developed theology and most clearly formulated "word of the cross" of all the twenty Restoration preachers studied here. Often he spoke in polemics, repeatedly he referred to the cross as the center of the faith and as a scandal.

Frank L. Cox was also unique in that he mentioned six of the eight metaphors of the atonement at least once each and twice he dealt with the Suffering Servant theme. But less than twenty percent of his sermons contained any reference to the cross. In one sermon the cross was presented as a threat to God's plan which was overcome in the resurrection. The church was really the hero of the story for Cox. Leslie G. Thomas recalled the cross even less often than Cox, only twelve percent of the time. He pointed to only three of the eight metaphors of the atonement, a sum total of five times in the one-hundred sermons. Especially noticeable is his ability to deal with key passages on the atonement without mentioning the cross at all. Fred Dennis mentioned the scandal of the cross twice and presented Jesus' death as incentive for evangelism and Christian living. But he mentioned the cross is only twenty-eight percent of his sermons, only two of those twelve references had any real substance. More than anything else he preached the church.

The loss of the cross from our preaching is most obvious in the sermons of Foy Wallace. In the one sermon in which he did state several aspects of the biblical doctrine of the atonement he turned away from the subject as "too majestic" and ended with an exposition of the church and man's part of salvation. In another place he said the cross was a part of the Old Testament "remedial system." Choosing to focus elsewhere, he asserted that the real "hub of the Bible" was Acts 2. Not in theory, but in practice the church was everything in his preaching, the cross was almost nothing. The identity of the church was found as over against other churches, not in relation to the person of Jesus Christ. He could summarize his own platform, the program of restorationism, and the first reformers' intent without mentioning the cross.

All in all, the fourth generation's sermons in the composite show further decline in mention of the core gospel, from 26% to 23%. This is the case even including Brewer's individual rate of 69%. If they are to be judged by their books of sermons the other four preachers believed that the main message of preaching is the church.

Such a judgment is not intended here to diminish the importance of that "blood bought institution." But I am suggesting that blood bought must always receive the accent in that phrase. The core gospel makes the church, not the other way around.

My own judgment is that the seeds of the first generation's church-centered "Reformation" had by this time taken root, come to full maturity and were bearing abundant fruit. Long since had the focus shifted from Golgotha to Pentecost.

NOTES

[1] G.C. Brewer, *Christ Crucified, A Book Of Sermons Together With A Lecture On Evolution.* (Cincinnati: F.L. Rowe, 1929) p.7.

[2] Brewer, p. 53.

[3] Brewer, p. 90.

[4] Brewer, p. 139.

[5] Brewer, pp. 154,155.

[6] Brewer, pp. 169,170.

[7] Brewer, pp. 226,227.

[8] Frank. L. Cox, *101 Sermon Outlines*, Revised. (Austin: Firm Foundation, 1971.) For a discussion of the advantages and disadvantages of using books of outlines in this kind of study see footnote number 13, chapter 3 above.

[9] Cox, pp. 42,43.

[10] Cox, pp. 15,16.

[11] Leslie G. Thomas, *One Hundred Sermons*, (Nashville: Gospel Advocate, 1940).

[12] Thomas, p. 74.

[13] Thomas, pp. 39-41.

[14] Thomas, pp. 210-212.

[15] Fred E. Dennis, *Fifty Short Sermons.* (Grand Rapids: Erdmans, 1944).

[16] Dennis, pp. 19,20.

[17] Dennis, pp. 34,34.

[18] Dennis, p. 48.

[19] Dennis, p. 130.

[20] Dennis, p. 165.

[21] "Gospel Advocate," March 6, 1980, p.131.

[22] Foy E. Wallace, Jr., *The Gospel For Today*, (Nashville: Wallace, 1967).

[23] Wallace, p. 140.

[24] Wallace, pp. 15, 25, 26.

[25] Wallace, pp. 97, 98.

[26] Wallace, pp. 245, 256.

[27] Wallace, p. 752.

[28] Wallace, pp. 589, 590.

[29] Wallace, p. 211.

Summary of Part 2

While I was in the writing stages of this book two appraisals of our preaching came to my attention. The first was entitled "A 70-Year Overview." It was written by F.W. Mattox and appeared in the "Gospel Advocate" (June, 1988, p.6). Brother Mattox looked back over the last few decades of our preaching I have attempted to analyze here. He spoke of the small beginning of the church as he first knew it in 1918. He believed the hard times were good for us. Every member was taught the Bible and the ability to teach it. "The church had a deep conviction that denominationalism was wrong and that we must work for unity to please Christ. The principle of the Restoration Movement offered the only hope." Then he made a statement about our preaching in the early part of our century, emphasizing our treatment of the atonement.

> We took for granted that the denominations had saturated society with the teaching of faith and grace and the atonement, and we went about straightening out their misunderstanding of the place, action and order of faith, repentance and baptism in obtaining church membership. We showed deep conviction in the reality of sin and its eternal consequences. Our faith in the

resurrection of Jesus and in the infallibility of the
Scripture was unshakable.

In a phone interview Brother Mattox (1/30/91) explained that the Methodists, Baptists and others had been preaching the atonement but not baptism. We had been preaching baptism but not the atonement; we assumed that others were covering that important topic. Mattox considers it a tragic mistake for preachers ever to assume the basic gospel of Christ crucified and raised. He also admonished me to sound a warning about the opposite extreme: we must not preach the cross of Christ without telling people how to receive that salvation in baptism. Mattox ended his article with a positive evaluation of today's preaching.

> Sin is still real. Its reality is in the existence of God. Sin is held against man in the mind of God. Forgiveness takes place in the mind of God. God not only has revealed His wrath against sinful man, He has revealed that He accepts the penitent sinner who trusts the atonement of Christ and accepts His Lordship.

> Our preachers now understand the relationship of the condition of salvation to the atonement better than ever before. When we get the world to see it, the church will grow faster than ever before.

In 1937 K.C. Moser published a tract entitled, "Are We Preaching The Gospel?" The typescript is preserved today in the Harding Graduate School of Religion Library. In the preface Moser explained that he sent the paper out with a great concern for the state of preaching in the Churches of Christ. He believed the gospel was not being preached. By the gospel he meant the good news that Jesus was crucified for man's sins and salvation was secure and available to all who would receive it.

In order to check up on this point, I have gone to considerable pains to read written sermons, to study sermon outlines, and to listen to sermons preached. But this has been done only after I had observed that the gospel was being neglected in many sermons which were supposed to be gospel sermons. Some years ago, I heard every sermon delivered in a three-Sunday meeting. I, as well as others, noticed that the gospel was not being preached. The meeting continued from night to night and from day to day and still the gospel was neglected. True, in his invitations the preacher might have made some statement about the death of Christ, but not one time in all that meeting was any emphasis put on the gospel. It was simply not "preached." More recently, I have had similar experience. It is tragic for one to preach for two weeks and never do more than make a brief reference to the gospel of Christ....

I have in my possession a book containing over fifty sermons. In not one of these sermons does the gospel receive more than a passing notice. Never is the gospel stressed, never is the subject of Jesus Christ really discussed. It would even appear to some that the author of these sermons had intentionally neglected the gospel. The subject of one sermon was John 3:16. Naturally one would expect the gospel to be preached with such a subject. But alas, it was not preached. According to the sermon, the death of Christ was merely for the purpose of displaying God's love for man and giving him a law to obey that would bring life. Christ is said to save by furnishing man an EXAMPLE. He simply showed man how to save himself!...

Moser went on to speak of another book of sermons, "more excellent in many respects." His only criticism was what the book did not contain: any reference to the death of Christ for the sins of man. He then quoted a critique of Harry Emerson Fosdick's book, *The Modern Use Of The Bible* in which the reviewer said that "Nowhere is there a shadow of a hint that he 'bare our sins in his body on the tree'..." Moser said he was not accusing his preaching brother of being a "Modernist" like Fosdick. But he did conclude with a strong statement. "If Mr. Fosdick has REJECTED the gospel, others have NEGLECTED it." Later he warned: "Mistakes have a way of becoming more serious than one suspects. Religious errors are no exceptions to this rule. A neglect to preach the gospel finally ends in the logical, if not the actual, rejection of the gospel." He anticipated disagreement and countered. "But someone objects, 'There is no such danger among us today.' Because I sincerely believe this danger is very evident among us is the chief reason for the whole study. Many able brethren share this opinion with me."

I quote these observations by two leaders in the church who witnessed the last generations of preaching because they seem to give eye-witness confirmation to my findings. They agree that we took the atonement for granted and preached other things. Moser asserted that "many able brethren" saw that something was wrong.

Looking back over this survey of four generations of preaching we seek patterns of change and development. All twenty of these men sincerely loved the Lord, his church, and the Scriptures. They must have made great contributions to thousands of lives. At the end of the twentieth century we who are their heirs have much of which to be proud and for which to be thankful. Their tenacious love of the Scriptures and confidence in the individual to understand the Bible are foremost among the blessings in our heritage. As their descendants we would continue returning to the New Testament to measure our preaching by the preaching we find there.

An overview of the New Testament preaching of the cross was attempted in section one. The core gospel of Christ crucified appears everywhere in story, picture, metaphor, admonition, vision of heaven. Jesus presented himself primarily as the Suffering Servant of God who would give his life a ransom for many and rise the third day. The church was born and nurtured on the core gospel of Christ crucified and raised. Paul set forth the scandal of the crucified Messiah.

In this second section we surveyed the first four generations Restoration preaching to see how this core gospel was handled. The first generation of Restoration preachers together made in one-hundred and nine sermons only six references to the scandal of the cross and no mention of the Suffering Servant theme. In only six instances use was made of the gospel story line to present the gospel. Slight use of the metaphors of the atonement appeared, the priest/sacrifice picture predominating. The paradox of the first generation's preaching was the difference between their theory of and preaching about the core gospel on the one hand and the legacy they left on the other. Without exception all five proclaimed that the death, burial, and resurrection of Jesus was the fountainhead of the faith. Their preaching often indicated how deeply they believed that assertion. At the same time each one in his own way cut the root of further study of the atonement. Campbell affirmed the cross as central to the faith, preached it as core gospel and at the same time urged the young preachers to assume the basics and give themselves to "the current Reformation" of church order for sake of Christian unity and the coming millennium. In eighty-two percent of his sermons Stone referred to the core gospel. He issued warm-hearted appeals to his hearers, assuring them that their salvation depended solely on the blood of the Lamb. At the same time he reacted so strongly to Calvinistic speculation and harshness on the atonement that he denied the wrath of God, reduced the New Testament metaphors to reconciliation, the meaning of the cross to God's love for man, and cautioned about the danger of division over discussion of the subject. Sewell mentioned the cross in seventy-five percent of his sermons. He understood that salvation was not something yet to be negotiated with God, that it was once and for all provided on Golgotha. On the other hand, he did not preach the atonement for its own sake. It was a polemical weapon against mourner's bench religion and especially against the Catholic doctrine of "mystery." Walter Scott gave his life to preaching the "golden oracle" that Jesus was God's Messiah. He preached Christ more than any other of the first generation preachers studied here. What happened on Golgotha and the open tomb were the proof of Jesus' divine sonship. On the other hand, he was against theologizing about the atonement. As an answer to excesses of experiential religion on the frontier Scott set out his six steps of salvation or "five finger exercise." While the last three of the original six (forgiveness of sins, the gift of the Spirit, and eternal life) were God's side of the gospel, Scott's emphasis was on the first three steps or man's side of salvation. And, one notices that the cross is not mentioned at all, even as the source of God's three priceless gifts to mankind. Scott claimed to have restored the ancient gospel in 1827. Ever so subtly the focus had changed from God to man, from the atonement to man's response. Benjamin Franklin had a firm grip on the core gospel. He could tell the crucifixion narrative in a moving way. The connection between the cross and baptism was made clear again and again. On the other hand, his main emphasis was on the authority of Jesus to issue the great commission. The resurrection confirmed Jesus' sonship and right to set in motion the order of salvation.

The real focus of attention was on the work of the apostles and the establishment of the church. At one point he even rejoiced that the threat posed to the Christian faith by the cross of Christ had been overcome in the resurrection.

To a man these five preachers would have resisted any attempt to substitute another gospel for the cross. But taken together they mention the cross in only sixty-one of one-hundred nine sermons or fifty-six percent of the time. The New Testament contains some reference to death, burial, and resurrection or and what that accomplished in one-hundred percent of its thirty-three sermon length units. Our first fathers did little better than half of that. The paradox remains: each man handed on the core gospel with one hand and took it back with the other. My judgment is that our deficiencies in preaching the atonement are rooted most of all in this first generation.

From the first to the second generation mention of the cross decreased from just over one-half of the sermons to less than one-half. References to the biblical metaphors were even more sparse than before. In one-hundred and fourteen sermons these preachers made no reference to the Suffering Servant, only one reference to the scandal of the cross and only three times did they employ the gospel story line to present the gospel.

These proclaimers did not all have a developed theology of the atonement as was true with the first generation. Theirs was a "cut flower" gospel of the cross. In many instances one can still see its beauty and fragrance. But it had no root. They would not pass it on to the next generation. Even in this generation it was not always present. In the preaching of Brents the theme is hardly present at all. Frazee made several meaningful comments on the atonement. And yet he could speak of salvation, spiritual growth, and the value of the soul without mentioning the cross. Larimore was the exception in content, tone and warmth. However, there was no mention of the scandal or the Suffering Servant in his preaching. Key figures for our study were Sweeney and McGarvey. Sweeney displayed a considered understanding of the literature on the atonement. But he said it was not wise to study the atonement, pointing out the danger of conflict over the subject and the threat to the Restoration program of unity. Besides, preaching the atonement was unnecessary. Only the "practical question" was important and that was: "What must I do to be saved?" McGarvey included several meaningful statements about the cross in his sermons. Nevertheless, our foremost scholar proclaimed the atonement an incomprehensible mystery. He considered studying it and trying to preach it unnecessary and unwise. No one could understand it. From the first generation's impulse to preach other matters to the second generation's discouragement of study and proclamation of the atonement we notice a steady decline of interest in the core gospel.

In the third generation the rate of mention drops still more. From 56% in the first generation to 46% in the second to 26% in the third. In three hundred fifteen sermons one finds no references to the Suffering Servant or the scandal of the cross and only twice is the gospel story line employed. Use of the metaphors declined further from the second generation. Even the low rate of mention does not indicate the poverty of these sermons regarding the cross. Borden mentioned aspects of the atonement in a bare handful of sermons. In the single sermon which promised an exposition of the cross he preached it to establish the necessity of baptism. Freed preached a sermon listing twenty-five of man's needs without mentioning the cross. The emphasis on man's side of salvation is now even more pronounced than in the previous generations. Tant used the cross as a polemic against those not in the Church of Christ, but never as a subject in itself. White preached a sermon on the "foolishness of preaching" without mentioning the cross. In only four of ten sermons Hardeman made reference to the core gospel. His main focus was on the church and not on the cross. We see in the third generation that more and more topics are handled without any reference to the cross while mention of the atonement narrows to a few themes. The core gospel is no longer the ground of all thought and preaching.

G.C. Brewer was the exception in the fourth generation. Cox, Thomas and Dennis preached a gospel of the church. This trend found its extreme expression in Foy Wallace who could summarize the faith, the Restoration plea, and his own personal faith without reference to the death, burial, and resurrection of Jesus. In one sermon he defined "preaching Christ" as preaching baptism. Acts 2, the establishment of the church, was for him the most important chapter in the Bible.

Over the four generations we have seen the rate of mention decline from 56% to 46% to 26% to 23%. Of eight hundred twenty-nine sermons two hundred sixty-one mentioned the core gospel. The composite percentage was 32%. Exceptions to the trends were: Stone, Scott, Larimore and Brewer. To visualize the severity of this decline in quantity and quality of Restoration preaching of the core gospel in comparison with New Testament preaching of the cross one may consult the chart below.

Explanation of Chart, Fig. II

The purpose of this chart is two-fold. First, it reports the findings regarding Restoration preaching of the core gospel. Second, it shows a comparison of New Testament and Restoration preaching of the cross.

Figure No. 2
SUMMARY OF PREACHING OF THE "CORE GOSPEL" BY REPRESENTATIVE PREACHERS OF THE FIRST FOUR GENERATIONS OF OUR RESTORATION MOVEMENT

Restoration Preachers		A. Campbell	B. Franklin	Walter Scott	J. L. Sewell	B. W. Stone	TOTALS	T. W. Brents	T. B. Larimore	W. D. Frazee	J. S. Sweeney	J. W. McGarvey	TOTALS	E. M. Borden	A. G. Freed	J. D. Tant	R. C. White	N. B. Hardeman	TOTALS	G. C. Brewer	F. Dennis	F. L. Cox	L. G. Thomas	Foy Wallace	TOTALS	Restoration totals Rate of mention All 4 generations	Restoration totals Rate of mention per 33 sermon unit (25 units)	New Testament Rate of mention 33 sermons
	Generation	1st Generation						2nd Generation						3rd Generation						4th Generation								
Frequency of mention of the themes	Sermons with mention	13	20	7	12	9	61	9	14	10	7	13	53	9	9	7	15	41	81	11	14	21	12	10	68	263		
	Total No. of sermons	26	42	14	16	11	109	21	27	25	17	24	114	25	27	60	103	100	315	16	50	101	100	24	291	829		
	Individual % of mention	50	48	50	75	82	%	43	52	40	41	54	%	36	33	12	15	41	%	69	28	21	12	42	%	95/36%	8.0	33
Composite % of mention in all sermons by generation		56%						46%						26%						23%						32%		
Treatment of themes	Substantial	9	7	5	3	8	32	4	3	3	4	6	20	2	2	1	5	7	17	10	2	10	3	1	26	95/36%	3.8	160/73%
	Incidental	4	13	2	9	1	29	5	11	7	3	7	33	7	7	6	10	34	64	1	12	11	9	9	42	168/64%	6.7	58/27%
KINDS AND OCCURRENCES OF NEW TESTAMENT MATERIALS																										32%	32%	100%
Atonement metaphors:																												
Priest/Sacrifice		7	4	1	2	4	18	1	2	4	2	1	10	1		2	2	2	7	1	3	1	2	2	4	39	1.6	36.0
Redemption/Ransom		5	1	4		1	11		2	1	1	2	6		2	2	2	3	7		3	2		1	7	27	1.1	25.0
Propitiation/Expiation		2	1	1	1	2	7			1		1	2					1	1	1						10	0.4	4.0
Reconciliation		1	1	1	2	3	8	1	1	1	1		4	2		1	2	3	7	1	2	2	2		3	22	0.9	16.0
Victor over Satan/Death		1	3	3	1		6						0			1	1	4		2	2	1			5	15	0.6	84.0
Suffering Servant							0						0						0							2	0.1	14.0
Justification (law court)		2		1	2	3	6		2				0			1		1	2	2	1	3	1	1	2	10	0.4	6.0
Example (pattern)		1	1			3	4		1	1	1	2	5					1	1			1				12	0.5	21.0
Scandal of the cross			1				3											1	1	3	2	2			6	11	0.4	57.0

A Comparison of Restoration and New Testament Preaching of the Core Gospel

Summary of Part 2

On the LEFT side one notices the same items which were listed on the New Testament chart, p.105. (See Appendix A for assumptions and methodology regarding the New Testament analysis and Appendix B for assumptions and methodology regarding the study of Restoration preachers.) ACROSS the top are the names of the five preachers chosen in the four generations of Restoration preaching. One can read each column from top to bottom and see how each preacher preached the core gospel. For example, Campbell mentioned the core gospel in 13 of 26 sermons, 50% of the time. Nine of those references were substantial and four incidental. He mentioned the priest/sacrifice metaphor 7 times, redemption/ransom 5 times, propitiation 2 times, reconciliation 1 time, victory over Satan 1 time, justification 2 times, example 1 time, the scandal of the cross 1 time and the gospel story line 1 time. To see the composite totals of the first five preachers in the first generation one can look down the "Totals" column. The composite percentage of mention of the core gospel in all sermons of the generation is listed just below individual percentages. In the case of the first generation that composite total is 56%. Moving from left to right one may compare the generations and mark the trends.

On the FAR RIGHT one finds a comparison of Restoration and New Testament Preaching of the core gospel. The first column is labeled: "Rate of mention Restoration totals, all 4 generations." That column shows the composite numbers and percentages of all four generations taken together. The cross was mentioned in 263 of 829 sermons or 32% of the time. Ninety-five or 41% of those references were substantial, 128 or 59% were incidental. All together, in all their sermons these preachers mentioned the priest/sacrifice metaphor 39 times, and other items as indicated. The next column "Rate of Mention Restoration Totals Per 33 Sermon Unit" breaks down these Restoration sermons in 33 sermon groups, corresponding to the New Testament which is a 33 sermon group. If all Restoration sermons are divided into 33 sermon groups, one sees 25 groups of 33 sermons each. This column, then, reports the per 33 sermon group totals. For example, Restoration preachers mentioned the cross 8.0 times per 33 sermon group across the 25 groups, or 32% of the time. There were 3.8 substantial references per 33 sermon group in these Restoration sermons. Per 33 sermon group the priest/sacrifice was used 1.6 times and so on.

The last column to the right reports the New Testament totals from the chart on p.105 for sake of comparison. In the New Testament the core gospel was preached in 33 of 33 sermons or 100% of the time. The priest/sacrifice metaphor was found 32.0 times and so on. By comparing the second to last and last columns one can see how Restoration preaching of the cross as a whole compares with the New Testament preaching as a whole. For example, Restoration preachers mentioned the priest/sacrifice 1.6 times per 33 sermon group whereas the New Testament mentioned it 32.0 times per 33 sermon group.

Possible Reasons For The Decline

This alarming rate of decline in our preaching of the core gospel cries out for explanation, especially as it compares with the New Testament totals. One might suggest that the New Testament church needed the cross in evangelism, apologetic, and edification in the early stages of its development. One might conjecture that the situation in nineteenth and twentieth century America was different. And enormous differences are obvious. On the other hand, it is not enough to say that times, situations, and issues changed. The New Testament itself was written over two or three generations and contains materials written to a wide range of situations and to a broad spectrum of issues. The death, burial and resurrection of Jesus and the "word of the cross" formed the basis for its evangelism, apologetic, and edification. That has not been the case with us. Why? It is difficult to analyze historical developments. Factors of influence are varied, curious, sometimes impossible to identify. I will offer my own judgment as to five factors which I believe contributed to our loss of the cross in our preaching.

This first cause was the time and place of our birth as a movement. The Restoration movement was born in the heady period of America's new independence and expansion westward. It grew up as a child on the frontier. We were a part of the original American dream. The air our early leaders breathed was charged with hope and optimism. Anything was possible. Barton Stone was an exception in not believing that human beings could accomplish anything given time and opportunity. With the Enlightenment view of man and the vast untapped resources of our rich land, nothing could stop us. Common sense and hard work could unite the churches on the basis of the Bible and bring in the millennium! Many other American religious traditions drank from this same well. Opportunity and optimism easily translate into self-reliance and the pride of humanism. There was, to be sure, a minority opinion like Stone's. When babies died at child birth, the crops failed and relations with the Indians turned brutal believers huddled together and sang "we'll understand it all by and by" "mansion over the hilltop" and "rock of ages." But the prevailing mood in our preaching was man-centered and self-reliant. The American frontier was neither the time nor the place when preachers in any tradition focused on man's inadequacy and need, on the Suffering Servant and the scandal of the cross.

A second factor must have been the spectacles through which our first leaders read the Scriptures. Steeped in the scientific method of Francis Bacon, saturated with the common sense rationalism of John Locke, Campbell, Scott and others had no use for mystery. The faith could be outlined, systematized, analyzed, and understood. This basic outlook was confirmed and developed even more when it came into contact with the excesses of subjective religion on the frontier. Rationalism allowed no place for story and metaphor. Consequently, two of the main New Testament channels for an appreciation of the atonement were blocked. We recognized mystery on God's side of salvation but saw no reason to study it in order to fulfill our side of the transaction.

Third, reaction to extreme and harsh Calvinism led us away from the biblical doctrine of the sovereignty of God and finally cost us the gospel narratives. A one-sided emphasis on man's freedom and responsibility made God a distant and minor player. He was held captive by his own system of salvation. Our debates and preaching on baptism and the thorny problem of the thief on the cross were devastating for our use of the gospels and the appreciation of the atonement. Our religious neighbors continued to set forth the thief on the cross as an example of one who was saved without baptism. We answered that he died before the kingdom was established on Pentecost, under the old covenant. When pushed on that argument we said that the gospels recorded events prior to Pentecost and so were not really important for the church. Perhaps a more biblical answer to questions about the thief on the cross would have been: "God is sovereign. He will save whomever he wishes however he will. But we preach Christ crucified and Jesus told us to receive the gift of Golgotha in the waters of baptism. God will receive the thief on the cross however he will. As for you and me, Jesus told us to meet him at baptism to receive the redemption he provided at

Calvary." When we lost the sovereignty of God we were obligated to answer all his questions for him according to the Bible as we read it. Since the thief on the cross was not baptized, since there are no cases of disciples' baptism in Jesus' name in the gospels, we pronounced the gospels irrelevant to the church. When we lost the gospels we lost the person of Jesus, who he was, why he died and was raised. Loss of the gospel story line was fatal to our understanding of the core gospel.

Fourth, a noble ideal became more important to us than the gospel. What greater vision could one have than the unity of all believers in one great church of God? Realizing that ideal would require that we set about fine-tuning the churches according to the Scriptures. That was so massive a task and so noble an ideal that the preachers had to leave the basics like the atonement to others. The proclaimers would rivet their attention on the church and the Bible. Our focus moved from Christ crucified to his church, a subtle but profoundly destructive shift. Perhaps Wallace was correct in summarizing the Restoration plea without mentioning the cross. Jesus' own plan for unity got lost in the shuffle: "If I am lifted up I will draw all men unto me." In John's parlance Jesus meant "lifted up" first on the cross and in then in proclamation. God would do the uniting, not man. Our first leaders were large-hearted men of great vision. The only goal greater than their noble ideal was God's cosmic plan to "unite all things in Christ." (Ephesians 1:10)

Fifth, once our sickness took hold, we grew weaker and weaker, more and more anemic. Those who suffer from anemia are always irritable and difficult to live with. We were caught in a vicious cycle. Without the gospels we lost touch with the source of our faith. Without the Suffering Servant we lost our will and reason to serve and suffer. Without the scandal of the cross we more and more sought respectability and popularity. Without a clearly focused central core gospel everything in the faith became equally important. Almost nothing was a matter of opinion, all was a matter of faith. Without the nutrition of the atonement we craved more and more the sweets of fads and methods. Without Jesus' death to unite human beings in a consciousness of sin and the joy of salvation we were powerless to bring about unity. Not only could we not unite Christendom, we could not even avoid division among ourselves. Without the cross of Christ there was nothing to check our pride, convict us of our sin, assure us of our salvation, infuse us with joy for evangelism, and steel us for Christian living in a harsh and cruel world. Without the resurrection there was no sure ground of hope for the peace that passes understanding.

Our communion meditations, hymns, and Sunday School lessons faithfully reminded us of Christ crucified. It was our preaching which was anemic. As we came to mid-twentieth century we in the Churches of Christ were enjoying the greatest material growth in our history. But a close look at the tradition handed us shows an alarming development. What we were preaching showed little correspondence to the richness, depth, and power of the New Testament core gospel. Our problem began with the first generation. The tradition which was just a degree or two off center in the beginning when extrapolated down four generations brought preaching in the Church of Christ to a point far away from the New Testament emphasis on the cross. There were a few laudable exceptions. But only a few. Our preaching, outstanding in so many ways, had a large void at the center. The core gospel was missing.

Part 3
Current Preaching of the Core Gospel

The purpose of this section is to provide encouragement. For members of the church who want a healthful diet it may be helpful to sample a number of sermons which center in the cross. Elders who have responsibility for what is preached may appreciate examples of lessons flowing out of the core gospel. All of us preachers, young and old, need inspiring models of gospel preaching. This section contains the substance of sermons from twenty preachers who are currently active in proclaiming the gospel. Their kind consent to my inclusion of their sermons does not mean that they necessarily endorse all the findings of this volume.

F. W. Mattox is quoted in the summary of the last section. "Our preachers now understand the relationship of the conditions of salvation to the atonement better than ever before." I believe that is true. One of the reasons is that we have had more teachers and preachers since mid-century who have pointed us back to Jesus Christ as the center of the faith. Representative of these leaders who have loved the church, have been devoted to the Restoration plea, and have treasured the Scriptures is *Frank Pack*. I mentioned earlier that he was among those who encouraged and instructed me during my college years.

Thousands of other men and women could say the same. In 1986 Jerry Rushford edited and Pepperdine University published a book in honor of Dr. Pack entitled, *We Preach Christ Crucified.* Twenty-five of Pack's former students submitted sermons for the volume. Every one expressed appreciation for the center and focus his teacher provided for the preaching ministry.

In 1982 Pack preached two sermons at the Culver Palms church in Los Angeles which centered in the core gospel. The first was entitled "The Cross" and the other "The Resurrection Of Christ." The first of these was based on Galatians 6:12-16, that passage in which Paul expressed his desire never to boast except in the cross of Christ. Pack began by surveying the many ways in which the cross appears in our society as an object of beauty and honor. It is found in beautiful jewelry, the Red Cross means care for the hurting, every nation has a medal of honor in the shape of the cross. He went on to explain how different the perception of the cross was in the first century. Crucifixion was scandalous to both Jew and Gentile. It was the most shameful death practiced, and according to Jewish law the curse of God rested on the one sentenced to the criminal's death on a tree. The physical pain was excruciating beyond belief. Then Pack affirmed that the cross was, nevertheless, the core gospel.

> See, you cannot preach the gospel without the cross of Christ; you cannot preach the gospel without the blood of Christ; you cannot preach the gospel without the story of one who laid his life down in order that we might live. One who was willing to go all way unto death has been raised by God's power, broke the power of death and came forth a victor. Because of this God exalted his name high, and gave him the name that is above every name. Through his death Christ broke the power of sin, and enabled the load of guilt to be taken away from our souls.

> Through his death he broke the power of the law which imprisoned and held men in bondage. He became the slave to make us free. He became poor that we might be made rich. He died that we might live. He became cursed that we might have the curse lifted from us. Fantastic, isn't it! This is the heart of the gospel.

In the other sermon on the resurrection Pack began by exploding the popular myth that the first disciples were just ignorant, gullible believers. From John 20 he explored the cases of Mary Magdalene, Peter, John, and Thomas. Each had an honest struggle to believe. Pack preached the sermon by telling the story, following John's narrative form. Capturing the human emotion of Mary Magdalene in the garden, he showed what a glorious victory God won in raising Jesus from the grave.

> Then she sensed that somebody was standing in back of her. She turned probably half way around, her eyes filled with tears, and she just noticed that some one was there but she did not recognize Jesus. Then he spoke to her and asked her virtually the same question the angels had asked. She answered as she did because she thought he was the gardener looking after the whole garden and the tomb that was there. In effect she said, 'If you have taken him away, if you have moved his body out of this place, then let me know where you have taken him and I will take it away. I will take care of it, I will give it the proper burial.' Then Jesus called her by name and all the difference in the world was in that name, Mary. I do not know how it sounded in her language nor why what Jesus addressed to her before he called her name did not reveal it to her, but it was only when Jesus called her by name that she knew who he was and offered him worship... Jesus gave her this impressive command, 'You

> go and tell my disciples that I am ascending to my Father and your Father, and to my God and your God.' So Mary Magdalene became the first emissary to tell the good news of Jesus Christ's resurrection from the dead.

The climax in John's story, according to Pack, was the confession of Thomas. Absent when the disciples first encountered their risen Lord, skeptical about the resurrection, Thomas finally came face to face with his Lord. He was invited to come see and touch the scars.

> Of all the confessions made in the Gospel, and there are a number of them, Thomas's confession is the most comprehensive one. He said, 'My Lord and my God.' We do not know whether Thomas did put his finger into the nail prints, and his hand into the side wound but we do know about his full confession. Thomas was just hard to convince. He was a realistic, hard-headed kind of person who would not accept other people's testimony. In Thomas's confession we have the climax of faith among those disciples. Jesus then reminded them all, 'Have you believed because you have seen me? Blessed are those who have not seen and yet believe.'

Pack concluded the sermon by calling his hearers to trust in Jesus crucified and risen, the Son of God. Not belief as a leap in the dark, but belief in Jesus Christ based on the story of John's gospel leads to life.

Other preachers active today have also been exploring the Christ crucified theme. I have asked several of my preaching brothers to share outlines and tapes with me for study. The sermons reviewed here were in most cases chosen from a random sample of lessons: the morning sermon for the first Sunday of each month during 1987. I am privileged to know these proclaimers personally. They represent a sizable army of preachers among us who are more and more giving themselves to discovering and proclaiming the cross of Christ. I could have asked another group at least this large even of my own acquaintances who are reclaiming the core gospel. Each May I attend a ministers' seminar with a hundred of my preaching brothers. My observation is that many are seriously pursuing a better understanding and stronger proclamation of the death, burial, and resurrection of Jesus.

Preaching at the White Station Church of Christ in Memphis, *Jim Howard* spoke on the courage of the apostle Paul. For his text he read Jesus' promise to Paul found in Acts 23:11: "Take courage, for as you have testified about me at Jerusalem, so you must bear witness also at Rome." First, he pointed to Paul's courage to endure criticism when he returned to Jerusalem and met accusations that he had sold out Moses and the Law. By joining several men in a vow, he agreed to the church leaders' plan for winning the favor of the Jews. Howard asked his brothers and sisters how willing they were to endure what they disliked for the cause of Christ. All should remember that Jesus endured the cross for God's kingdom. Second, Paul had the courage to communicate to hostile audiences. Seven times between Acts twenty-one through twenty-six he witnessed to his Lord. He demonstrated the truth of Jesus' promise in Matthew 10 that the appropriate words would be given if one stands firm to witness to his faith. Paul spoke of a resurrected Lord to those who did not want to hear it. Howard confessed for himself and the church timidity in witnessing for Jesus. Third, Paul had the courage of a great companionship. He said "It is no longer I that live but Christ lives in me," and "I am crucified with Christ." Men do not die for dead legends, said Howard. Jesus had appeared to Saul on the Damascus road. Ever after he knew his Lord as a present friend. His Lord stood beside him and promised that he would yet preach the gospel in Rome. Howard brought the message home.

> I do not know that Jesus continued to appear to Paul...but I do know that for Paul Jesus was as close as his own heartbeat... Paul says 'It's because of the resurrection of Jesus that I stand before you this day.' And he went on to talk about a living Lord, a resurrected Savior...Jesus was just that real, just that genuine, and just that authentic with him. He really did walk with Paul...he stood beside him...he gave him his presence and his powerful message.
>
> Someone has said if we have no story to tell we have no reason to talk to others. If Jesus is no more real to us than a figment of our imagination or a name out of ancient history or someone about whom we read and about whom we know...we have nothing to share with a lost world. But if Jesus Christ stirs within us, and if he is alive, and if we feel the power of his redemption and the enormity of our sin forgiven and if he walks with us daily and we love him and feel the warmth of his presence why not share your faith with someone else? If he's never done anything for you, if you've never had the openness of heart to receive him you don't have anything to say, you're speechless before a lost world. But if Jesus died for you and if he's been raised for you, if he lives in your heart and life why not tell somebody about it?
>
> ...The power of the early church was not in a doctrine or a dogma, the power was in a living person, the resurrected Christ. It's not one whit different for us today. As long as we are tied up with a theology or a

> dogma or a doctrine as the essence of life we will find
> deadness not aliveness. But when our life becomes the
> person of Jesus, when he becomes that real to us, that
> resurrected to us, that alive to us in a world of deadness
> we've got a message. Let's proclaim it, let's tell it...!

Jack Reese preached a sermon at the Oak Hills church in San Antonio entitled, "Bearing The Burden of the Crucified Christ." From I Corinthians 1:18-25 he stressed Paul's words "...but we preach Christ crucified, a stumbling block to Jews and folly to Gentiles, but to those who are called, both Jews and Greeks, Christ the power and the wisdom of God."

Reese commented on the joy of worshiping in hymns of praise. The early church sang such hymns, as is evidenced by fragments in Philippians 2 and Ephesians 5. He observed that the congregation had just sung together the simple, moving hymn: "Jesus Is Lord." To enjoy such worship together is a privilege we take for granted. It was not so for the early Christians. To sing hymns of praise to a crucified God was absurdity. The Gentiles believed the one advantage the gods had over mere men was their immortality. How unthinkable that a god would come here to die, to say nothing of dying a criminal's death! The Jews would have nothing to do with the idea of a crucified Messiah. Popular opinion put pressure on the church's confession. Some had become embarrassed about their faith. The story seemed crude and offensive.

The Corinthian Christians dealt with the problem by diving headlong into spirituality, states of feeling, competition among the gifted, etc. Paul warned them that they could not run away from the scandal of the cross. Without sharing Christ's burden there is no power, no redemption, no salvation, no life, and no church.

Reese suggested that modern Christians escape the burden of the cross in ways different from the Corinthians. Some give their loyalty to legalism and moralism. They live their lives for the externals of the faith. Others are caught up in themselves, their own ministries and activities in the church, in dreaming great things for the church. Some focus on the social aspects of the faith, giving themselves completely to "body life." While the ministries of the church are important, the faith is not centered in these. He then applied the painful message to himself and his hearers.

> The thing that concerns me the most about churches in general, and perhaps too much in this church, is that what we claim is most attractive about the church — is the church. The activities of the church, the relationships in the church, the facilities of the church, the classes of the church, the people in the church. We will proclaim the living, urgent message of God only when we see the clear irony that what is most unattractive is what we put forth to attract. It is the immortal God who became mortal, the exalted Christ who became humiliated, the God who suffered with us, the Jesus who died. Not only died, but called us to participate in his death. Not just to remember his death and resurrection, but to share in it. A God who calls us to lay our possessions aside and to give our lives with that crucified Christ. It is a Jesus who has called us to climb up on that cross with him. And until and unless we are able to proclaim with boldness and courage that extraordinarily unattractive message we will never be the kind of church that God calls us to be. Because there is no power in ourselves, in our plans, in our programs, in our lives, in our people, in our social networks. There's only one power in the church and that is the crucified Christ. Him we proclaim. In him we live.

> And, remarkably, as in the earliest church, as we proclaim that unattractive message through what the world perceives as foolishness (which is God's wisdom) the people in the world begin to see the message they must hear and perceive. And as they see it in its clarity they are drawn to the Savior who suffered and died for their sakes.

Reese then returned to Paul's statement in I Corinthians 2 that he came determined to preach only Christ crucified, not all of the secondary things. He challenged Christians who had for years enjoyed the fruits of their religion but not the life given to the crucified Lord. He promised them God's grace to live and to know Christ as never before. He then spoke to those not yet in Christ. He invited them to accept God's gift at Golgotha, to respond to Jesus' death and resurrection in their own going down in baptism and coming up for new life in him.

From the favorite Restoration passage, Acts 2:36-41, *Wayne Dockery* preached the sermon, "Repent and Be Baptized" at the Fellowship Church of Christ in Denton, Texas. To an audience of God's chosen people Peter proclaimed Jesus, a man who came doing signs and wonders, whom God appointed for sacrifice, whom they had crucified. "Let all of the house of Israel know assuredly that God has made him both Lord and Christ, this Jesus whom you crucified." Dockery emphasized Peter's reply to the plaintiff plea of the Pentecost crowd: "What shall we do?"

> And Peter said, 'Just pray that Jesus shall come into your heart.'

> No, that is not what Peter said. For Peter knew that the sinfulness of this people of God was no simple matter to be simply overlooked or excused— 'Just let Jesus come into your heart.' No, they had radically offended God.

They had murdered the Son of God. Peter said, "Repent and be baptized, everyone of you, for the remission of your sins, and you shall receive the gift of the Holy Spirit.'

He called for radical action. Their lives were to be totally reoriented. They were to be overwhelmed with water, washed with the washing of God. Otherwise they could never stand in his presence.

But with the washing of God, they were purified according to his grace through the death of his son. He could receive them into his presence. Their sins were swept away and they received the Spirit of God, power to live in a way pleasing to God.

This is the root meaning for baptism in the New Testament. Paul deepens the meaning of baptism in his writings (talking about incorporation into the body of Christ, dying and rising with him), but in Paul's writings as well this is the way baptism is first understood, as a cleansing. God acts in baptism, really acts on behalf of the believer to cleanse him or her of their sin, once and for all, so that they can enter his presence.

This is no mere symbol; this is no quaint rite. What happens in baptism is a purifying encounter with the living God. God has given us baptism in which we surrender ourselves to him in trust, placing ourselves not only at the mercy of the one who is doing the baptizing, limp in his hands, but also at the mercy of God. And the wonderful and holy God whom we in our sinfulness could never approach, washes us in his mercy, cleanses us of our guilt, receives us into his new age, and causes us to

> stand sinless before him, making us a part of his new people.
>
> There are signs that we are beginning to forget the life and death significance of baptism. But let this be affirmed this day: when each of us — even followers of God since childhood, as were these ones at Pentecost — comes face to face with the way that we have crucified the Son of God ourselves in our lives, what is called for is not some pious prayer — this is an altogether too serious situation for that. What is called for is the radical event of baptism in which we are plunged beneath the water, and in which God freely chooses to wash away all sin, and present us spotless in his presence.
>
> Thanks be to God for his incomparable gift in Jesus Christ!

Dockery then addressed several problems related to the doctrine and practice of baptism. He referred to the "alienness" of the rite in the modern world. He spoke of the way baptism has been diminished in importance over the long history of the church in many traditions. He noted that many Churches of Christ are wrestling today with the best way to teach baptism to those coming from other traditions, and with closely related questions of admission to "church membership." He pointed out that the difficulty of these questions may tempt some to de-emphasize the significance of baptism. "But that I am not willing to do," Dockery said. "Baptism is a great gift of God; to simply disdain it and lay it aside as unimportant would be sacrilege." For him the rite is of primary importance, not in and of itself, not as a distinctive mark of our tradition, but because God is at work in the event of baptism cleansing us and filling us with his Spirit through the same power that sustained him in death and raised him to life.

Another familiar Restoration text was chosen by *Lanny Henninger* for a sermon he preached at the University Avenue church in Austin. The sermon was entitled: "Doing Good." Many times in Restoration preaching the story of Cornelius has been used to illustrate how the centurion's goodness was not enough without baptism. Henninger affirmed that there is a goodness which is good enough, and that goodness is what lies behind baptism. In verses 34-43 of Acts 10 Luke records Peter's words:

> ...how God anointed Jesus of Nazareth with the Holy Spirit and with power; how he went about doing good and healing all that were oppressed by the devil, for God was with him. And we are witnesses to all that he did both in the country of the Jews and in Jerusalem. They put him to death by hanging him on a tree; but God raised him on the third day and made him manifest; not to all the people but to us who were chosen by God as witnesses, who ate and drank with him after he rose from the dead.

Henninger began his sermon by commenting on how threadbare the word "good" has become. We use it in so many ways that it means almost nothing. Sometimes it is used as an insult, for example in the label, "do-gooder." And yet the text says Jesus went about doing good. That proclamation evokes memories of Jesus' inaugural sermon in his own home synagogue. He said he was anointed to preach good news to the poor, to proclaim release to the captive, recovering of sight to the blind, to set at liberty the oppressed and to proclaim the acceptable year of the Lord. One is reminded of the time John sent messengers asking if Jesus was the promised one and he sent back a report in the same terms. Jesus was a good man in a robust sort of way, Henninger said. It is his very goodness which is unsettling to us in our cynical world. We expect dishonesty, greed, self-service, vengeance. The headlines are full of the evil men do.

> But authentic goodness makes us do a double take. A firefighter climbs a swaying ladder, breaks into a room dense with smoke, carries a child to safety...Gandhi confronts his wayward teenage son, hands him a whip, and says: 'Beat me for failing to be a better father'...A couple with children of their own open their home to other children, disenfranchised, going, going, almost gone...A teacher whose message was peace and love climbs up on a cross as he prays for his executioners, 'Father, they don't know. Forgive them.' Such goodness is a rare item. Whenever we meet it we ask: 'Where did it come from? Why can't I be more like that?'
>
> Early in his letter to the Romans, that most profound letter of them all, Paul drops this intriguing line: '...Do you not know that God's kindness is meant to lead you to repentance?' I would have thought something else: wrath, vindication, the pangs of Hell! But instead he insists the sheer goodness of the Almighty is what brings us to our knees. Long years before a psalmist caught the sound of it. 'He does not deal with us according to our sins, nor requite us according to our iniquities.' What a remarkable truth: grace, not judgment, is at the heart of the gospel! God chose to win us — not with threats or bribery — but from a cross: 'God so loved the world that he gave his only son...'
>
> What do we do in the face of this? Isaac Watts knew. Do you remember the words from his old hymn? "Were the whole realm of nature mine, that were a present far too small! Love so amazing, so divine, demands my soul, my

life, my all.' Which is to say, we cannot be expected to bring more that we have to the altar. But dare we bring any less and lay it at the feet of him who is so good, who loves us so? A great Japanese Christian once said: 'I read in a book about a man who went about doing good. It is disconcerting that I am so content with just going about.' From a life of aimlessness and tyranny of self Jesus has come to rescue us. Won't you say 'yes' to him?

John Wright preaches for the Burke Road church in Pasadena, Texas. The sermon cited here was preached in August of 1987, two weeks after a busload of young people from a church in Dallas was caught in a ferocious storm in the Texas hill country and one third of them perished in the flash flood. One mother whose son escaped said she had prayed fervently that he would survive. Why, Wright asked, was her boy saved and others were not? Had she prayed more or in a better way? Was her son a better boy than the others? He then mentioned a national AIDS telethon in which a minister appeared on a panel and said, "Since I'm a Christian, God is my Protector. He won't let me get AIDS. I have no fear..."

Wright chose for his text the story from Acts 12 about Herod beheading James while Peter went free. Was Peter more faithful, valuable to God, sincere, holy? Was Peter prayed for by large groups of Christians while no one prayed for James? Of course, someone might just as well ask the question about Peter and Jesus. Why was Peter spared when facing the same religious authorities who crucified Jesus? What does that fact say about the prayer, faith, and loyalty of Jesus?

Many of our questions arise out of our presumptions about Scriptures, Wright said. He pointed to several strong affirmations of faith in Scripture, passages which pictured God as the one who rescues and protects. He especially highlighted Psalm 91 and Habakkuk 3:17-19. But Israel had never believed these passages to contain such guarantees. Nor had Jesus and his apostles taught it that way. Instead, we are called to "take up our cross" and follow Jesus, to "bear one another's burdens" and to "weep with those who weep." Finally, Wright set forth the Christian's only true comfort: God's unfailing love.

> All we have to do is look about us to see Christians who have disease, who experience cancer, who have tragedy in their lives. Or just look at the teaching and life of Jesus Christ. He was goodness incarnate. And he was not only tempted in all points as we are, he suffered adversity. Mental and physical. Ultimately dying on a cross.

> ...men and women are always getting themselves into trouble, just as Peter was constantly getting himself in and out of prison. Sometimes God gets them out of it. The light shines in the cell, the chains fall off. We can never tell when or where something like that might happen. Neither can we assume that we are lost or that our case is hopeless. Because at any moment the angel of deliverance may appear. And yet, it is also true that God does not always get us out of our trouble, whether it's of our own making or external circumstances. Sometimes he just sees us through it. He did not get Jesus out of it. But he saw him through it... Sometimes he chooses another way...It is nevertheless true that God is with us, he stands by us and he will see us through the worst that comes. That we can count on. Because he is our Protector.

At the Cole Mill Road church in Durham, North Carolina, *Paul Watson* spoke on "Jesus, The Mediator." He chose for his text I

Timothy 2:1-7. His lesson centered in three words from the text. First, the word "mediator." He recalled an event from the headlines two weeks before in November of 1987. The Cuban Archbishop of Miami had mediated between Cuban prisoners and prison officials in Atlanta and Louisiana. Watson pointed up several features of that event which paralleled Jesus' mediation for us. Even if authorities had given provocation, the prisoners bore the responsibility for beginning the incident. We human beings have no such provocation for our rebellion against God. Secondly, there was no question who had the power. The government had all the means necessary to squash the rebellion by force. They chose another way, partially in consideration of the hostages. Thirdly, like the prison officials God provided a mediator.

The second word Watson highlighted from the text was "man." The one who became our mediator was the "man Christ Jesus." In writing to Timothy Paul stressed Jesus' identification with us. He was one of us, understood our predicament, spoke our language. As the Archbishop had literally spoken for and to the prisoners, Christ "spoke our language." He entered the world as we do, breathed our air, ate our food, shared our company and died our death. Watson confirmed the value of marking the birth of Jesus each year in December, but stressed that Jesus did not remain in the crib. He went through childhood, adolescence, and manhood to become one of us. He has "shown us the Father" and has "presented us" to the Father.

The third word Watson underscored was "ransom." The mediator has to be willing to take risks. Watson pointed to the Anglican churchman, Terry Waite, who had disappeared in Lebanon in the process of trying to negotiate freedom for the hostages. He then explained the price Jesus paid to ransom us.

> And so it was with Christ. He was a message bearer, he was a go-between, he showed us the Father, he is our advocate with the Father. But more than that he paid the price necessary for our deliverance — with his own blood. A ransom is something which covers up or cancels an incurred claim that one person or group has on another.

Watson then quoted an article by Harold Hazelip in which the gift of Golgotha is pictured in many ways. In banking terminology we were in debt and Jesus paid our obligation. Before the court we stood condemned and he bore the penalty. In temple terms we were defiled and he was our sacrifice. In domestic terms we were children of disgrace and he restored us to the family circle. We were prisoners of war; he broke in and set us free. We were slaves at the slave market and he paid our ransom.

> And note that this was the only way that the new agreement could have been put into effect, the only way the new covenant could have been ratified and made available to us. For all the negotiations would otherwise have failed. Our past performance was not satisfactory. Our future promises were not acceptable. None of us can ransom ourselves, even as the psalmist says: 'Truly no man can ransom himself or give to God the price of his life. For the ransom of his life is costly and can never suffice, that he should continue to live on forever and never see the pit.' (Psalm 49:7-9)

> And so a ransom was necessary to end the stalemate. The man Jesus Christ gave himself as that ransom. And that is why there is one and only one mediator between God and man.

Ken Durham preached a sermon entitled, "Heroic Vulnerability" at the Church of Christ in Stamford, Connecticut. The text was Philippians 2:5-11. His main concern was the question: how can Christians share their faith with those who do not know Christ? He answered that we Christians must make ourselves available to others, and that means risking vulnerability.

God sends to us a gospel that must be communicated person-to-person. But our society seems to specialize in impersonal messages. Junk mail, the automatic "Have a nice day," the bumper sticker with the smiley face that says, "Smile, God Loves You!" are the rule of the day. What is missing is the warmth of the human touch.

But offering the human touch will always be costly. Jesus, always our mentor and model, shows us that in his heroic vulnerability. He had this wonderful way of getting beneath the surface, of talking more than just "news, weather, and sports." What keeps us so often at the surface-level is the fear of getting hurt, of being unloved, of being vulnerable to others. Vulnerable means woundable, open or exposed to injury. "Superman is invulnerable; you can't hurt him. But we are not supermen and superwomen. We can be hurt, and hurt deeply."

Durham went on to say that vulnerability is an essential quality of love itself. Love is a risk, an adventure, a leap of faith. He paraphrased C.S. Lewis. "The only sure way to make certain that your heart will never be bruised or broken is never to give it to anyone. You can wrap it up safe in a coffin of selfishness. But there it will become hard, unbreakable, and irredeemable." Then he quoted, "The only place outside Heaven where you can be perfectly safe from all the dangers...of love...is Hell." (The Four Loves) Durham then held up the supreme example of vulnerable love.

One of the most profound truths, I think, that Scripture has to offer is the vulnerability of God in Christ. We see it so wonderfully in this passage from Paul in Philippians two. This one who was in nature God, in the company of God, in equality with God found a way to turn loose of it. And to come in human form in the nature of a servant. To humble himself and become vulnerable to the cross. What a wondrous thing that is!...To be found in form of a fetus, to go through nine months of development, and to be born among the most vulnerable of all offspring on this planet. Red and wrinkled and crying and un-potty-trained. For God, for God to be so vulnerable to us!

And for Christ to take those risks and to receive those wounds. Not just the wounds of the cross, which are considerable and painful in our consideration of them, but the wounds of rejection. The wounds we read of in the gospels from those who followed him for a time and said, 'Ah, it's not what I'd hoped for,' or 'He's too tough,' or 'He's not the real Messiah.' And even to have those who stayed with him misunderstand him, stumble, and show the weakness of little faith! And yet Isaiah told us long before he came, that one would come who would be "wounded for our transgressions." To be wounded, you first have to be woundable. And he was.

So we shouldn't be surprised to see Jesus displaying that vulnerability in the way he related to people. Communicating a special kind of openness to people, as he built relationships with them. I don't think people laid down their nets to follow Jesus just because he was charismatic and interesting; I think it was because he was compassionate and interested.

At the 11th and Willis congregation in Abilene, Texas, *Tony Ash* addressed three important problems by a study of Paul's writings on the cross. The first was the problem existing in the church at Rome regarding Christian morality and the grace of God. Christian standards of living are not based on arbitrary rules, but on the loving nature of God himself. The Roman Christians were rationalizing, finding religious justification for immorality. "Since God looks the best when he's forgiving us, let's give him plenty to forgive." Ash read Paul's answer in Romans 6:1-11 and then commented.

> Paul was saying…'What did you intend, what did you mean, what did you have in mind when you were baptized?… Don't you remember when you were baptized that this was a radical decision in your life, a time when you resolved to give up the way you were living when you just sinned without concern for justification? Don't you remember…that kind of life held you enthralled, you were in bondage to it? …and you died so that you might live? Don't you remember that, in the very act of baptism, the death and burial of Christ and that was what was happening in your life, you were burying the old lifestyle to take on a new lifestyle?… Don't you recall that back then you were given the hope of resurrection and that your life was no longer a dead-end item, that you now had something that drew you on, a bright reality, a victory, something that was yours and was already working in your life? That decision you made back then ruled out any playing games with God ("How close can I get to the edge? How much can I get by with? Where is the area of God's concern?")..that whole frame of mind was ruled out back there.' Paul is saying, 'If you go back to look for reasons to justify your sinning you are denying what you did back then.'

The second abuse Paul addressed was a magical view of baptism which produces pride and false confidence in the Christian. In I Corinthians 10 he reminded Christians that the Hebrews were also "baptized" in the sea and "ate the spiritual food and drank the spiritual drink" and still perished in the wilderness. Paul's point was: "Let him who thinks he stands take heed lest he fall." Ash told of a couple who rushed in to the church building early one Sunday morning, took a pinch of bread and a sip of grape juice in order to get going on a trip. He asked what such a magical view of the Lord's Supper, devoid of any spiritual meaning or communal dimension, meant for their lives and the lives of others around them.

The third problem Ash called a "blight" on both the early and modern church: division among believers. In Corinth parties loyal to their favorite teachers used baptism as a point of identity. He referred to I Corinthians 1 for Paul's answer.

> Paul is saying it is a contradiction of the very purpose of baptism for that to be the way people are drawn into parties. Baptism is an act which, by its very nature, implies humility and giving and so in this context Paul connects baptism with the cross. What is the cross? Does Jesus go up on a cross so people will think he's someone great? Should we say that we know very little about a cross. It is the extreme of service, it is the extreme of suffering for the sake of other people. And baptism is connected with that...in which one accepts that servant status, that life of service that characterized Jesus himself. And if anyone takes baptism, which has those themes woven into its meaning, and makes it an instrument of personal glorification then one has inverted the very sense of it. And that's why Paul says: 'If you're going to do that with it that's why I'm glad my personal policy was not to baptize many people with my own hands.'

Ash went on to talk of I Corinthians 12 and Ephesians 4 in which Paul again connected baptism with the unity of Christians in Christ. On this point he commented that it is ironic that a people who have said so much about baptism over the years have forgotten what it means in relation to fellowship. Ash stressed the vital connection of baptism with the cross of Christ on the one hand and Christian living on to the other.

The next sermon we review was preached by *Rubel Shelly* at the Ashwood church in Nashville. He began by talking about riddles in the Bible and then proposed one of his own: "When is an end a beginning?" He cited four examples in the life of a Christian.

First, and obvious to all believers, the death of Christ was a beginning which seemed like an end. In John 14 Jesus spoke of his going away and coming back. That whole conversation was a riddle to the disciples since he was saying: "the prince of this world is coming."

> Satan didn't do to Jesus on that cross what he thought he was doing. He thought he was whipping him. He thought he was putting it all to an end. He thought that he had defeated Jesus and that all he was trying to do...would be crushed. ...Jesus said 'Satan has no hold on me.' ...Jesus and the Father had agreed how salvation was going to be achieved... Jesus said, 'The Father and I have worked that out and when I go to that cross it's not Satan's doing. He has no hand in this except as something of a bit player.'

The second time when an end is a beginning is the believer's baptism, said Shelly. Baptism is a glorious event because the cross and resurrection were glorious. But the believer must take the act of obedience seriously.

> If you don't want to change, don't be baptized. If you don't want something to be different in your life, don't come to baptism. Don't desecrate it, don't mock it... Because baptism is an end of the old and unregenerate and alienated and the beginning of the new, the redeemed, the life of fellowship in Christ's own life. ...the cross that ended Jesus' life on earth now puts this sinner to death and a new creature is raised to life. Not the old one revivified, but new, brand new. The same power that raised Jesus out of the tomb the third day raises you to new life and then lives in you to make the new life possible.

In the third place, Shelly said personal failure and defeat can be a beginning. In II Corinthians 12 Paul said he had asked three times for a removal of his "thorn in the flesh" and finally heard the answer: "My grace is sufficient for you." Paul then spoke a riddle of his own: "When I am weak then I am strong." When we give up that which is most precious to us, when we are "stripped of our Isaac" as Abraham was, whether it is love of money, a forbidden relationship, or whatever we are holding back and come to emptiness...then we can know God.

Shelly pointed to a fourth time when an end is a beginning: death itself. He acknowledged the natural, inevitable fear of death, that the Bible itself speaks of death as man's enemy. But he gives strong reassurance based on Jesus' passion, quoting Hebrews 2:14-15.

> When Jesus died he turned death on the fellow who'd brought it, he turned it back on the devil and he destroyed the devil and by his resurrection he conquered death....when Jesus comes again he will destroy the last enemy, which is death. (I Corinthians 15:24-26.) 'Death

will be swallowed up in victory,...' We know death isn't the end, those of us who are believers...And, death, whatever else you are, my enemy, my Nemesis, you are not my conqueror! As surely as Jesus went into the tomb and came out, I'm going into the grave and I'm coming out, too.

"Imitate What You Admire" was the challenge issued to the Sunset Ridge church in San Antonio by *Roy Osborne*. He said he had been amazed and thrilled to see so large a crowd the day before at the funeral of one of their own, Greg Westerman. Some in this world might have considered him an "insignificant man," much in the same way they would have considered Jesus an "insignificant man." Jesus never wrote a book, received a college degree, made a fortune or travelled far from where he was born. Pondering all of that Osborne had written an observation: "It is too bad that most of us do not have the moral courage to imitate that which we admire."

Osborne applied the insight to two areas of Christian living. First, the matter of grace. He told of a little boy who shot out a streetlight, repented to his father, but was chagrined that he would still have to save up his money to pay for the repairs. In Christ God paid the price for us. But we must receive the gift and extend it to others. What we admire we must imitate.

> Let me tell you something: forgiveness is free, and forgiveness is easy for God. But, unfortunately, forgiveness is not easy for you. It is necessary for you to dedicate yourself to forgiveness. The Jewish nation lived for centuries on the hope of a Messiah...that would come to restore the glory of Israel, that would give them back what they had once had. And they gave it all up because they were not willing also to take along with them the

scandal of the cross. The humiliation of being equal with all men. The responsibility of loving and caring for everybody in the world.

Secondly, Christians should imitate Jesus' love for the church. Jesus said, "Upon this rock I will build my church." Many people in our society, especially in Hollywood, disdain Christians and the church. Christians themselves are found either consciously or unconsciously denigrating the church. Do Christians love all their brothers and sisters or only those of their social group and theological set? Do members of the church even miss others who are absent from worship?

> We are part of the club, aren't we? We expect those who are in charge to run the ship...Jesus said, 'Upon this rock I will build my church.' Do you know what the rock was? Peter had just said, 'Thou art the Christ, the son of the living God;' he did not found the church on a set of words or a motto...he founded it upon the significance of the fact that God, Creator of heaven and earth, had come to this earth because he loved us enough to go through the indignity, the sacrifice, and the pain of the cross. Because he was willing to be an insignificant carpenter. He was willing to be nobody, and yet to persevere. He was willing to be ignored, to be laughed at. But he loved even those who ignored him and laughed at him enough to persevere and to hope for them, and to pray in the final, gasping breaths of the cross: 'Father, forgive them, for they know not what they do.'

Osborne went on to say that Christ himself the king invites all into the church. To disparage the church is not to degrade the elders, leaders, or even the hypocrites. It is to insult the Lord himself.

God loved the world so much that he gave his only begotten Son to suffer the scandal of the cross... And we treat it with such disdain as though it were something created by men. Our dedication to the church is so small because we have allowed ourselves to be hypnotized by the world's concept of the church as cathedrals set on corners in the metropolis, preachers robed who stand in the pulpit to orate, and pious leaders who march on Sunday morning but the rest of the week they spend with the Devil. ...I'm afraid that when Christ gave himself for the church it was not for that concept.

And every once in a while we are allowed to glimpse the life of an individual who is not a part of the hierarchy, not a part of the cathedral church, but who loved...cared...served...worked and never wanted any thanks or any glory. And isn't it a shame that we...do not have the moral courage to dedicate ourselves to the simple things of life that the exalted is made of?

Bob Hendren preached a sermon from John 11 at the Donelson church in Nashville. He began by remarking how many television seminars promise instant wealth to those who follow their advice and subscribe to their programs. The spokesmen have so much to say, unless they face an issue like death.

In John 11 the evangelist tells us that a friend of Jesus became ill and died. One might expect that such a good friend would have been exempt from suffering and death. Some TV preachers assure their listeners' escape from sickness, that their stocks will go up, that people will be nice, that they will always find a parking place at work. It's all unrealistic. Friends of Jesus also struggle with life. This life, after all, is not the final answer, the final place. Jesus, himself, went through suffering.

Even more difficult to understand than the suffering of Lazarus was Jesus' delay in coming to Bethany. It's the problem of the absence of God. Where is God when we need him? Many have earnestly prayed and have heard only silence. Mary and Martha were irritated. "Lord, if you had been here..." Perhaps Jesus chose not to come because he had a deep reason. Maybe they would not have understood even if he had told them.

The disciples had no better understanding than Mary and Martha. After the delay he told them it was time to go. Thomas said, "Well, let's go up that we may die with him." But Jesus' attitude was different.

> Knowing that it's a calculated risk and that his own life will be in danger he doesn't go up to throw his life away. He goes up because he knows he will lay it down voluntarily. Thomas, on the other hand, has a kamikaze view of his cause... But when Jesus dies there will be enormous purpose in what he does.

Having arrived at Bethany, Jesus found a typical funeral scene. He told Martha he was the resurrection and the life.

> Martha, like a lot of us, thinks that because she has faith in some idea, some doctrine of the resurrection that that's about all she has to get by on. And she thinks, I believe, that Jesus is saying to her...what we...say as we try to comfort people...'Well, everything is going to be all right. There, there, now, don't cry. After all, this person is victorious...' And we only say those things because we really don't know what to say. We are filling the space with what we think are nice, pious words...So Jesus is not just making a pious statement...he comes back instantly, almost as if to say to her: 'Oh, you believe in the

resurrection of the dead...? ...Let me tell you...what you must believe in is not so much that doctrine, but in me the guarantor of that action. I will see that through,...'

In the next scene Jesus goes to the tomb. He observes the grief and is "very deeply moved." He is enraged. The word in classical Greek sometimes referred to a war horse snorting, almost impossible to restrain in the face of battle. Jesus sees the enemy and everything within him cries out to enter the conflict. So "Jesus wept" is more than a curiosity, the shortest verse in the Bible. Even though he will raise Lazarus in the next five minutes, tears course down his cheeks. He is not like those who piously say, "Don't cry." He weeps because he sees what death does to people. We are no more upset than Jesus is when we lose a loved one. He understands how utterly repugnant death is. For Jesus would die in less than a week.

Hendren described Jesus taking his position opposite the grave. He recalled the television program, "You Were There," which attempted to reenact great historical moments for the viewers as eyewitnesses. But more than any of those, Hendren said he would choose to be present that day in the suburbs of Jerusalem when Jesus called forth Lazarus. He concluded with the strong assurance that a funeral will never be the last word for one who believes in Jesus.

At Highland in Abilene, Texas, *Lynn Anderson* preached on Mark 10, calling the sermon, "I Want To See." The disciples didn't see who Jesus was or where he was going. Intoxicated by intertestamental rhetoric of a conquering warrior Messiah, they had trained in guerrilla camps for war. They would be ready when Messiah came. Now Messiah had come and they were anxious to charge into battle. They had no clue what he was about.

> They didn't understand why he spent so much time with children, lepers and blind folks, with poor people. But they were impressed by the miracles so they followed. ...he was on his way to a cross. In their minds they were headed toward Jerusalem and a crown. He wanted them to be servants. They wanted to be soldiers. They wanted power, but he was concerned about people...

Anderson highlighted three points in the narrative of Jesus and disciples on the way to Jerusalem. First, Jesus was ahead of them on the road toward Jerusalem. Behind him were the astonished disciples and then the confused crowds. Already having rejected an easy kingship just over the Jews, having denied self in favor of God's will, the solitary Jesus moved on toward Jerusalem. The disciples had not even been able to hear his two predictions of suffering. They were ready to go to war. One more time Jesus explained in vivid detail what would happen to him at Jerusalem. Second, James and John came asking "Jesus, do for us whatever we ask...let us sit on your right and left hands in your glory." Jesus told them they were thinking like Gentiles; among his followers service would be the hallmark.

From Mark Twain's "Soldier's Prayer," Anderson pointed to the horrors of war and showed how selfish the requests of James and John were. He then asked:

> Have you ever prayed any prayers like that? 'Give me my way, O God, no matter what it costs someone else. Give me happiness though I destroy my marriage and my children. Give me prosperity though I take food out of the mouths of those already hungry. Give me spiritual blessings, though it costs me no cross.' Jesus explained that the Son of man didn't come to get served, but to serve and to give his life a ransom for many...'What I want is not soldiers but servants.'

Third, Anderson told the story of the blind man at the outskirts of Jericho. Blind Bartimaeus called repeatedly, "Son of David, have mercy on me." Always one to help the helpless, Jesus stopped and healed him. Jesus was making a point for the disciples. "You cannot see that you cannot see. He understands more about the Messiah than you do." Anderson asked how many of us restorationists actually read the Bible and see Jesus.

> ...we interpret it psychologically. 'Well, I know the Lord says that but it is not sound mental health; that stuff you said about sticking in marriages that are uncomfortable, is not healthy. A person has to look out for number one. Certainly Jesus is interested in the person's welfare; don't give me this stuff about running over your own feelings.'

> Jesus said, 'If you don't give yourself away you lose yourself.'

> Or we look at it like entrepreneurs look at the market. 'Well, now, we are going to build the kingdom of God...we have got to test the market and see what kind of religion sells nowadays.' Then we draw from the text those bright, attractive tidbits we can market in the name of the gospel. And in so doing...we preach something that is not the gospel...and further addict people to something that is not bread...and finally, disillusion them. Or we go to the Evangelical bookstores...looking, not for Jesus and his will, but for Bible verses that will "touch us." Jesus said, 'Listen to me...you guys aren't listening. I'm headed for a cross. If you follow me you take it up...my agenda is people...you need to learn to be servants.'

Anderson confessed that he and the church need to learn the lesson; we seek a religion that blesses our lives with little concern for serving others.

At the Burlington, Massachusetts church *Jim Woodroof* preached a series of sermons on Jesus' approach to the cross. The emphasis was a study of the heart of Jesus, what made him choose the cross. In previous lessons he had discussed four features of Jesus' ministry which offended the Jewish leaders: he went out of his way to disregard the heaped up human traditions regarding the Sabbath; he ignored the emphasis placed on external cleanliness, the washing of hands; he befriended sinners; and he welcomed Gentiles into the kingdom of God. But most of all Jesus offended because he claimed to be the Son of God, the offense discussed in this fifth sermon.

Woodroof began by showing how determined Jesus was to go to Jerusalem. "His face was set toward Jerusalem" (Luke 9:51-53). He walked ahead of the disciples on the road, a man obsessed with his mission (Mark 10:32-34). Next, he turned to Jesus' claims themselves. The gospels present testimony supporting Jesus' divinity. His claims were substantiated by the witness of others and by his own words. Even before his birth an angel told Mary, "He shall be called the Son of the Most High." Later his contemporaries confirmed the announcement: John the Baptist, Nicodemus, the man healed of blindness in John 9, and the disciples themselves.

Then there was Jesus' testimony about himself that he was God's Son. He made private statements, mostly to his disciples. But he also told outsiders. To the woman at the well in John 4 he said, "I who speak to you am he." To Martha in John 11 he said "I am the resurrection and the life." Sometimes indirectly he claimed to be divine. In Mark 2:5 he asserted the right to forgive sins. "I am the living bread...from heaven," he said in John 6. Jesus made forthright statements of his relationship with the Father which sent the religious authorities into a rage.

The growing conflict climaxed with Jesus' own statement at his trial. When witnesses could not agree and their false stories clashed, the High Priest asked him specifically: "Are you the Christ?" "I am," Jesus said. They screamed, "He has made himself the Son of God!" Woodroof read from John 19 about their leading Jesus out to be crucified, and from Mark 15 about his godforsaken cry and the centurion's statement: "Surely, this man was the Son of God." Jesus went to the cross because he claimed to be God's son.

> We're about two thousand years removed from that. You will have to make your own decision about it, about him, and about what he claimed. Nobody can make that one for you. But I do think you have the right to know...that this is why he died. If he had just simply said, 'Wait, you misunderstood what I said about being the Son of God...I'm no more than you are, we're all sons of God, that's all I meant, he would have died at about seventy, retired in Nazareth. But this man who violated the Sabbath traditions in order to show people that God is not an angry ogre and that people are more important than days, this man who refused to go along with their ceremonial washings because clean hearts are more important than clean hands, this man who came down on the side of sinners and publicans and outcasts like you and me, and this man who took his place beside Gentile people — this man, when he was given the chance to deny or affirm that he claimed to be God on earth,...looked right at them and said, 'I am.' And they killed him. And we are going to observe something he

> said the night before he died: 'Take this bread and eat it, this is my body. Take this cup and drink it, this is my blood of the new covenant.' And you and I today stand where we are with feelings of forgiveness and grace because this man came showing us the Father. And they killed him for it.

"When Life Does Its Worst" was the title of a sermon *Dan Anders* preached at the Malibu church. His text was Romans 8:31-39. Anders began by observing that many crises are not really crises at all; they are only minor inconveniences. He mentioned the adjustment involved in his switching back to glasses after living twenty-one years with contact lenses. But there are real trials in life, rugged tests to be endured. They come on like a rushing freight train to broadside our lives. "What do you do when real trouble comes?" he asked. Romans 8 presents a potent prescription. In the NIV there are six questions in three pairs. The answers provide an antidote to doubt and despair.

"What shall we say in response to this?" Paul asked. The "this" could be the whole message of God's grace as set out in Romans or the liberating Spirit mentioned in chapter 8, or the single promise just given that God works in all things to produce the ultimate good for those who love him. In this passage Paul affirmed God's grace and God's justice.

> To clinch his point, Paul uses a word that was rich in the history of Israel. He says that God did not 'spare' his own Son. Paul is thinking of the story of Abraham and Isaac, where the same verb is used. Abraham did not 'spare' his own 'beloved son'. (Gen. 22:12 LXX)
>
> In a similar, but grander way, God did not spare Jesus Christ. God 'delivered up' his own Son so that we might

> know his saving grace. To what did God 'deliver' Jesus? To the experience of being human — 'the Word became flesh and lived among us.' To the trial of temptations — 'tempted in every way as we are.' To suffering — 'he himself suffered for us.'
>
> Most of all, God gave Jesus up to death in our place. That word 'deliver up' is used over and over in Scripture to point to Calvary. There, supremely, God gave his Son in bloody death so that we might know the riches of his redeeming grace...
>
> ...So whatever troubles come our way, however steep or dark the path, we can rely on this grand fact: God is for us. He has proven it once-for-all in the grace-gift of Jesus Christ.

Anders then followed Paul's discussion in affirming God's justice. "If God has justified us, who can prosecute our case?" Not Satan, not one's opponents, not even one's own conscience. No one can indict us because God in Jesus has declared us 'Not guilty.'

> In one pregnant sentence Paul summarized the good news of Christ — died, raised to life, seated with God, interceding for us. This is the heart of the gospel. Here is the whole story in capsule form. It is as if Paul wanted with one stroke of his pen to say all that needs to be said.
>
> Christ died for us. Without Calvary there is no redemption. Apart from Christ's cross there is only condemnation. But Jesus' saving death is not the end of the story! 'More than that,' he was 'raised to life.' It is the resurrection that validates the crucifixion. Because Christ lives, we know the meaning and power of his death.

> And he does not merely live. Christ continues to serve us. He is 'at the right hand of God'...Jesus still ministers to us — he is 'interceding for us' with his Father.
>
> Paul's questions affirm a grand truth: God is just. We have stood before the Supreme Court of the universe. The Chief Justice has declared us 'Not Guilty' because of Jesus Christ. And no one can overturn God's verdict!

With Paul, Anders joyfully asked the question "Who shall separate us from the love of God in Jesus Christ?" Is there any physical force that can pull God's love away from us? Any discouragement? Disappointment? Defeat? Can any spiritual power strip us of Jesus' love? The Scriptures are full of stories of heartache and loss. But God is good and faithful. We are more than conquerors through him who loved us!

At the Glenwood church in Tyler, Texas, *Charles Siburt* preached the sermon, "How The World Was Won." Matthew reports that the disciples were astonished at Jesus' resurrection. But he told them to go out and preach the news to all the nations: "Jesus came to bring the kingdom. The resurrection means that nothing can stop it now. Not even death can stop it now." The Jews were in bondage to a kingdom of legal rules and interpretations. The Greco-Roman world was enslaved to fatalism. They feared "angels," "principalities," and "powers." Since they practiced astrology, their lives were filled with fear and despair.

Siburt quoted from Paul's letter to the Romans: "If God is for us, who is against us? For Christ Jesus who died is now resurrected and sits at the right hand of God to make intercession for us."

> That was the message that won the world. It put an end to fear and fatalism and despair. It said the world belongs

> to God, and to nothing else. And, therefore, nothing else need control us in this life. The resurrection proved it, as even the last enemy of life, death itself, had been conquered. For God has the last word, and the last word is 'life.'

He observed that, although the modern world has advanced beyond the first century world in many ways, in other ways men and women still feel trapped. Some are even trapped by a view of grace as license or a voracious appetite for emotional highs.

> You see, the resurrection does not say that we will always win; it says that our suffering now can be for good, and not for nothing. It doesn't say that because we are raised with Christ, we will always be on a perpetual high. It says that when you get depressed, that's just the way you are; it's not the way the world is.

> The resurrection means you are never trapped. That's what Jesus preached before the resurrection, and that's what he commissioned the apostles to preach after the resurrection. The apostles preached it to a society that was locked into an understanding that life was controlled by fate. Jesus preached it to a similar society, a Jewish society. They...believed that you were locked into a destiny because of what they called 'the law.' If you sinned, you were forever branded as a sinner. If you were diseased, you were branded as cursed. If you were of a different race, you were branded as unclean. So it was no accident that during his life Jesus made it a point to go to the sinners, the outcasts, the foreigners, and forgive them, and heal them, and eat with them. And he told parables in which the sinners, the outcasts and the foreigners march into heaven first, ahead of those who

thought they had reserved seats there. The point that he was trying to make was that nobody, nobody is trapped in his life. We thought that who the world tells us we are is who we must always be. Jesus said, who God created you to be is who you can become.

Siburt applied this good news to women who continually punish themselves because they do not conform to the society's image of beauty. He spoke to men who see themselves as failures by to the world's standards of success. The problem is not that we have to change our human nature. "Our problem is that our human nature is in bondage to superstitions and to myths about who we really are." He closed with a story from Fred Craddock about an old man who interrupted a pleasant meal the Craddocks were having while on vacation. The old man from the Smoky Mountains of eastern Tennessee told his own story. As a bastard son he had been ostracized by everyone in his home town, especially by the good Christians. He was always fearful of meeting people, knowing that they were always trying to guess who his father was. One Sunday the preacher tapped him on the shoulder and said, "'Well, boy, you're a child of uh...You're a child of God!...Go claim your inheritance, boy!'" Craddock asked the old man his name. "Ben Hooper" was the reply. "I remember," Craddock concluded, "my father had told me of the time when for two terms the people of Tennessee had elected an illegitimate boy named Ben Hooper as Governor."

Rick Atchley preached a sermon at the Southern Hills church in Abilene entitled, "Preparation For Proclamation." It was based on Mark 1:9-13. He began by observing that preparing the preacher is always a bigger task than preparing the sermon. He noted that Jesus prepared for thirty years before he began his public ministry. From the text he proceeded to point out what preparation for ministry really means, as exemplified in Jesus.

The listener was asked to mark what Jesus came to do. He did not present himself as a miracle-worker first of all. First he came proclaiming the good news that God was near, the kingdom was at hand. He also came to prepare good men, to call some to be "fishers of men." "Declaring and discipling were his mission, and isn't it also the goal of all of the ministries of the church?" Atchley asked. Often we feel inadequate and guilty in our ministries. The need is not to feel more guilt but to get better prepared. Not the preparation of training, as important as that is, but the preparation of heart and character. To see what is involved we can look at Jesus' preparation.

First, Jesus accepted his ministry in submission. He came and was baptized by John in Jordan. He did it to validate John's ministry, to identify with the common crowds on the river's bank, to comply with his own destiny he submitted to baptism. Atchley stressed that baptism in Jesus' mind was a pointer to Golgotha. From the first, Jesus was willing to surrender to God's will for his ministry, whatever that meant. Second, Jesus had the assurance of the Spirit. He came up from the water anointed for his ministry. Christians must see that the same Spirit who anointed Jesus anoints them for their ministries. The reason for the anointing is ministry. In our history we have virtually eliminated God's action in our salvation. Walter Scott's original "five finger exercise" listed three actions of God's and two of man's. When we made the five steps all man's doing we "pulled the plug to power" in our ministries. Third, Jesus had a firm knowledge of his sonship to the Father. We, too, are sons and daughters of God and heirs of his promise. We are privileged to cry out, "Abba, Father." The devil will do his best to make us doubt that sonship because it is a vital secret to our fruitful ministry.

Fourth, Jesus accepted suffering. The Spirit drove him into the desert of temptation. We are prone to believe our baptism is not valid if we then have hard times and heavy temptations. But trouble is sure proof that we are God's children.

Atchley then asked what Christians should do to appropriate the lesson. First, they should learn to apply the Word of God as Jesus did in the temptations. Second, they should affirm the cross from the beginning.

> The first thing Jesus did to begin his ministry was to choose the cross. He could have chosen the devil's way, the devil said: 'You want the world, I can give you the world...' But Jesus rejected that way and we've got to reject the world's way, folks. We've got to reject that way that calls for self-exaltation and self-promotion and we've got to choose the path of self-denial. We've got to choose Golgotha. Our lifestyle is going to speak louder than our lessons. And if when people see us, if they don't see Christ, but they see ourselves our message is diminished.

Third, Atchley concluded by suggesting that Christians who would minister effectively must accept God's love. Why did Jesus stand on the river bank? Why did he go into the temptations? Why did he go to the cross? "Because, he loves you so...nothing would so empower your ministry as deciding to believe that."

On the first Sunday of the year at the College Church in Portland, Oregon, *Dave Bland* issued a call for unity on the basis of Philippians 2. He noted that the church at Philippi had a problem maintaining oneness. In chapter 1, verse 27 Paul hinted at the problem when he urged his brothers and sisters: "Only let your manner of life be worthy of the gospel of Christ, so that whether I come and see you or am absent, I may hear of you that you stand firm in one spirit, with one mind striving side by side for the faith of the gospel." In the fourth chapter he admonished Euodia and Syntyche to "agree in the Lord."

Paul's aim was to encourage humility and concern for others. These new Christians may not have realized how important this attitude is. With our background in the Church of Christ we understand. Selfishness is not easily rooted out of our lives. It is a problem we all have and it lies behind much of the world's problems: wars, killings, robbery, prejudice, destruction of marriages and families, etc. One might try reading the morning paper just to notice how many of our tragedies grow out of basic selfishness.

> Paul's resolutions should be of great interest to us because we all can say 'Yes, I struggle with selfishness.' But notice that Paul doesn't scold them. He does not give them a pop solution or come back with a quick-fix response. Even for such a seemingly small incident, for example, as the one between Euodia and Syntyche, Paul uses the strongest argument he can summon. He holds up Christ and the model of his life. He became a servant. And Paul discloses what Christ did through this hymn.
>
> First, he renounced himself (vv. 6,7). Christ, though equal with God, did not count that equality as something to be held onto. So he emptied himself; he denied himself the privileges that were his as God's only son. Then he adapted himself to humanity (vv. 7-8). He thoroughly identified with people. He did not do so in order to find out what it was like to be human. He did so because he already knew what it was like and desired to show us how to live. Jesus was incarnated not into the upper echelon of society but among the poor and the outcast; he became a servant. And in humility he

> surrendered himself (v.8). He became obedient to His Father. Finally, he sacrificed himself in death (v.8). But this was not just any death; this was death on a cross. He went from God's throne to death by crucifixion.
>
> Paul's reason for emphasizing this movement is that the attitude that Christ had was the attitude the Philippians were to have in their dealings with each other. Christ's mindset was to express itself in their lives.

Bland said the point of it all was Paul's admonition in verse 5: "Have this mind in you," the mind of humility, the heart of a servant, one who has concern for others. Another possible rendering might be: "think this way among yourselves which you think also in Christ." The solution is to think in the right way, to saturate one's mind with Christ. Bland recalled his experience in learning Greek and Hebrew. One has to go over it again and again, he can never repeat it too much. Christians can never think too much about who Jesus was, what he did, and why.

Paul gives even more help with this principle in holding up examples and models of selflessness: himself in verse 17, Timothy in verses 19-21, and Epaphroditus in verses 25, 29-30. In conclusion Bland answered an important question. What does it take to love and have the servant mind? He told the moving children's story of "Skin Horse and The Velveteen Rabbit." As the story suggests, only giving self makes one "real." Jesus shows us how to be real.

On that same first Sunday, a few miles up the road north *David Fleer* preached on "The Word Of The Cross: The Power To Change" at the church in Vancouver, Washington. He began with musings about the curious fact of change. In "Annie Hall" Woody Allen went back in memory to his first grade class, wondering what each of his classmates had become. They had all changed, no doubt. On the television show, "Little House On The Prairie" two rowdy boys grew up to amount to something after all. One became a minister, the other a doctor. The powers that change us are time, the influences which play upon our lives, and the guidance of God, Fleer observed.

When change happens one can be sure a power has been in effect. Fleer groaned about being in the fourth month of winter and looking forward to February and March. But Spring would come because the power of nature works the wonder every year. He led his listeners to his text: I Corinthians 1:18-31.

> This passage refers to a power that can bring about change. More significant than that which causes seasonal resurrection of green leaves, buds and flowers in the Spring. This is a power more significant than the mighty Bonneville Dam which converts the waters of the Columbia River into electrical power that illumines the Portland area. This is a power even more significant than time and influence that allows children to grow up and personalities to develop.
>
> What then is the word of the cross? The cross was the execution tool often used in Jesus' day. It was the popular means to rid society of its dregs. Today the electric chair, the gallows or the gas chamber are the execution tools.
>
> In the first century the cross brought to criminals a terribly painful and embarrassing death. Can you imagine hearing of someone in Florida who has been put to death in 'the chair.' What do you think? There are exceptions, but likely you'd assume this person did something horrible to deserve the punishment. When

> you read that someone has died in the gas chamber in California you usually connect that death with some crime. Now, think of your reaction if someone told you, 'Gerald from Spokane was hung for you.' Ugh!
>
> Ironically, this 'word of the cross' has power to change lives.
>
> The death of Jesus, on the cross, is given in some detail in Luke's narrative. Hanging between two criminals, Jesus was mocked and tormented (Luke 23:32-33, 35-37). But at his death some wonderful things happened. The power of the cross darkened the sky (v. 45) and tore in two the veil of the temple (v. 45). The power of the cross caused the centurion guard to believe (v.47). The power of the cross caused bystanders to become emotionally distraught. They had gathered to 'view a spectacle' but, because of the power of the cross, left 'beating their breasts' (v.48). This is the power that can change a life. My life. Your life.

Fleer went on to talk of the power of the cross to redeem lives here and now. A lonely, neglected little girl who became a rebellious young lady later sang the blues. But she is perhaps best remembered for singing: "His eye is on the sparrow and I know He watches me." Her name was Ethel Waters. Then there was the young man who had no equal in cursing, swearing, and lying. He was found by God in the crucified and later wrote *Pilgrim's Progress*.

And, not only does the cross redeem lives, it also has power to sanctify what it ransoms. Fleer quoted Albert Schweitzer's statement of dedication to serve the wretched blacks in Africa. The example of the Suffering Servant did that. That same power can save us from pride, lust, bad habits, bitterness and a sense of abandonment. Many Christians have never allowed the power of the cross to work fully in their lives. Fleer said he counted himself among that number. The Christian message is simple, he said, it is the cross of Christ.

The last sermon reviewed here was preached by *Mike Cope* at the College Church, Searcy, Arkansas. Introducing a series on the cross, he entitled his lesson: "The Fulcrum Of The Faith." Cope began by relating the reflections of then Vice President George Bush on the funeral of Leonid Brezhnev in 1982. Bush remarked that the service contained no mention of eternity, hope, or the Creator. Dignitaries filed by the casket. Finally Mrs. Brezhnev came alone, stood until she thought no one was watching, leaned over and traced something on his chest. A small cross, a Christian cross.

Cope called the church's attention to I Corinthians 15:1-11. The problem in Corinth was confusion about the resurrection, some did not have confidence that the dead would be raised. Paul set forth the death, burial, and resurrection of Jesus as the matter "of first importance." Cope saw two important truths.

> One truth is that there is a center of our faith...While all Christian teaching is important these are the things you must hold on to...I think we need to hear that because many of us have been victimized by a view of the Bible that sees everything of equal importance. We passed from correctly saying that all is important to incorrectly saying that all is of equal importance. Paul wouldn't agree with that. Paul would say these were the things that were most critical. This was the heart of the matter. This was the fulcrum of the faith, this is what it all goes back to. 'I preach these things as of foundational importance.'

The second truth Cope saw in I Corinthians 15 was that the cross was the absolute center of that gospel message. Paul had said in I Corinthians 2 that he was "determined not to preach anything but Christ crucified." The truth that Jesus died for our sins, a substitutionary atonement, was long ago foretold in Isaiah 53. Cope reviewed as many New Testament books as time allowed, showing how the cross was vital to each. He drew his lesson together and challenged the church to consider the importance of recovering the cross as central in the faith.

> The cross is the heart of our faith. It is the central part of what we must stand for. It's the only reason we can gather as a community of faith...There's a modern parable that tells the story of too many individuals and too many churches. A church erected a new building. Behind the podium was a large sign, reading: "We Preach Christ Crucified." Off to the side they put a potted, creeping vine. The vine began to grow, the congregation began to mellow. Eventually the vine covered the last word so all they could see was: "We Preach Christ." Not so much the cross, but the nice little Jesus who meets human needs. But the vine kept growing so that it covered the next word so that all the sign said was: "We Preach." Eventually we just forget about Christ. It's a human religion and you're responding out of human need, searching for anything whether it be from God and Christ or from some aspect in anybody. But the vine continued to grow, till all that was left was the word, "We."

> I pray to God that in your life you still proclaim Christ crucified. Three quick questions. Does the cross bring you to your knees in thankfulness? Does the cross free you from guilt? Does the cross cause you to surrender daily to God, dying on your own cross, letting Christ live in you?

Cope ended with these words from the hymn, "Rise Up, O Men Of God."

> *Lift high the cross of Christ!*
> *Tread where his feet have trod;*
> *As brothers of the Son of man,*
> *Rise up, O men of God!*

Summary of Part 3

It is important to understand what is *not* being said in this book and what *is* being said. I am not saying that the cross was never preached among us until 1950 and that it is always preached now. I have attempted to trace *trends* in our preaching of the cross. From Campbell and Stone to the mid-twentieth century the general trend was away from the cross toward a gospel of the church. I am convinced that, since mid-century, more of our preachers have been moving back toward a Christ-centered gospel. Now we are beginning to ask an even more carefully focused question: what about Jesus is most important to understand and tell, what is the core gospel? We are just beginning to ask questions about what preaching Christ crucified really means. The inquiry is not yet common enough among us to be called a trend. But if we continue this quest by disciplined study, prayer, thought and sharing of insights we will develop a stronger "word of the cross" than our Restoration Movement has ever known. None of these preachers just quoted would claim to have restored the core gospel in its full New Testament power, depth and beauty. That's because they have truly come into contact with the cross and have seen vistas yet unexplored. I certainly would not make any such claim for my own preaching. But this interest in the cross is the right direction.

A story is told of the novelist, Lloyd C. Douglas, which seems to have meaning just here. He went to visit a musician friend in his studio. "What's the good news today?" Douglas asked, half joking. His friend picked up the triangle and struck it. "Do you hear that?" he asked. "That's 'A.' The baritone across the hall often flats his high notes. The soprano upstairs sharps the low ones. The violin next door is sometimes out of tune. But that's 'A.' It was 'A' yesterday; it's 'A' today; and it will be 'A' tomorrow and forever. That's the good news for today."

If the church were a symphony orchestra what would the role of the preacher be? Is he to write the score? Does he play all the instruments? Should he solo while everyone else plays softly in the background? Does he conduct the orchestra? It seems to me that none of these is his role. His calling is to do what the first violin does when the orchestra is tuning. As the "Concertmaster," (a title of great honor) he stands, having gotten his own instrument in tune, and sounds the "A". The whole orchestra listens for that pitch and tunes accordingly. His is a limited but important role. When he sounds the note every one who has learned to hear it says, "Yes, that's it. If we tune to that we will be ready to play the score under the conductor in full harmony."

That is the preacher's role in the congregation. His first responsibility is the considerable task of keeping his own heart in tune with the crucified and risen Lord. His second task is to speak the word of the cross clearly and repeatedly. Christians and unbelievers alike need to hear the right note; they must hear the core gospel to live. We have briefly sampled twenty-one sermons in which the preachers sounded clearly the right note. When those lessons were delivered hearers who were listening for the right note could say, "Amen! That's the gospel." They could leave worship with their hearts tuned to be God's people and to do his will in the power of his Spirit. They could go out into the world as the church under the cross.